High-Speed Networking with LAN Switches

Gilbert Held

WILEY COMPUTER PUBLISHING

John Wiley & Sons, Inc.
New York • Chichester • Weinheim
• Brisbane • Singapore • Toronto

Executive Publisher: Robert Ipsen
Editor: Theresa Hudson
Managing Editor: Angela Murphy
Text Design & Composition: Publishers' Design & Production Services, Inc.

Designations used by companies to distinguish their products are often claimed as trademarks. In all instances where John Wiley & Sons, Inc., is aware of a claim, the product names appear in initial capital or ALL CAPITAL LETTERS. Readers, however, should contact the appropriate companies for more complete information regarding trademarks and registration.

This text is printed on acid-free paper.

This publication is designed to provide accurate and authoritative information in regard to the subject matter covered. It is sold with the understanding that the publisher is not engaged in rendering legal, accounting, or other professional service. If legal advice or other expert assistance is required, the services of a competent professional person should be sought.

Library of Congress Cataloging-in-Publication Data

Held, Gilbert.
    High-speed networking with LAN switches / Gilbert Held.
        p.   cm.
    Includes index.
    ISBN 0–471–18444–6 (paper : alk. paper)
    1. Telecommunication—Switching systems.   2. Local area networks (Computer networks)   3. Wide area networks (Computer networks)
I. Title.
    TK5103.8.H45   1997
    004.6′8—dc21   97–15450

Printed in the United States of America
10 9 8 7 6 5 4 3 2 1

Contents

Preface

This book is a comprehensive reference to high-speed networking through the use of LAN switches. Although LAN switches are only a few years old, their effect upon the ability to support the networking requirements of organizations is nothing less than profound. Today you can use LAN switches to obtain a migration path for supporting multimedia applications while maintaining a significant portion of an existing networking infrastructure. Even if your organization has no intention of migrating to multimedia, you can use LAN switches as a mechanism for avoiding or delaying a more costly upgrade to a new networking infrastructure to support an increase in network activity.

In spite of the considerable benefits obtainable through the use of LAN switches, they are similar to other communications products in that there are many vendors manufacturing a variety of products that incorporate various features whose operational characteristics are important to understand. Thus, the primary objective of this book is to provide you with a comprehensive guide to the operation and utilization of LAN switches to obtain a high-speed networking capability within your organization. To accomplish this objective we will cover in detail the general operational characteristics of LAN switches as well as the specific operational characteristics of various types of switches, ranging in scope from a variety of Ethernet and Token-Ring products to ATM LAN switches. In doing so we will note the operational characteristics and features associated with various types of switches which will provide you with a mechanism to evaluate a variety of products as well as compare and contrast the use of various switches under various operating environments.

As a professional author I truly value reader feedback. You can write to me via my publisher, whose address is located on the back cover of this book. Let me know if there are topics you would like to see in a revised edition or if topics in this edition need further elaboration. Your comments and suggestions for improvements are sincerely welcome.

Gilbert Held
Macon, Georgia

Acknowledgments

Although the author receives primary credit for a book due to the placement of his or her name on the cover, the actual publication effort is a team effort that warrants acknowledgment of the work of many individuals. First and foremost, I would like to thank my family for their understanding and patience as I hibernated in my office on weekends and long evenings preparing the manuscript and reviewing galley pages for the book you are now reading. As an old-fashioned author I prefer the use of pen and paper, especially due to my extensive travel and the inability of most of my collection of electronic plugs and receptacles to match electrical outlets in some rather interesting hotels I have stayed at. Once again, I am indebted to Mrs. Linda Hayes for her fine effort in interpreting my handwriting and converting my notes into an acceptable manuscript. Concerning that manuscript, I would like to express my appreciation to Terri Hudson and Katherine Schowalter at John Wiley & Sons for supporting this project and to Angela Murphy for her effort in guiding the manuscript through the production process.

The Evolution
of the Switching
Revolution

1

The use of LAN switches is similar to other communications devices in that they represent an evolution of network design technology based upon changing end-user network applications. Thus, in this introductory chapter we will focus our attention upon changes in networking technology and how a variety of communications products such as LAN switches were developed to satisfy the networking requirements of various types of organizations. In doing so we will note the rationale for the use of switches, obtain an overview of their networking capability, and become familiar with some of their features that can justify their use. Although this is an introductory chapter, it forms the basis for obtaining an appreciation for the evolution of the switching revolution and provides a foundation for the material presented in succeeding chapters. Thus, readers that might otherwise be tempted to skip or skim the material in the first chapter of a technical book are encouraged to read this chapter.

THE COMPUTING EVOLUTION

Since networks are established to provide access to data stored on computers, any discussion concerning the evolution of networking technology must consider the evolution of computer technology. In this section we will briefly examine how computing has evolved from glass-enclosed mainframe rooms to desktop computers and the networks that were developed to support different types of computer access. As we examine each type of computing method, we will also examine some of the applications placed on different types of computers and the amount of transmission capacity, a term more commonly referred to as bandwidth, required to support those applications. By gaining an understanding of how changes in computing and computing applications changed bandwidth requirements, we will also gain an appreciation for one of the key roles obtained from the use of LAN switches—an ability to provide users with additional bandwidth capacity.

Mainframe Centric Computing

The first group of computers developed during and after World War II were based upon the use of vacuum tube technology. Requiring enough electricity to power a neighborhood and weighing several tons, such computers were only affordable for very large companies and government agencies. Although the incorporation of transistor technology significantly reduced the size, cost, and power consumption of computers during the 1960s, most were still fabricated in cabinet frames (which resulted in their name), and they still required a significant amount of floor space to install. In addition, their cost remained high enough to preclude their use by medium and smaller-size companies, resulting in the development of service bureaus that purchased mainframes and resold clock time on those computers to other firms that could not afford their own.

The primary use of mainframe computers through the 1970s was restricted to a core set of applications, primarily financial in nature. Those applications included payroll, accounts payable, accounts receivable, and a limited amount of forecasting. The dominant mainframe vendor through the 1980s was the IBM Corporation, although competition from RCA, Burroughs, NCR, Honeywell, Sperry Rand, and other companies attempted to penetrate the market for large-scale computers. Due to IBM's domination of the mainframe computer market, its networking strategy dominated the method by which remote users obtained access to mainframe computers.

IBM Networking

The original IBM networking strategy was known as 3270 networking and was based upon the use of a series of communications hardware products that were assigned numeric designators in the 3000 range. As computing applications changed, IBM's networking strategy evolved, with the introduction of its System Network Architecture (SNA) followed by a modification to SNA known as Advanced Peer-to-Peer Networking (APPN).

3270 Networking.   IBM's original networking strategy, which was followed by other mainframe manufacturers, resulted in a hierarchical network in which remote terminals were connected to control units. Control units in turn were connected to a front-end processor or communications controller, which was a special type of computer developed to off-load communications functions from the mainframe. The front-end processor in turn was directly cabled via a communications channel to the mainframe.

Figure 1.1 illustrates the hierarchical structure of a typical mainframe network. In examining Figure 1.1, you will note IBM's use of two different types of control units. A local control unit can be directly attached to a mainframe computer channel, bypassing the front-end processor. This networking scenario allows a group of terminals within a building to be supported by one connection to the mainframe via the use of a local control unit. In comparison, a remote control unit extends the ability of a front-end processor to support a group of terminals in a remote location via an analog modem or data service unit connection. For either networking situation, the control unit provides the mechanism by which a group of terminals share a

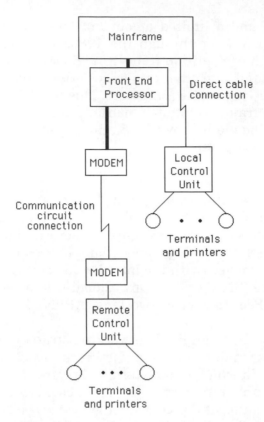

FIGURE 1.1 Network access to IBM mainframes is based upon a hierarchical network structure.

common communications facility. Thus, the initial IBM 3270 networking strategy introduced the concept of shared bandwidth as common communications facilities were shared by groups of terminal devices.

Bandwidth Utilization. Within the data center, the connection of local control units to mainframe computer channels is primarily achieved through the use of a coaxial cable connection. Although this connection can operate at data rates up to approximately 2 Mbps, the actual connection is shared by a group of terminal devices that can include both terminals and printers. The first series of control units supported up to 16 devices, while more modern control units support a maximum of either 32 or 64 devices. Thus, on a per-device basis, the 2-Mbps channel bandwidth is reduced to approximately 2 Mbps/64 or 31 Kbps when a 64-port local control unit is used. When networking is extended to remote locations, control units are commonly connected to the distant front-end processor via analog leased lines operating at 19.2-Kbps or 56-Kbps digital leased lines. Due to the significantly lower operating rate of analog and digital leased lines than that obtainable by a coaxial cable connection, most remote sites limit the use of a control unit to 32 attached terminals and printers. Even so, on a per-device basis, the available bandwidth per terminal device is reduced to between 600 and 1750 bps.

Although the amount of bandwidth per remote terminal device in a 3270 network appears low in comparison to that obtainable on more modern LANs, we must consider the applications those networks support prior to judging their level of support to end-users. Most mainframe-based applications are text based, with an average of 32 characters transmitted as a query and with an average response of 1000 characters being displayed. Thus, a typical query-response involves the transmission of 1032 characters. Figures 1.2 and 1.3 illustrate typical mainframe-generated screen displays. Figure 1.2 shows the login screen for accessing an IBM Virtual Memory (VM) mainframe computer. Note the use of asterisks (*) to generate the name of the organization via groups of characters instead of a raster image that might show a picture of a campus, a building, or person. Figure 1.3 illustrates the display of a news release placed on the mainframe. Note that all information displayed is based upon the use of common characters. Although the top portion of each screen shown in Figures 1.2 and 1.3 appears to represent a graphics display and does indeed represent graphics, those graphics are generated by a communications program operating on a PC linked to the mainframe via a coaxial cable connection.

Since the probability of more than a handful of users initiating a query at the same time is minimal, a 19.2-Kbps analog line which supports slightly over two simultaneous query-responses is usually sufficient to support text-based applications. For exam-

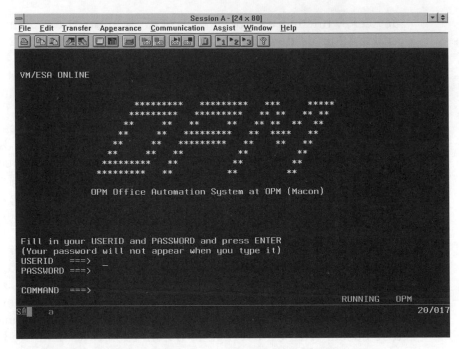

FIGURE 1.2 A text-based login screen generated by a mainframe.

ple, consider the news display shown in Figure 1.3. Although the screen size for the established session is 24 × 80 characters, there are several blank lines as well as partially completed lines. Preferring not to count the actual number of characters on the screen and knowing that a full screen will contain 1920 characters, we can come up with a reasonable estimate of 1500 characters transmitted by the mainframe to the PC functioning as a terminal. If only two remote users are simultaneously retrieving data from the mainframe via a low-speed 19.2-Kbps analog leased line, each user obtains 9600 bps of bandwidth. Since characters are transmitted as eight-bit bytes, this means 1200 characters per second could be downloaded from the mainframe to the PC. Thus, a 1500-character screen similar to the one shown in Figure 1.3 would require 1.25 seconds of transmission time, which is very reasonable for a text-based application. In addition, control units

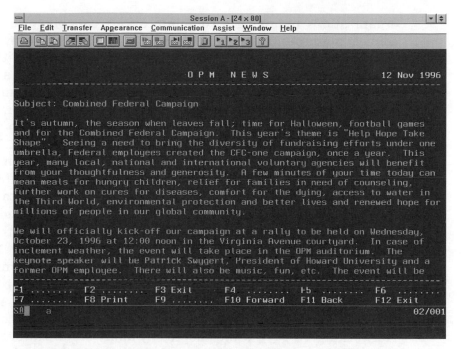

FIGURE 1.3   Viewing a news file maintained on a mainframe computer.

developed for use in the IBM 3270 network infrastructure have the ability to store screens and compare portions of new screens with previously transmitted screens, sending only those portions of a screen that changed. This limited type of compression further enhances the ability of control units to support multiple interactive query-response terminal-to-mainframe transmission sessions, and allows more simultaneous activity from text-based applications to be supported.

SNA Networking

As the number of applications developed for use on mainframes increased, the ability of a single mainframe to support the computing requirements of an organization diminished. By the late 1960s and early 1970s, many organizations began to acquire multiple mainframe computers. This in turn resulted in such organizations requiring a communications capability to inter-connect mainframes as well as provide terminal users connected in a hierarchical network structure to one mainframe with the ability to access applications on other mainframes. IBM's solution to evolving networking requirements was its System Network Architecture, better known by the mnemonic SNA. SNA maintained the hierarchical terminal-to-control-unit-to-front-end processor structure previously illustrated in Figure 1.1, but added the capability for users in one mainframe-centric hierarchical network to access applications on another mainframe-centric hierarchical network. This capability required data to be routed between two mainframes even if two terminals simply required the ability to communicate with one another. Although IBM periodically revised SNA, it wasn't until the early 1990s that it added the ability for terminal devices that now primarily are personal computers to communicate with one another without requiring communications to be routed through mainframes. This capability, in the form of Advanced Peer-to-Peer Networking (APPN), while adopted by many organizations with large SNA networks, achieved only a limited acceptance as a mechanism for supporting the communications requirements of organizations since most organizations turned to other networking solutions.

Distributed Computing and Minicomputer Networks

Although we can paraphrase Mark Twain and note that reports of the death of the mainframe era are premature, the era of mainframe-centric networking began its gradual descent during the mid-1970s. Minicomputers, which first appeared in the commercial marketplace during the 1960s, began to be used to support distributed processing. Such processing was originally focused upon moving portions of key mainframe applications, such as payroll, accounts receivable, and accounts payable, to the regional and branch organization locations. Within a short period of time minicomputer manufacturers and third-party software developers introduced a variety of minicomputer-based software packages which included support for networking hardware, allowing clusters of terminals connected to minicomputers to access applications on the same or a distantly located minicomputer. In fact, one of the earliest local area networks, Ethernet, was developed based upon the connection of terminal devices to minicomputers and the interconnection of minicomputers via a coaxial-based LAN operating at 10 Mbps.

Network Utilization

Transmission of data on mainframe and distributed minicomputer networks established during the late 1970s through the mid-1980s was similar with respect to the type of traffic transported even though there were key differences in their topology or network structure. Although minicomputers were used to develop mesh-structured packet networks to provide economical communications between remote users and mainframes, the traffic transported over such networks was primarily text based. In addition, the use of electronic mail and the growth of information utilities, such as CompuServe and (the now-defunct) The Source, whose access was primarily accomplished via minicomputer-based packet networks, were also primarily for text-based applications. Thus, the use of interactive terminals and the advent of personal computers using 300-, 1200-, and 2400-bps modems was usually sufficient for most applications developed during the late 1970s through the mid-1980s.

Personal Computing and LANs

Although the first PC in the form of a kit reached the market during the 1970s, it wasn't until 1981 when IBM introduced its PC and the following year when the hard drive–based IBM PC XT reached the market that personal computing was accepted as a business tool. With the introduction of word processing, electronic spreadsheets, and database management software for use on PCs, distributed processing finally arrived on the desktop. Accompanying the introduction of PCs into the business community was the requirement to share data between PCs as well as PCs and the corporate mainframe or minicomputer. Initially this requirement was satisfied by emulation cards installed in PCs along with software which turned the personal computer into a specific type of terminal supported by the mainframe or minicomputer. Then, PC users would share data through a connection between each PC and the mainframe or minicomputer, using the mainframe or minicomputer as a temporary storage facility. Through the mid-to-late 1980s it was common to see PCs with coaxial cables which were routed into ceilings and then disappeared on their way to a connection with a control unit hidden in a closet.

While mainframes and minicomputers filled a need for connectivity, they were only suitable for medium to large organizations. In addition, since the PC was extremely affordable, a significant amount of program development work began to occur on personal computers as business, financial, personnel, and other types of software were developed. Ethernet, which was initially developed before the personal computer, found a major market in the ability to network PCs together. During the late 1980s continuing through the 1990s, several versions of Ethernet were standardized whose use satisfied tens of millions of PC users. Although Ethernet satisfies the local area networking requirements of a large number of organizations, access to an Ethernet LAN is not predictable. This is due to the Carrier Sense Multiple Access with Collision Detection (CSMA/CD) protocol scheme used to gain access to an Ethernet network, and whose operation will be described later in this section. Recognizing the need for greater access predictability, IBM developed a token-passing-based LAN. This LAN, in which the token rotates around a ring, is (as you would expect) referred to as a Token-Ring LAN. Both Ethernet and Token-Ring LANs are shared-bandwidth networks, a technology that warrants a degree of investigation to obtain an appreciation for the role of switches and their effect upon network performance.

Shared-Bandwidth LANs

Accompanying the growth in personal computing was a recognition that the networking of PCs was required to provide a mechanism for data sharing. This recognition resulted in the development of network operating systems and client/server technology which supported the use of Ethernet and Token Ring networks.

Ethernet. The original Ethernet network structure was based upon the use of coaxial cable. Workstations are attached to a common coaxial cable via the use of a transmitter-receiver (transceiver) connected to the cable at one end and cabled to a network adapter installed in a computer. Since coaxial cable is relatively bulky, not exactly easy to install, and difficult to place under carpeting, further developments resulted in what is now referred to as 10BASE-T, a 10-Mbps Ethernet networking technology based upon the use of twisted-pair wiring. Both the earlier coaxial cable–based Ethernet and the more modern twisted-pair version (in which stations attach to hubs) operate at 10 Mbps using the CSMA/CS technology.

Under the CSMA/CD access protocol, a station that has data to transmit first listens to determine if there is activity on the network. If no activity is heard, the station assumes it is safe to transmit and does so. If another station with data to transmit also listens to the network at the same time, it also assumes there is no activity and begins to transmit, resulting in the occurrence of a collision.

When a collision occurs on a CSMA/CD network, the voltage level doubles, providing a mechanism for stations to detect its occurrence. When a collision is detected, the transmitting station will cease the transmission of data and initiate the transmission of a jam pattern. The jam pattern, consisting of 32 to 48 bits, is placed on the network to ensure that the collision lasts long enough to be detected by all stations on the network. Figure 1.4 illustrates the Ethernet collision detection process.

Once a collision is detected, the transmitting station waits a random number of slot times before attempting to retransmit. The term *slot* represents 512 bits on a 10-Mbps network, or a minimum frame length of 64 bytes. The actual number of slot times the station waits is selected by a randomization process, formerly known as a truncated binary exponential backoff. Under this randomization process, a randomly selected integer r defines the number of slot times the station waits before listening to

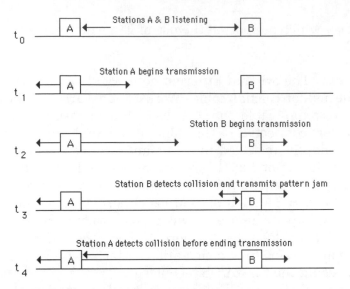

FIGURE 1.4 Collision detection.

determine whether the channel is clear. If it is, the station begins to retransmit the frame, while listening for another collision.

If the station transmits the complete frame successfully and has additional data to transmit, it will again listen to the channel as it prepares another frame for transmission. If a collision occurs on a retransmission attempt, a slightly different procedure is followed. After a jam signal is transmitted, the station simply doubles the previously generated random number and then waits the prescribed number of slot intervals prior to attempting a retransmission. Up to 16 retransmission attempts can occur before the station aborts the transmission and declares the occurrence of a multiple collision error condition.

The previously described CSMA/CD access protocol, which utilizes the mechanism whereby stations initiate a random delay after a collision prior to retransmitting, reduces the probability of a subsequent collision occurring from the next sequence of workstation transmissions. However, the CSMA/CD access protocol also restricts transmission from source to destination to one originating device at a time. Thus, the bandwidth is shared among a group of stations connected to the network.

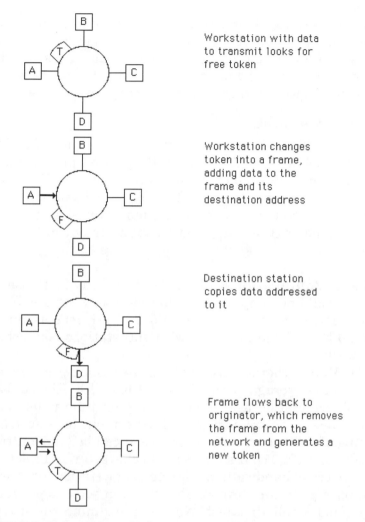

Workstation with data
to transmit looks for
free token

Workstation changes
token into a frame,
adding data to the
frame and its
destination address

Destination station
copies data addressed
to it

Frame flows back to
originator, which removes
the frame from the
network and generates a
new token

FIGURE 1.5 Token-Ring operation.

Token Ring. In a Token-Ring network a token circles the ring until a station that has data to transmit acquires it, converting the free token into a frame. Figure 1.5 illustrates the general operation of a Token-Ring network. In examining Figure 1.5 note that at any time only one token or one frame can be circulating the network. Thus, similar to Ethernet, a Token-Ring network represents a shared-bandwidth or shared-media LAN to which network users contend for access. Now that we have an appreciation for the term "shared bandwidth" or "shared media," let's examine the evolution of applications data transported on shared-media networks and their effect upon the average bandwidth available to Ethernet and Token-Ring network users.

The Effect of Multimedia

Through the 1980s and into the early 1990s, the use of 10-Mbps Ethernet and 4- and 16-Mbps Token-Ring LANs provided a reasonable level of performance for most organizations. There were many reasons for this acceptable level of performance; however, the primary reason was the continuation of text-based applications as the major type of application supported by most organizations.

Text-based Applications.   To understand why text-based applications could be supported on shared-bandwidth LANs, let's perform some elementary computations. First, let's assume we have a 10-Mbps Ethernet LAN with 100 stations connected to the network.

A 10-Mbps Ethernet LAN with 100 stations provides each station, on the average, with 10 Mbps/100 or 100 Kbps of bandwidth. If each station user is performing an interactive query-response operation requiring a full screen of information consisting of 1920 characters, that screen can be transmitted or received using 1920 characters × 8 bits/character or 15,360 bits. With an average bandwidth of 100 Kbps per station, each workstation user could flip through almost seven screens per second if they could scroll that fast. Now let's examine the use of a shared-bandwidth LAN for conventional e-mail operations, assuming a Token-Ring LAN with 200 stations is used.

On a 16-Mbps Token-Ring LAN with 200 users the average bandwidth per user becomes 16 Mbps/200 or 80 Kbps. Assuming the average length of a text-based e-mail message is 5000 characters, each station user could send and receive two messages per second, which is beyond their capability to read and absorb the contents of. If we look at the capacity of the total LAN, a 16-Mbps Token-Ring LAN could transport 16 Mbps/(5000 characters/message × 8 bits/character) or 400 messages per second.

Multimedia Applications.   Beginning in the late 1980s and gaining momentum through the early 1990s was the emergence of a variety of multimedia applications. Multimedia can be considered to represent the merging of text, audio, and video, with video ranging from a single image to frames of images that provide motion. A multimedia application can include any two or all three types of information. Today, the most common multimedia application is the use of browsers to connect to the World Wide Web servers. To illustrate the effect of multimedia upon shared-bandwidth LANs, let's examine a typical sequence of browser operations.

Figure 1.6 illustrates the use of the Netscape browser to access an online auction of computer equipment. In examining Figure 1.6, note the use of a series of images in the form of a large rectangular notice that informs Web surfers of the name of

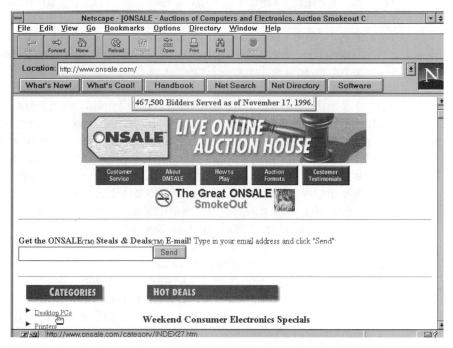

FIGURE 1.6   Viewing the World Wide Web home page of the ONSALE auction house.

the organization (ONSALE) and its business (Live Online Auction House), and a series of smaller rectangular images labeled "Customer Service," "About ONSALE," "How to Pay," and so on. Concerning those rectangular images, each image is linked to a Uniform Resource Locator (URL) which enables a user to click on the image and invoke a hyperlink to a Web document previously associated with the hyperlink. Although there is a minimal amount of text displayed in Figure 1.6, we would be severely mistaken if we assumed that that portion of the Web page shown through Netscape's viewing area represents less than the 1920 characters associated with a full screen of text. The reason we would be mistaken is due to the fact that each image can require more characters to be transmitted from the Web server accessed to the computer the browser is operating on than the number of characters required to fill a screen. To illustrate this let's examine a portion of the composition of the screen display illustrated in Figure 1.6. In addition, let's also discuss the HyperText Transmission Protocol (HTTP) to obtain an appreciation for another problem associated with the use of images on Web servers.

From the Netscape browser view menu you can select the source entry to display the HyperText Markup Language (HTML) statements used to generate the Web page you are viewing. Figure 1.7 illustrates the source coding used to generate the ONSALE home page previously displayed in Figure 1.6. In examining the statements contained in Figure 1.7 you will note the statement beginning <IMG SRC= "/newgif/onsale.gif" that starts approximately halfway down the screen. That statement is followed by a series of five statements that begin <A HREF=. The first line just referenced results in the transmission of the large rectangular image shown at the top of Figure 1.6, while the series of five statements that begin <A HREF= results in the transmission of five smaller rectangular-shaped images that are displayed under the larger rectangular image shown in Figure 1.6. Each of the images is stored on the Web server as a GIF file, which is ascertained from the extension .gif listed in Figure 1.7 for each image. Thus, approximately the top one-third of the Web page shown in Figure 1.6 represents the transmission of six GIF images from the Web server to the browser. This sequence of

```
┌────────────────────────────────────────────────────────────────────────┐
│═                    Netscape - [Source of: http://www.onsale.com/]    ▼ ♦│
│                                                                         ▲│
│ <HTML>                                                                   │
│ <HEAD>                                                                   │
│ <TITLE>ONSALE - Auctions of Computers and Electronics. Auction Smokeout Compaq.</TITLE>│
│ </HEAD>                                                                  │
│ <BODY BGCOLOR="#ffffff"><center>                                         │
│ <table border="3">                                                       │
│     <tr>                                                                  │
│         <td align="center" bgcolor="#COCOCO"><font                       │
│                                                                          │
│         color="#400080"><strong>467,500 Bidders Served as of             │
│         November 17, 1996.</strong></font></td>                          │
│     </tr>                                                                 │
│ </table>                                                                 │
│                                                                          │
│ <IMG SRC="/newgif/!onsale_.gif" border=3 ALIGN="BOTTOM"><br>             │
│ <A HREF="/cgi-bin/remap.cgi?https:/custserv.htm"><IMG SRC="/newgif/Service.gif" ALIGN="TOP" ALT =│
│ <A HREF="about.htm"><IMG SRC="/newgif/b_about.gif" ALIGN="TOP" ALT = "About ONSALE"></A>│
│ <A HREF="howto.htm"><IMG SRC="/newgif/b_howto.gif" ALIGN="TOP" ALT = "How To Bid or Buy"></A>│
│ <A HREF="format.htm"><IMG SRC="/newgif/b_format.gif" ALIGN="TOP" ALT = "Auction Formats"></A>│
│ <A HREF="testimon.htm"><IMG SRC="/newgif/!testimo.gif" ALIGN="TOP" ALT = "Testimonials"></A>│
│                                                                          │
│ </center>                                                                │
│ <CENTER><A HREF="/BLOOD/GREAT5.HTM"><IMG SRC="/BLOOD/SMOKEHP.GIF"></A></CENTER>│
│ <HR>                                                                     │
│ <FORM METHOD="POST" ACTION="/cgi-win/Register.exe">                      │
│ <strong>Get the ONSALE<font size =-2>(TM)</font> Steals & Deals<font size =-2>(TM)</font> E-mail!│
│ <hr>                                                                     │
│                                                                          │
│ <TABLE>                    <! start the table>                           │
│ <TR valign=top>            <! define the first - and only   row.>        │
│ <TD>                       <! This begins the data for the first column - it contains a title gif a│
│                                                                          │
│ <img src="newgif/!categor.gif" align="absmiddle" Alt="Categories"> <! The BRs space down a bit>│
│                                                                          │
│◄│                                                                     │►│
└────────────────────────────────────────────────────────────────────────┘
```

FIGURE 1.7 Viewing the source code used to generate the Web page shown in Figure 1.6.

transmissions represents two distinct problems that adversely affect client/server operations—multiple sessions and traffic.

Multiple-Session Problems. HTTP can be considered to represent a start-stop protocol. That is, after a client transmits a request the HTTP protocol treats text and each graphic on a requested page as a separate entity. Thus, the six graphics at the top of Figure 1.6 would require six separate HTTP sessions as well as synchronization between client and server. Since one HTTP session terminates prior to another one beginning, there are delays between the termination of one session and the beginning of the next. If you have a corporate intranet with many Web browsers accessing a help desk Web server, the use of a large number of images on each Web page will result in additional Ethernet or Token-Ring frames being transmitted to carry synchronization data as well as the contents of each image. This in turn will result in an increase in network traffic that can adversely affect the ability of other network users to access the Web server or perform other network activity. Now that we have an appreciation for the problems resulting from multiple sessions resulting from multiple images on a Web page, let's probe a bit deeper and examine traffic problems caused by the use of images.

Traffic Problems. There are two areas where the use of images commonly results in network traffic problems. The first, which many people are quite familiar with from personal experience, is associated with the use of World Wide Web browsers. A second area, which may not be as noticeable but whose effect on network performance can also be significant, results from e-mail attachments. In this section we will examine both areas to obtain an appreciation for how multimedia can affect our network.

Browsers: If you are familiar with the use of a browser you may remember a little trick you can use to note the dimensions

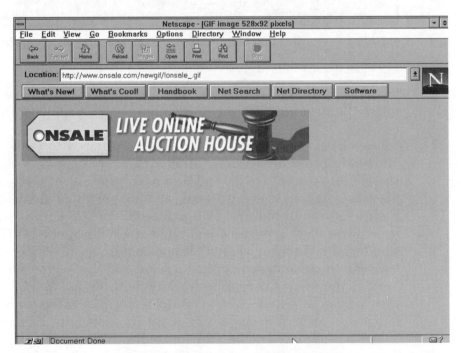

FIGURE 1.8 Using the Web browser to display the dimensions of the large rectangular image shown at the top of Figure 1.6.

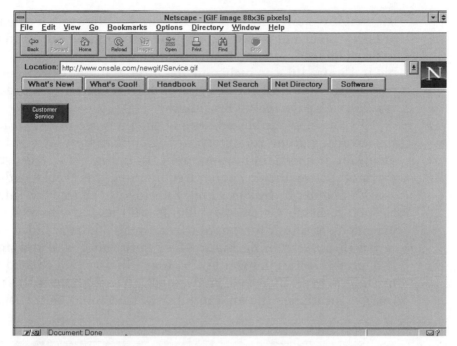

FIGURE 1.9 Using the Web browser to display the dimensions of one of the smaller rectangular images on the ONSALE Web home page.

of an image. By moving the cursor over an image and clicking on the right mouse button, you obtain the ability to display an image by itself. When you do so the browser will also display the size of the selected image in pixels.

Figures 1.8 and 1.9 illustrate the effect of the previously described operation to display the large rectangular image at the top of Figure 1.6 and the first smaller rectangular-shaped image under the larger image. In examining Figure 1.8, note that the dimension of the large rectangular image is 528 by 92 pixels, representing a total of 48,576 pixels or 6,072 (48576/8) bytes, without considering the effect of the color depth of the pixels or the effect of Lempel Ziv Welch (LZW) compression used by the GIF image file format. Since the color depth of a GIF image is 8 bits/pixel, without considering the effect of LZW compression the display of the image would require the transmission of 48,576 bytes from the server to the browser. Similarly, the small rectangular image illustrated in Figure 1.9 consisting of 88 by 36 pixels would require the transmission of 3168 bytes to be displayed. Although only a portion of the Web page is visible in Figure 1.6, the inclusion of a large number of graphics can easily grow the number of bytes of data required to represent a typical Web page to 100 K or more.

To continue our observation of the increase in network traffic resulting from relatively new applications, let's turn our attention to another browser application. Figure 1.10 illustrates a typical screen display generated by the Lycos World Wide Web search engine. In this example I decided to search for information on a popular movie of 1996 as well as the name of a past president of Argentina popularized by an Andrew Lloyd Weber musical. In examining Figure 1.10 note the use of graphics in the form of rectangles containing text which, when clicked upon, initiate a hyperlink to a predefined URL. Although the use of images multiplies the amount of data that must be transmitted

FIGURE 1.10 Using the Lycos World Wide Web to search for pictures of Evita.

to display a screen of data, the use of images represents a fact of life resulting from the evolution of computing to the use of GUI interfaces. This becomes more apparent when you note the label of rectangular image number 3 in Figure 1.10, which allows you to search the Web for images, further increasing the amount of traffic networks are handling. To illustrate this method of searching, let's click on the second search item provided by the Lycos search engine.

Figure 1.11 illustrates the picture of "Young Evita in Buenos Aires" stored on a Web server at the University of Michigan. Note that the browser tells us that the image is stored in JPEG format and its dimensions are 410 by 394 pixels. Since JPEG uses three bytes per pixel for color depth, without considering the effect of the compression technique used by JPEG-based images, the display of the photograph of young Evita would require the transmission of $410 \times 394 \times 24/8$ or 484620 bytes.

FIGURE 1.11 Viewing a digitized picture of young Evita in Buenos Aires that was stored on a server located at the University of Michigan.

Even though JPEG compression is very effective, as your network users begin to flip through screens requiring the transmission of 100 Kbytes of data or more, the effect of such operations on shared-bandwidth networks becomes very pronounced.

E-mail: Until the early 1990s most e-mail applications were text based and very rarely were documents attached to a message. Today most e-mail applications are GUI based and permit the attachment of various types of files. Figure 1.12 illustrates the use of Novell's GroupWise e-mail system to attach a large document to a relatively short message. If the 235-page attached document contains images, the resulting file can easily represent several Mbytes of traffic. Now that we have an appreciation for the traffic being generated by modern computer applications, let's examine their effect upon shared-bandwidth networks.

Network Operation.   The conversion of data, whether in the form of files or typewritten queries for transport by a local area network, requires information to be placed in a predefined location

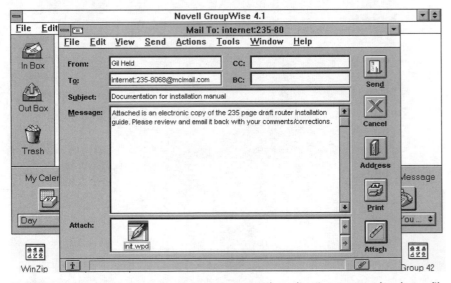

FIGURE 1.12   Using Novell's GroupWise e-mail application to attach a large file to a relatively short message.

in the LAN frame. On an Ethernet network the maximum length of the information field used to transport data in a frame is 1500 bytes. For Token-Ring networks the maximum length of the information field depends upon the operating rate of the LAN as well as the setting of the control field within the optional *routing information field* (RIF) when bridges are used. On a 4-Mbps Token-Ring network, the maximum information field length is 4500 bytes, while on a 16-Mbps Token-Ring network the maximum length of the information field within a frame is extended to 18000 bytes. Both of those numbers are substantially reduced when a Token-Ring network is transparently bridged to an Ethernet LAN. Since the maximum length of the information field on an Ethernet LAN is 1500 bytes, when transparent bridging is used each Token-Ring workstation must be configured to allow a maximum of 1500 bytes in its information field. Otherwise, bridging would result in the loss of data when the information field of a Token-Ring frame exceeds 1500 bytes as there is no mechanism at the bridging layer of operations to fragment the information field.

In addition to the constraint associated with the length of a frame's information field, there are additional constraints that govern the maximum data transfer capability on a LAN. For example, on an Ethernet LAN there is a 9.6-ms gap between frames. In addition, each frame contains a degree of overhead in the form of fields containing the source and destination addresses of the frame, its type, and a frame check field which holds a four-byte cyclic redundancy character computed to permit an integrity check of the data carried in the frame. Based upon those constraints, a 10-Mbps Ethernet LAN can support the transmission of a maximum of 812 maximum-length frames per second, with each frame containing a 1500-byte Information field.

To illustrate the effect of large file transfers in the form of images, audio recording, or even e-mail attachments, let's examine the operation of a typical Ethernet LAN. Figure 1.13 denotes a conventional hub-based 10BASE-T Ethernet network consisting of several hubs interconnected to one another. In this example workstation 1 is in the process of transmitting a request to a server located on a different hub. Hub A receives

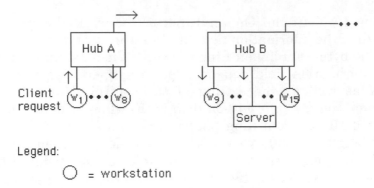

Legend:

◯ = workstation

FIGURE 1.13   How network bottlenecks occur.

the frame containing the request and broadcasts it to every port other than the originating port, since a hub can be considered to represent a repeater. Hub B receives the frame and performs a similar action, broadcasting the frame onto all ports other than the port it was received on. As each hub broadcasts the frame originated from workstation 1, the other stations and the server are barred from placing traffic on the network. Assuming a few network users are working with image-based applications, sending e-mail with large files attached, or performing other applications that require the use of the server, network bottlenecks will occur. The primary cause of those bottlenecks is the fact that the servers must contend for access to the network with the workstations. Since the maximum number of maximum-length frames that can be transmitted on a 10BASE-T network is fixed at 812, as additional workstations initiate activity that requires server action, queues begin building in the server. For example, assume one workstation user working on a personnel database clicks on the name of an employee to retrieve a screen display of information that includes a photograph of the employee. At nearly the same time a second workstation user initiates an e-mail with an attached 5-Mbyte document, while a fraction of a second later a third network user initiates a short query to a server-based application. If the response to the personnel database query requires the transmission of 200 Kbytes, the server will have to pack the response into 133 frames (200K/1500). As the server begins transmission of the first few frames, it receives the request for the e-mail transfer and begins to place the e-mail and its attached 5-Mbyte file in the computer's output queue. This action will result in the server having to place a minimum of 3334 maximum-length frames on the network. Thus, the server will have to transmit a total of 3467 frames. If no other activity occurs on the network, a total of 3467/812, or 4.3 seconds, would be required until the server could respond to the next client/server request. Of course, it is highly doubtful that no other activity is occurring on the network. Thus, the response to the third query could take a minimum of slightly more than 4.3 seconds and could take significantly longer. As response time increases, users may get frustrated and initiate another query, adding to the traffic load on the network. In addition, the absence of a response to a query after a predefined period of time can result in a query timeout, causing the workstation user to re-initiate his or her query. Now that we have an appreciation for the reasons why shared-bandwidth networks may not be able to handle modern applications, let's turn our attention to modern networking trends and the role of local area network switches.

MODERN NETWORKING TRENDS

Over the past few years there have been two pronounced trends in local area networking—upgrading to faster LAN technologies and the use of LAN switches. As we will shortly note, both technologies can be used together, and in one case have been merged in the form of Asynchronous Transfer Mode (ATM).

Faster Networks

Today network managers and administrators have a significant choice in selecting a higher-speed LAN. You can consider two 100-Mbps variants of Ethernet, referred to as 100BASE-T and 100VG-anyLAN, the 100-Mbps fiber optic–based Fiber Data Distributed Interface (FDDI), or ATM, which can operate at either 25 or 155 Mbps.

Advantages and Disadvantages of Use

The primary advantage associated with the use of a 100-Mbps network is its increased bandwidth, multiplying the capacity of a 10-Mbps Ethernet LAN by a factor of 10 and a 16-Mbps Token-Ring LAN by a factor of 6.25. Although the additional capacity may be sufficient for many network applications, there are several problems you must consider that are associated with their use. Those problems include the necessity to change network adapter cards, hubs, and possibly network cabling if you already have an older network in place. Even if you are considering the installation of a new 100-Mbps network, those networks still represent shared-bandwidth LANs; therefore, only one frame at a time can flow on the network. Thus, although the use of faster LAN technology may be an acceptable solution to the requirements of many organizations, if network traffic increases due to additional users, additional applications, or a mixture of the two, the use of LAN switches deserves consideration as a supplement to a current infrastructure or as a complement to the migration to a higher-speed infrastructure.

LAN Switches

While LAN switches represent relatively recent communications product offerings that are only a few years old, the actual concept the technology is based upon was developed during the early 1900s. At that time telephone companies developed electromagnetic switches which allowed a central office serving a large number of local subscribers to route locally generated calls onto long distance trunks as well as to receive long distance calls and route those calls to local subscribers. By examining the operation of telephone company switches developed during the 1920s, we can appreciate the advantages associated with modern LAN switches. Let's return to the era of the flapper for a few moments and examine how telephone company switches operate.

Telephone Switch Operations. Figure 1.14 illustrates the use of two central office switches to provide subscribers with the ability to directly call other local subscribers or to contend for access to trunk lines that interconnect telephone company offices. In the example illustrated in Figure 1.14, at city A telephone subscriber 1 is assumed to have dialed subscriber 3 in the local exchange. The switch would note the lack of an area code to determine that it is a local call. Then, by examining the three-digit prefix of the dialed number the switch would note if the dialed number is served by that switch. If so, the switch would route the call to the line associated with the four digits following the three-digit prefix. Thus, by examining the dialed number the switch in city A knows to cross-connect subscriber 1 to subscriber 3, and the dialed number results in the telephone ringing at subscriber 3's location.

If an area code was included in the dialed number or the prefix does not match those supported by the local switch, that switch knows the call must be routed to another switch. The local switch would then examine routing information previously stored in the device to determine the trunk onto which to place the call. In the example illustrated in Figure 1.14, subscriber 2 in city A is shown being routed through the switch in city B to subscriber 1 in city B. At that city the switch examines incoming calls received on trunk lines and routes those calls onto other lines, such as the routing of the call from subscriber 2 in city A to

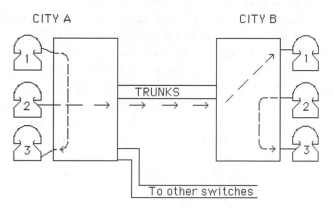

FIGURE 1.14 Using the central office switches to connect telephone subscribers. The LAN switch can be considered as a modern incarnation of the central office telephone switch.

subscriber 1 in city B. The switch in city B also allows calls with an exchange number associated with local subscribers to be routed through the switch from one subscriber to another in the local calling area. This is indicated by subscriber 2 shown connected to subscriber 3 in city B.

Operational Advantages. If we consider the operation of the telephone switch we can note several advantages associated with its use. First, note that several cross connections can be performed simultaneously, enhancing the ability of switches to support subscribers. Second, note that only those calls destined for a different telephone number prefix are placed onto a trunk line. This means that switches can be interconnected to service a wider area as long as the switches operate in a similar manner. Now that we have an appreciation for the operation of telephone switches, let's focus our attention on the more modern LAN switch.

LAN Switch Operations. If we replace the telephone subscribers shown in Figure 1.14 with ports that connect to LANs or individual LAN workstations, we can develop a more modern networking infrastructure based on LAN switches. Figure 1.15 illustrates an example of a LAN switch-based network showing the interconnection of two LAN switches, with each switch supporting several Ethernet network segments as well as individual workstations. In examining switch A, note that it has 5 ports, with port 1 connected to an Ethernet segment containing its own server. Ports 2 and 3 support individual workstations, while port 4 supports the direct connection of a server operating at 100 Mbps and port 5 provides an interswitch connection to port 5 on switch B. Concerning that switch, ports 1 and 4 support directly connected workstations, port 2 supports a directly connected server operating at 100 Mbps, and port 3 supports the connection of a network segment with its own server.

Assuming each port, with the exception of port 4, operates at 10 Mbps, let's examine the network activities that are occurring on the network formed through the use of two LAN

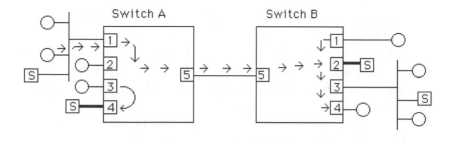

Legend:

○ = workstation

○ = segment with workstation

S = server

n = port n

—S = server connected at 100 Mbps

FIGURE 1.15 Creating a networking infrastructure based upon the use of LAN switches.

switches and the total bandwidth of activity occurring on the network. A workstation on the Ethernet segment connected to port 1 on switch A is shown being routed through the switch, output on port 5, and received by switch B and routed to port 2. Another connection on switch A allows a directly connected workstation connected to port 3 to be cross-connected to port 4, providing that workstation with access to the server. Although the server can transmit and receive data at 100 Mbps, since it is being accessed by a workstation operating at 10 Mbps the switch will act as a speed converter between ports operating at different data rates. When the workstation on port 3 transmits to the switch on port 4, the switch outputs data faster than it was received. When the server responds to the query at 100 Mbps, it is able to rapidly output its response into a buffer which is used by the switch for transmitting data to the workstation at 10 Mbps. However, since the server can complete its network responses at 100 Mbps, it becomes available to service another query faster than if it was connected to the switch at 10 Mbps. Based upon the preceding, switch A can be considered to be supporting two simultaneous cross-connections at 10 Mbps, doubling the bandwidth in comparison to providing the two individual workstations and servers on one network segment.

Turning our attention to switch B, we note the incoming connection from switch A that is routed to the server on port 2 on the switch. Since the server is connected to the switch via a 100-Mbps connection, it will also be able to respond quickly to queries and become available for responding to additional queries quicker than if the server was connected at 10 Mbps. In addition, the workstation connected to port 1 on switch B is shown connected to the workstation on port 4. Although there is no activity on port 3, note that a connection could be in progress between a workstation and server on the segment connected to port 3 on switch B. Thus, in addition to supporting 20 Mbps associated with two simultaneous cross-connections through switch B, that switch also allows activity local to a segment to occur without affecting the operation of the switch.

Based on the operations in progress on the two-switch network illustrated in Figure 1.15, we can note several direct advantages associated with the use of LAN switches. First, their use expands available bandwidth as switches support multiple simultaneous cross-connections. Second, existing network segments or individual workstations can be directly connected to switch ports without having to scrap a previously developed infrastructure. Third, and most important to many organizations, the use of LAN switches provides a migration path to newer technologies. This was illustrated by connecting a server to each switch at 100 Mbps, allowing each switch to respond fast to network requests, which enables a subsequent request to be responded to more quickly than if the server was connected at 10 Mbps. Thus, the LAN switch represents a relatively new tool for use by network managers and administrators to fix congestion caused by graphics—intensive applications, additional network users, or a combination of increased applications and an increase in network users. This tool enables you to break the shared-bandwidth barrier of conventional LANs as well as use network segments with limited traffic growth as is. In addition, by supporting high-speed ports most LAN switches provide a migration path from low-speed 10BASE-T and Token-Ring networks to high-speed Ethernet and ATM without requiring the replacement of an existing infrastructure. Due to this capability the general category of LAN switches has evolved in a few years to a multi-billion-dollar market. Although from a conceptual basis the LAN switch is indeed a formidable tool, similar to any communications device its features and operational capability must be carefully analyzed to ensure you obtain an appropriate product that will satisfy your organization's networking requirements—topics we will explore in subsequent chapters as well as examining specific types of LAN switches.

2

Switching Basics

Switches designed for use on local area networks have a wide range of functions, features, and capabilities. Although we will examine the operation and utilization of various types of switches in subsequent chapters, it is important to obtain an appreciation for their basic functions and features prior to examining specific types of products that may be designed to support a particular type of local area network or the integration of two or more specific types of networks. Thus, the purpose of this chapter is to provide you with detailed information concerning the general operation of LAN switches, including their basic functions and features. Although a description of certain features requires the reference of a particular type of LAN switch, most of this chapter will focus on generic switch features, with references to a particular type of local area network switch or switching module occurring only when necessary. Since the basic operation of switches as well as many constraints associated with their use are highly related to the bridge, which we can consider as its predecessor, in the first section of this chapter we will focus our attention upon the operation of transparent and translating bridges. Once this is accomplished, we will turn our attention to examining the general operational characteristics of LAN switches.

BRIDGE OPERATIONS

As noted in the first chapter in this book, intelligent switching hubs represent an evolution of communications technology dating back to early telephone technology. Similarly, bridges represent an evolution of telephone switching technology. However, bridges can also be considered to represent an elementary type of switch due to their limited number of ports and simplistic switching operation. That switching operation is normally based upon whether the destination address in a frame "read" on one port is known to reside on that port or on another port.

Bridges operate at the data link layer of the International Standards Organization (ISO) Open System Interconnection (OSI) Reference Model. That layer is bound by the network layer above and the physical layer below, and was subdivided by the Institute of Electrical and Electronic Engineers (IEEE) into logical link control (LLC) and media access control (MAC) sublayers as illustrated in Figure 2.1. The logical link control sublayer provides a link between network layer protocols and media access control, while the media access control sublayer is responsible for controlling access to the network. When a host has data to transmit, information flows down a protocol stack from an application layer at the top of the OSI Reference Model. Such information may be subdivided into multiple frames based on the number of characters to be transmitted and the maximum length of the information field in the frame. A prefix and suffix is added to each frame prior to its placement on the media, with the prefix containing the destination address of the frame, the address of the station transmitting the frame (which is referred to as the source address), and other information that can vary based upon the type of LAN. The suffix contains a *cyclic redundancy check* (CRC) which is used as a mechanism to verify the integrity of the contents of the frame and may contain

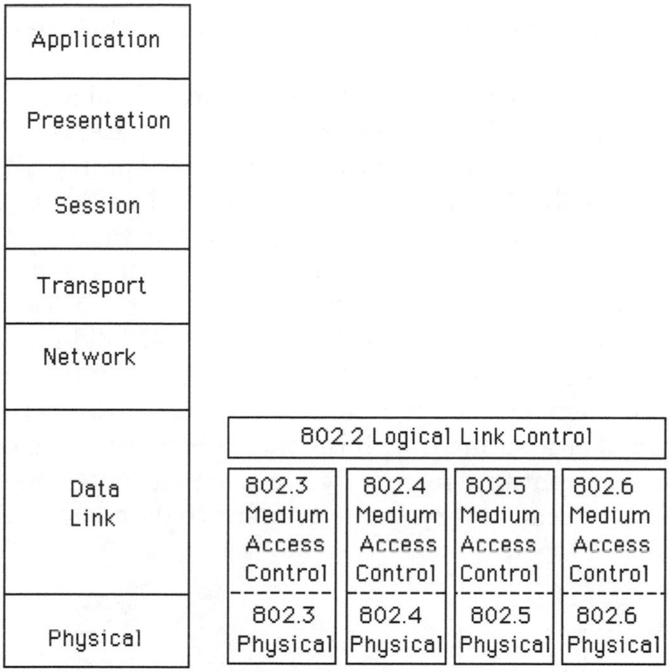

| Application |
| Presentation |
| Session |
| Transport |
| Network |
| Data
Link |
| Physical |

802.2 Logical Link Control			
802.3 Medium Access Control	802.4 Medium Access Control	802.5 Medium Access Control	802.6 Medium Access Control
802.3 Physical	802.4 Physical	802.5 Physical	802.6 Physical

FIGURE 2.1 Bridges operate at the data link layer of the OSI Reference Model. That layer was subdivided by the IEEE into logical link control and medium access control sublayers.

one or more additional fields, again depending upon the type of LAN. To illustrate how bridges operate, we will restrict our examination of the contents of frames to their source and destination addresses.

Transparent Bridges

The first type of bridge we will examine is referred to as a transparent bridge. This is the most basic type of bridge and, as its name implies, its use is transparent to the networks it connects. That is, a transparent bridge is a plug-and-play device that does not require the setup or configuration of any hardware or software. You just plug cables from each transparent bridge port into an appropriate network connector and the bridge operates or "plays."

To illustrate the operation of a transparent bridge requires at least two networks. Let's create several simple LANs so we can examine how a transparent bridge operates. The top portion of Figure 2.2 illustrates the use of a transparent bridge to connect workstations on two LANs. For simplicity we will assume that source addresses of stations on each LAN are represented by the letter contained in the squares attached to each network. In actuality source addresses are contained in a 48-bit field represented by 12 hex characters, of which the first 6 represent the manufacturer of the network adapter card, while the last 6 represent a unique number associated with the manufacturer of the card.

A transparent bridge operates in promiscuous mode, which means that it reads every frame transmitted on each LAN it is

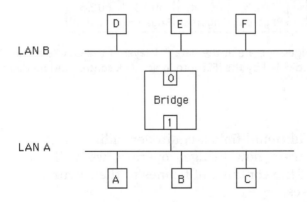

Steady State Port Address Table

Port	Address
0	D
0	E
0	F
1	A
1	B
1	C

FIGURE 2.2 Using a transparent bridge to connect two networks.

connected to. In the network example illustrated in Figure 2.2, a two-port bridge is shown connected to two LANs, with three stations shown connected to each network. Once the bridge is connected to each network and powered on, it examines each frame and either discards or forwards it. This decision is performed by the bridge using the destination address of the frame and comparing it to an address-port table it maintains. That table is constructed by the bridge noting the source address contained in each frame received on a port and using those addresses to construct the table. For example, assume a frame with source address A and destination address B is received on port 1. If this is the first frame received on port 1, the bridge enters address A into its address-port table. Since the frame is destined to address B, which is not in the table, the bridge at this point in time does not know where the destination resides. Thus, it "floods" the frame, a term used to reference its transmission onto all ports other than the port it was received on. Since the bridge in Figure 2.2 is a two-port bridge, this means that the frame is forwarded onto port 0 even though the destination resides on LAN A. However, the frame will not be received by any station on LAN B and its forwarding does not affect its transmission on LAN A. Thus, the forwarding operation has no adverse effect on the two networks other than using some bandwidth on LAN B that might otherwise be used more productively. Next, let's assume station B transmits a frame to station A. The bridge reads the frame on port 1 and stores the source address in the address-port table. Since address A is already in the address-port table, the bridge knows the frame is destined to a station on the LAN connected to port 1 and discards it.

Although the previously described sequence of operations can be used as a decision criteria for forwarding or discarding frames, address tables are constructed faster using a reverse learning process. Due to this, transparent bridges use a *backward learning algorithm*.

The Backward Learning Algorithm

Under the backward learning algorithm, a bridge examines the source address of frames flowing on each port to learn the addresses of destinations reachable on that port. Returning to Figure 2.2, eventually the bridge would associate source addresses D, E, and F to port 0 and A, B, and C to port 1. Then, by examining the destination address of each frame against the addresses stored in its port-address table, the bridge can determine whether to discard or forward the frame.

Frame Forwarding

There are two types of forwarding operations a bridge can perform—specific and flooding. A specific forwarding operation occurs when the bridge can match a destination against an entry in its port-address table. Then, the bridge can determine the specific port onto which it should forward a frame. In comparison, flooding represents the forwarding of a frame onto all ports other than the port the frame was received on. This action is performed by a bridge when it does not have an entry in its port-address table that matches the destination address contained in a frame. Since the destination address may not have been learned at this point in time, the bridge sends the frame to all possible locations via flooding.

To illustrate how a flooding operation can occur, consider Figure 2.3 in which a second bridge was added to the network previously illustrated in Figure 2.2. In this network expansion the second bridge is used to connect LANs C and D to LAN A, which in effect results in LANs C and D being linked to LAN B.

Suppose station D on LAN B transmits a frame to station G on LAN C. If station G did not previously transmit any frames to LAN A or LAN B, its address is known only to bridge 2. Thus, the port-address table in bridge 1 does not have an entry for address C. This means that bridge 1 forwards the frame onto port 1 where it is received by port 0 of bridge 2. If station G was active on port 1, bridge 2 would know to forward the frame onto port 1. However, if station G just powered up, bridge 2 would not have an entry in its port-address table. Thus, bridge 2 would then flood the frame, forwarding it onto both ports 1 and 2 which represent all connections other than the connection the frame was received on.

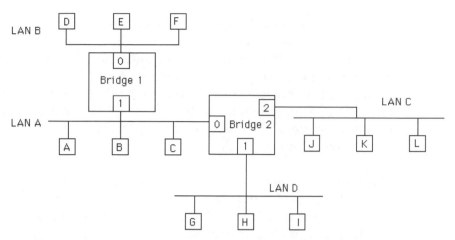

FIGURE 2.3 An expanded network using two bridges to interconnect four LANs.

Table Entry Considerations

As networks connected via bridges add workstations, this results in an expansion of the number of entries in their port-address tables. Although a variety of routines, such as storing entries in memory and using a hashing algorithm to perform matching or attempted matching of destination addresses against table entries, has significantly improved search time, as the number of entries increases so does the search time. This in turn can degrade bridge performance and even result in the dropping of frames if buffer areas in the bridge fill as it temporarily stores frames while performing a searching algorithm against its tables. Recognizing this problem, as well as the fact that a topology is dynamic and stations can be moved or powered on and off throughout the day, a bridge will include the current time with the entries in its port-address table. When a frame with a previously known destination is read the bridge updates only the time associated with the address. Thus, the bridge maintains a last-used time which is associated with each address stored in memory. Then, it periodically uses a timer to initiate a process which purges all entries older than a predefined time. This process enables port-address tables to shrink when users power off their stations or are not performing LAN-related activities. In addition, it allows the bridge to automatically adjust itself to adds, moves, and changes, which is why another name for this type of bridge is the *self-adjusting bridge*. However, this process also results in a bridge periodically having to flood frames when a station is simply quiet for a period of time and another station needs to send data to that station.

We can summarize the operation of a bridge as follows:

1. If the destination and source addresses are on the same LAN, discard the frame.
2. If the destination and source addresses are on different LANs, forward the frame.
3. If the destination location is not known, flood the frame.

Figure 2.4 summarizes the operation of a two-port bridge. Although a destination address that is unknown results in the bridge flooding the frame, in actuality a two-port bridge would simply forward the frame onto the port other than the port it was received on.

Loops

Although the use of bridges plays an important role in extending networks and enabling two or more segments to operate as an entity, they also represent a critical point of failure. Thus, to increase reliability, you would probably expect network managers and administrators to use two or more bridges in parallel to interconnect pairs of networks. Depending upon the type of networks being interconnected, the use of parallel bridges may or may not be possible. If transparent bridges are used, only one bridge out of two or more used in parallel can be operational at any point in time. The reason for this is to preclude the creation of closed loops, which could result in frames continuously circulating through interconnected LANs and which would literally consume their bandwidth. To illustrate this, consider Figure 2.5, which shows two LANs connected by a pair of parallel transparent bridges.

In examining Figure 2.5, let's assume station A generates an initial frame (A_1) at time t = 0. If this is the first frame trans-

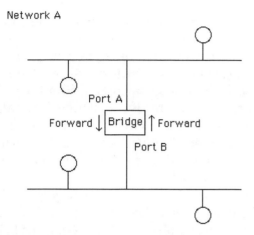

Network A

Port A

Forward ↓ Bridge ↑ Forward

Port B

Port A Operation

1. Read source address of frames on LAN B to construct a table of destination addresses.
2. Read destination address in frames and compare to addresses in port address table.
3. If destination address on same LAN, do nothing; if destination address in table, forward onto port B; if destination address unknown, flood the frame.

Port B Operation

1. Read source address of frames on LAN A to construct a table of destination address.
2. Read destination address in frames and compare to addresses in port address table.
3. If destination address on same LAN, do nothing; if destination address in table, forward onto port A; if destination address unknown, flood the frame.

FIGURE 2.4 Bridge switching operation.

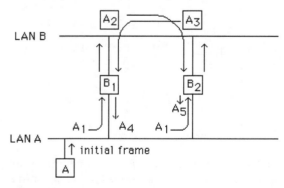

LAN B

A_2 A_3

B_1 B_2

A_5

A_1 A_4 A_1

LAN A

↑ initial frame

A

FIGURE 2.5 Active parallel transparent bridges would continuously copy frames between networks.

mitted and there are no entries in the port-address table, each bridge uses flooding, resulting in two initial frames, A_2 and A_3, being received on LAN B. Once frame A_3 is copied onto LAN B, bridge 1 sees it but does not know its destination. Thus, it copies the frame back onto LAN A, generating A_4. Similarly, A_2 generated by bridge 1 is received by bridge 2, which generates frame A_5. This cycle would continue, which, if frames represented money, would make bankers happy. Unfortunately, frames represent network activity and this repeated cycle of activity would not be appropriate for networks.

The solution to this problem is to allow only one bridge from multiple parallel bridges to be active and in a forwarding state at any point in time. To accomplish this, transparent bridges use a spanning tree algorithm and communicate information about their position in the tree using Bridge Protocol Data Units (BPDUs).

Through the use of the spanning tree algorithm, a unique path is logically defined between each interconnected network. Those paths preclude the use of closed loops, and any bridges in a network that would form a physically closed loop are then placed into a standby state. To illustrate the formation of a logical spanning tree upon a physical network topology, consider Figure 2.6, which illustrates six LANs interconnected via the use of six bridges. Note that bridges B, D, E, and F result in the formation of a closed loop. By breaking the loop by placing either bridge B, D, E, or F in a standby mode of operation, we can

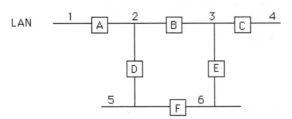

FIGURE 2.6 Interconnecting six LANs with six bridges. Four spanning trees are possible for this network configuration by placing either bridge B, D, E, or F into a standby mode of operation.

ensure there is a unique path between each LAN without the formation of a loop. Since either bridge B, D, E, or F could be made inactive to satisfy providing one path from every LAN to every other LAN, we need a methodology by which bridges can communicate with each other to enable them to decide which bridge or bridges must go into a standby mode of operation. Let's turn our attention to the method used by the spanning tree algorithm to construct a spanning tree without loops.

Constructing the Spanning Tree

As with any tree, a spanning tree has a root; however, it is used as a mechanism for paths to branch out instead of forming the kind of branches associated with natural trees. Thus, the initial process required to form a spanning tree is to identify the root.

When there are multiple bridges in a network one will have to be selected as the root bridge. Since each bridge has a unique serial number the bridges will use BPDUs to exchange serial numbers, with the lowest serial number associated with a bridge in the network resulting in the selection of that bridge as the root. Next, the shortest path from the root to each bridge and LAN in the internetwork is constructed to form the spanning tree. Since network topology can be altered due to the failure or addition of bridges, those devices periodically exchange BPDUs to update the spanning tree. Thus, the failure of an active bridge operating in parallel with a bridge previously placed in a standby mode of operation could result in the standby bridge being placed into a forwarding or active state the next time the spanning tree is constructed.

Source Routing Bridges

Source routing bridges use a scheme developed by IBM known as source routing to make forwarding decisions. Source routing is applicable only to Token-Ring LANs and is based upon the inclusion of an optional routing information field (RIF) in a Token-Ring frame.

Operation

Under source routing a station that does not know the path to the destination beyond its LAN transmits a discovery frame that can be considered an all-routes broadcast message. That message is transmitted on every path through the network, with each bridge inserting the ring number from the LAN the frame arrived on and its bridge number into a portion of the RIF. The first frame that arrives at the destination is transmitted back to the originating station with the contents of the RIF functioning as a path identifier.

The RIF, which will be described in more detail when we examine Token-Ring switches in Chapter 4, contains 2 bytes of control information and up to 16 bytes of routing information. Since 12 bits are used for the LAN identifier and 4 bits for the bridge identifier, a route can cross up to eight bridges.

Under source routing bridges examine the contents of the RIF to make forwarding decisions. Since the path is in the RIF, this means you can use source routing bridges to form loops without fear of the continuous circulation of frames since bridges operate on the contents of the RIF. In addition, Token-Ring LANs automatically purge a frame that circulates a ring more than once, a situation that would occur if, for example, a destination workstation was powered off before a frame sent to that station arrived.

Locating Process

In a Token-Ring network, the use of source routing bridges moves the locating process from bridges to hosts. In doing so source routing bridges require the network manager or administrator to configure the ring and bridge number for each port connection, a process which removes it from being a plug-and-play device. Now that we have a general overview of the operation of bridges, let's turn our attention to the basic operation of a highly related device—the LAN switch, also referred to as an *intelligent switching hub*.

THE INTELLIGENT SWITCHING HUB

As previously indicated, bridges were developed for use with shared-media LANs. Thus, the bandwidth constraints associated with shared-media networks are also associated with bridges. That is, a conventional bridge can route only one frame at a time received on one port onto one or more ports, with multiple-port frame broadcasting occurring during flooding or when a broadcast frame is received.

Recognizing the limitations associated with the operation of bridges vendors incorporated parallel switching technology into devices known as intelligent switching hubs. This device was developed based upon technology used in matrix switches, which for decades have been successfully employed in telecommunications operations. By adding buffer memory to store address tables, frames flowing on LANs connected to different ports could be simultaneously read and forwarded via the switch fabric to ports connected to other networks.

Basic Components

Figure 2.7 illustrates the basic components of a four-port intelligent switch. Although some switches function similar to bridges that read frames flowing on a network to construct a table of source addresses, other switches require their tables to be preconfigured. Either method allows the destination address to be compared to a table of destination addresses and associated port numbers. When a match occurs between the destination address of a frame flowing on a network connected to a port and the address in the port's address table, the frame is copied into the switch and routed through the switch fabric to the destination port, where it is placed onto the network connected to that port. If the destination port is in use due to a previously established cross-connection between ports, the frame is maintained in the buffer until it can be switched to its destination.

To illustrate the construction and utilization of a switch's port-address table, let's assume we are using a four-port switch,

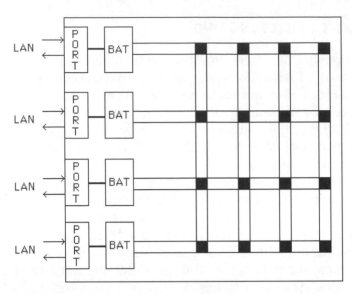

FIGURE 2.7 Basic components of an intelligent switch. An intelligent switch consists of buffers and address tables (BAT), logic, and a switching fabric which permits frames entering one port to be routed to any port in the switch. The destination address in a frame is used to determine the associated port with that address via a search of the address table, with the port address used by the switching fabric for establishing the cross-connection.

with one station connected to each port. Let's further assume that the MAC addresses of each station are A, B, C, and D as indicated in Figure 2.8. If ports 0, 1, 2, and 3 are associated with addresses A, B, C and D, then the table in the lower portion of Figure 2.8 indicates how the port-address table associated with each port learns the addresses to place in its port-address table. For example, when address A needs to send a frame to address C after the switch is initialized, the port-address table for each port is filled with nulls. Since port 0 cannot find a destination address, the switch floods the frame onto all other ports than the port it was received on, just like a bridge. This action, coupled with internal switch logic, enables ports 1, 2, and 3 to note that address A is associated with port 0. Similarly, when station C next transmits a frame destined to station B, port 0 cannot find station B in its port-address table. Therefore, it floods the frame onto ports 0, 1, and 3, and those ports now associate sta-

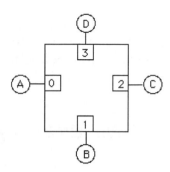

Function to Perform	Operation Performed
1. A sends frame to C.	Frame sent to ports 1, 2, 3 as destination unknown. Ports 1, 2, 3 update port-address tables and now know address A associated with port 0.
2. C sends frame to B.	Frame sent to ports 0, 1, 3 as destination unknown. Ports 0, 1, 3 update their port-address tables and now know address C associated with port 2.
3. C sends frame to A.	Port-address table for port 2 has entry for destination A (see function 1) and causes cross-connection to port 0.

FIGURE 2.8 Switch functions versus switch operations.

tion C with port 2. Thus, when the third function listed in the table in Figure 2.8 occurs (C sends frame to A), port 2 has the entry 0-A in its port-address table and can tell the switch to establish a cross-connection between port 2 and port 0.

Delay Times

Switching occurs on a frame-by-frame basis, with the cross-connection torn down after being established for routing one frame. Thus, frames can be interleaved from two or more ports to a common destination port with a minimum of delay. For example, consider a maximum-length Ethernet frame of 1526 bytes comprising a 1500-byte data field and 26 overhead bytes. At a 10-Mbps operating rate each bit time is $1/10^7$ seconds or 100 ns. For a 1526-byte frame the minimum delay time if one frame precedes it in attempting to be routed to a common destination becomes:

$$1526 \text{ bytes} \times \frac{8 \text{ bits}}{\text{byte}} \times \frac{100 \text{ ns}}{\text{bit}} = 1.22 \text{ ms}$$

The previously computed delay time represents blocking resulting from frames on two service ports having a common destination and should not be confused with another delay time referred to as *latency*. Latency represents the delay associated with the physical transfer of a frame from one port via the switch to another port and is based upon the architecture of the switch which adds additional delay above and beyond the delay associated with the physical length of the frame being transported through the switch. In comparison, blocking delay depends upon the number of frames from different ports attempting to access a common destination port and the method by which the switch is designed to respond to blocking. Some switches simply have large buffers for each port and service ports in a round-robin fashion when frames on two or more ports attempt to access a common destination port. This method of service is not similar to politics as it does not show favoritism; however, it also does not consider the fact that some attached networks may have operating rates different from other attached networks. Other switch designs recognize that port buffers are filled based upon both the number of frames having a destination address of a different network and the operating rate of the network. Such switch designs use a priority service scheme based upon the occupancy of the port buffers in the switch.

Key Advantages of Use

A key advantage associated with the use of intelligent switching hubs results from their ability to support parallel switching, permitting multiple cross-connections between source and destination to occur simultaneously. For example, if four 10BASE-T networks were connected to the four-port switch shown in Figure 2.7, two simultaneous cross-connections, each at 10 Mbps, could occur, resulting in an increase in bandwidth to 20 Mbps. Here each cross-connection represents a dedicated 10-Mbps bandwidth for the duration of a frame. Thus, from a theoretical perspective, an N-port switching hub supporting a 10-Mbps operating rate on each port provides a throughput up to N/2×10 Mbps. For example, a 128-port switching hub would support a throughput up to (128/2)×10 Mbps or 640 Mbps, while a network constructed using a series of conventional hubs connected to one another would be limited to an operating rate of 10 Mbps, with each workstation on that network having an average bandwidth of 10 Mbps/128 or 78 Kbps.

Through the use of intelligent switching hubs you can overcome the operating rate limitation of a local area network. In an Ethernet environment, the cross-connection through a switching hub represents a dedicated connection so there will never be a collision. This fact enabled many switching hub vendors to use the collision wire-pair from conventional Ethernet to support simultaneous transmission in both directions between a connected node and hub port, resulting in a full-duplex transmission capability that will be discussed in more detail in Chapter 3. In fact, a similar development permits Token-Ring switching hubs to provide full-duplex transmission since if there is only one station on a port there is no need to pass tokens and repeat frames, raising the maximum bi-directional throughput between a Token-Ring device and a switching hub port to 32 Mbps. Thus, the ability to support parallel switching as well as initiate dedicated cross-connections on a frame-by-frame basis can be considered the key advantages associated with the use of intelligent switching hubs. Both parallel switching and dedicated cross-connections permit higher bandwidth operations. Now that we have an appreciation for the general operation of switching hubs, let's focus our attention upon the different switching techniques that can be incorporated into this category of communications equipment.

Switching Techniques

There are three switching techniques used by intelligent switching hubs: cross-point, also referred to as cut-through or "on the fly"; store-and-forward; and a hybrid method which alternates between the first two methods based upon the frame error rate. As we will soon note, each technique has one or more advantages and disadvantages associated with its operation.

Cross-Point Switching

The operation of a cross-point switch is based upon an examination of the destination of frames as they enter a port on the switching hub. The switch uses the destination address as a decision criterion to obtain a port destination from a look-up table. Once a port destination is obtained a cross-connection through the switch is initiated, resulting in the frame being routed to a destination port where it is placed onto a network on which its frame destination address resides.

As noted earlier in this chapter, a switch can be considered to represent a more sophisticated type of bridge. Thus, it should come as no surprise that a cross-point switch which is limited to providing cross-connections between similar type LAN stations commonly uses a backward learning algorithm to construct a port-address destination table. That is, the switch monitors the MAC source addresses encountered on each port to construct a port-address destination table. If the destination address resides on the same port the frame was received from, this indicates that the frame's destination is on the current network and no switching operation is required. Thus, the switch discards the frame. If the destination address resides on a different port, the switch obtains the port destination and initiates a cross-connection through the switch, routing the frame to the appropriate destination port where it is placed onto a network where a node with the indicated destination address resides. If the destination address is not found in the table, the switch floods the frame onto all ports other than the port it was received on. Although flooding adversely affects the capability of a switch to perform multiple simultaneous cross-connections, the majority of this activity occurs when a switch is powered on and its port-address table is empty. Thereafter, flooding occurs periodically after an entry is purged from the table due to aging and a new request to a purged destination occurs or when a broadcast address is encountered.

Figure 2.9 illustrates the basic operation of cross-point or cut-through switching. Under this technique the destination address in a frame is read prior to the frame being stored (1). That address is forwarded to a look-up table (2) to determine the port destination address which is used by the switching fabric to initiate a cross-connection to the destination port (3). Since this switching method only requires the storage of a small portion of a frame until it is able to read the destination address and perform its table look-up operation to initiate switching to an appropriate output port, latency through the switch is minimized.

Latency functions as a brake on two-way frame exchanges. For example, in a client/server environment the transmission of a frame by a workstation results in a server response. Thus, the minimum wait time is $2 \times$ latency for each client/server exchange, lowering the effective throughput of the switch. Since a cross-point switching technique results in a minimal amount of latency,

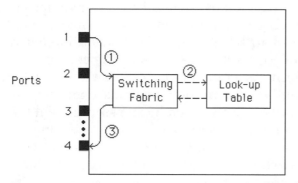

FIGURE 2.9 Cross-point/cut-through switching. A cross-point or cut-through operating switch reads the destination address in a frame prior to storing the entire frame (1). It forwards that address to a look-up table (2) to determine the port destination address which is used by the switching fabric to provide a cross-connection to the destination port (3).

the effect upon throughput of the delay attributable to a switching hub using this switching technique is minimal.

Store-and-Forward

In comparison to a cut-through switching hub, a store-and-forward switching hub first stores an entire frame in memory prior to operating on the data fields within the frame. Once the frame is stored, the switching hub checks the frame's integrity by performing a cyclic redundancy check (CRC) upon the contents of the frame, comparing its computed CRC against the CRC contained in the frame's frame check sequence (FCS) field. If the two match, the frame is considered to be error-free and additional processing and switching will occur. Otherwise, the frame is considered to have one or more bits in error and will be discarded.

In addition to CRC checking, the storage of a frame permits filtering against various frame fields to occur. Although a few manufacturers of store-and-forward intelligent switching hubs support different types of filtering, the primary advantage advertised by such manufacturers is data integrity and the ability to perform translation switching, such as switching a frame between an Ethernet network and a Token-Ring network. Since the translation process is extremely difficult to accomplish on the fly due to the number of conversions of frame data, most switch vendors first store the frame, resulting in store-and-forward switches supporting translation between different types of connected networks. Concerning the data integrity capability of store-and-forward switches, whether or not this is actually an advantage depends upon how you view the additional latency introduced by the storage of a full frame in memory as well as the necessity for error checking. Concerning the latter, switches should operate error-free, so a store-and-forward switch only removes network errors which should be negligible to start with.

When a switch removes an errored frame, the originator will retransmit the frame after a period of time. Since an errored frame arriving at its destination network address is also discarded, many persons question the necessity of error checking by a store-and-forward switching hub. However, filtering

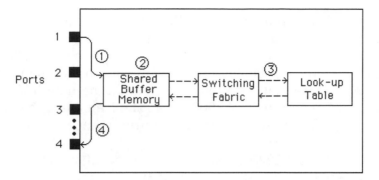

FIGURE 2.10 Store-and-forward switching. A store-and-forward switching hub reads the frame destination address (1) as it is placed in buffer memory (2). As the entire frame is being read into memory, a look-up operation (3) is performed to obtain a destination port address. Once the entire frame is in memory a CRC check is performed and one or more filtering operations may be performed. If the CRC check indicates the frame is error-free, it is forwarded from memory to its destination address (4), otherwise it is disregarded.

capability, if offered, may be far more useful as you could use this capability, for example, to route protocols carried in frames to destination ports far easier than by frame destination address. This is especially true if you have hundreds or thousands of devices connected to a large switching hub. You might set up two or three filters instead of entering a large number of destination addresses into the switch. When a switch performs filtering of protocols, it really becomes a router. This is because it is now operating at layer 3 of the OSI Reference Model.

Figure 2.10 illustrates the operation of a store-and-forward switching hub. Note that a common switch design is to use shared buffer memory to store entire frames which increases the latency associated with this type of switching hub. Since the minimum length of an Ethernet frame is 72 bytes, then the minimum one-way delay or latency, not counting the switch overhead associated with the look-up table and switching fabric operation, becomes:

$$96 \text{ } \mu s + 72 \text{ bytes} \times 8 \text{ bits/byte} \times 100 \text{ ns/bit}$$

or $\quad 9.6 \times 10^{-6} + 576 \times 100 \times 10^{-9}$

or $\quad 67.2 \times 10^{-6}$ seconds

Here 9.6 μs represents the Ethernet interframe gap, while 100 ns/bit is the bit duration of a 10-Mbps Ethernet LAN. Thus, the minimum one-way latency of a store-and-forward Ethernet switching hub is .0000672 seconds, while a round-trip minimum latency is twice that duration. For a maximum-length Ethernet frame with a data field of 1500 bytes, the frame length becomes 1526 bytes. Thus, the one-way maximum latency becomes:

$$96 \text{ μs} + 1526 \text{ bytes} \times 8 \text{ bits/byte} \times 100 \text{ ns/bit}$$

or $9.6 \times 10^{-6} + 12208 \times 100 \times 10^{-9}$

or .012304 seconds

Hybrid

A hybrid switch supports both cut-through and store-and-forward switching, selecting the switching method based upon monitoring the error rate encountered by reading the CRC at the end of each frame and comparing its value to a computed CRC performed on the fly on the fields protected by the CRC. Initially the switch might set each port to a cut-through mode of operation. If too many bad frames are noted as occurring on the port, the switch will automatically set the frame processing mode to store-and-forward, permitting the CRC comparison to be performed prior to the frame being forwarded. This permits frames in error to be discarded without having them pass through the switch. Since the "switch," no pun intended, between cut-through and store-and-forward modes of operation occurs adaptively, another term used to reference the operation of this type of switch is *adaptive*.

The major advantages of a hybrid switch are that it provides minimal latency when error rates are low and discards frames by adapting to a store-and-forward switching method so it can discard errored frames when the frame error rate rises. From an economic perspective, the hybrid switch can logically be expected to cost more than a cut-through or store-and-forward switch as its software development effort is a bit more comprehensive. However, due to the competitive market for communications products, upon occasion its price may be reduced below competitive switch technologies.

Port Address Support

In addition to being categorized by their switching technique, switching hubs can be classified by their support of single or multiple addresses per port. The former method is referred to as port-based switching, while the latter switching method is referred to as segment-based switching.

Port-based Switching

A switching hub which performs port-based switching supports only a single address per port. This restricts switching to one device per port; however, it results in a minimum amount of memory in the switch and provides for a relatively fast table look-up when the switch uses a destination address in a frame to obtain the port for initiating a cross-connect.

Figure 2.11 illustrates an example of the use of a port-based switching hub. In this example M user workstations use

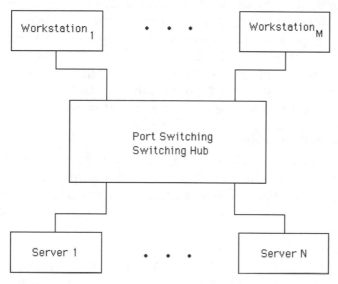

FIGURE 2.11 Port-based switching. A port-based switching hub associates one address with each port, minimizing the time required to match the destination address of a frame against a table of destination addresses and associated port numbers.

the switch to contend for the resources of N servers. If M > N, then a switching hub connected to Ethernet 10 Mbps LANs can support a maximum throughput of N/2 × 10 Mbps, since up to N/2 simultaneous client/server frame flows can occur through the switch.

It is important to compare the maximum potential throughput through a switch to its rated backplane speed. If the maximum potential throughput is less than the rated backplane speed the switch will not cause delays based upon the traffic being routed through the device. For example, consider a 64-port switch that has a backplane speed of 400 Mbps. If the maximum port rate is 10 Mbps, then the maximum throughput assuming 32 active cross-connections were simultaneously established becomes 320 Mbps. In this example the switch has a backplane transfer capability sufficient to handle the worst-case data transfer scenario. Now let's assume that the maximum backplane data transfer capability was 200 Mbps. This would reduce the maximum number of simultaneous cross-connections capable of being serviced to 20 instead of 32 and adversely affect switch performance under certain operational conditions.

Since a port-based switching hub has to store only one address per port, search times are minimized. When combined with a pass-through or cut-through switching technique, this type of switch results in a minimal latency (the overhead of the switch) in determining the destination port of a frame.

Segment-based Switching

A segment-based switching technique requires a switching hub to support multiple addresses per port. Through the use of this type of switch, you achieve additional networking flexibility since you can connect other hubs to a single segment-based switching hub port.

Figure 2.12 illustrates an example of the use of a segment-based switching hub in an Ethernet environment. Although two segments in the form of conventional hubs with multiple devices connected to each hub are shown in the lower portion of Figure 2.12, note that a segment can consist of a single device, resulting in the connection of one device to a port on a segment-

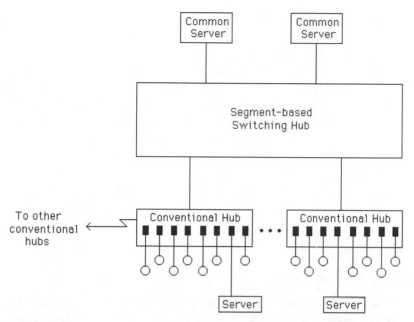

FIGURE 2.12 Segment-based switching. Through the use of a segment-based switching hub, you can maintain servers for use by workstations on a common network segment as well as provide access by all workstations to common servers.

switching hub being similar to a connection on a port-switching hub. However, unlike a port-switching hub that is limited to supporting one address per port, the segment-switching hub can, if necessary, support multiple devices connected to a port. Thus, the two servers connected to the switch at the top of Figure 2.12 could, if desired, be placed on a conventional hub or a high-speed hub, such as a 100BASE-T hub, which in turn would be connected to a single port on a segment-switching hub.

In Figure 2.12 each conventional hub acts as a repeater and forwards every frame transmitted on that hub to the switching hub, regardless of whether or not the frame requires the resources of the switching hub. The segment switching hub examines the destination address of each frame against addresses in its look-up table, forwarding only those frames that warrant being forwarded. Otherwise, frames are discarded as they are local to the conventional hub. Through the use of a segment-based switching hub, you can maintain the use of local servers with respect to existing LAN segments as well as install servers whose access is common to all network segments. The latter is illustrated in Figure 2.12 by the connection of two common servers shown at the top of the switching hub. If you obtain a store-and-forward segment switching hub which supports filtering, you could control access to common servers from individual workstations or by workstations on a particular segment. In addition, you can also use the filtering capability of a store-and-forward segment-based switching hub to control access from workstations located on one segment to workstations or servers located on another segment.

Switching Architecture

The construction of intelligent switches varies both among manufacturers as well as within some vendor product lines. Most switches are based upon the use of either Reduced Instruction Set Computer (RISC) microprocessors or Application Specific Integrated Circuit (ASIC) chips, while a few products use conventional Complex Instruction Set Computer (CISC) microprocessors.

Although there are a large number of arguable advantages and disadvantages associated with each architecture from the standpoint of the switch manufacturer that are beyond the scope of this book, there are also some key considerations that warrant discussion with respect to evolving technology, such as virtual LANs (vLANs). Both RISC and CISC architectures enable switches to be programmed to make forwarding decisions based upon either the data link layer or network layer address information. In addition, when there is a need to modify the switch such as to enable it to support a vLAN standard when the standard is promulgated, this architecture is easily upgradable.

In comparison to RISC- and CISC-based switches, an ASIC-based device represents the use of custom-designed chips to perform specific switch functions in hardware. Although ASIC-based switches are faster than RISC- and CISC-based switches, there is no easy way to upgrade this type of switch. Instead, the vendor will have to design and manufacture new chips and install the hardware upgrade in the switch.

In early 1997 most switches used an ASIC architecture as its speed enabled the support of cut-through switching. While ASIC-based switches provide the speed necessary to minimize latency, readers should carefully check vendor upgrade support as most vLAN standards can be expected to require modifications to existing switches.

Now that we have an appreciation for the general operation and utilization of switching hubs, let's obtain an appreciation for the high-speed operation of switch ports that enables dissimilar types of networks to be connected and that can result in data flow compatibility problems, along with methods used to alleviate such problems.

High-Speed Port Operations

There are several types of high-speed port connections intelligent switches may support. Those high-speed connections include 100-Mbps Fast Ethernet, 100-Mbps FDDI, 155-Mbps ATM, full-duplex Ethernet and Token-Ring, and fat pipes, with the latter referencing a grouping of ports treated as a transmission entity. The most common use of one or more high-speed connections on an intelligent switching hub is to support highly used devices, such as network servers and printers. Figure 2.13 illustrates the use of an Ethernet switch, with two 100BASE-T Fast Ethernet adapters built into the switch to provide a high-speed connection from the switch to each server. Through the use of high-speed connections the cross-connection time from a server to client when the server responds to a client query is minimized. Since most client queries result in server responses containing many multiples of characters in the client query, this allows the server to respond to more queries per unit of time. Thus, the high-speed connection can enhance client/server

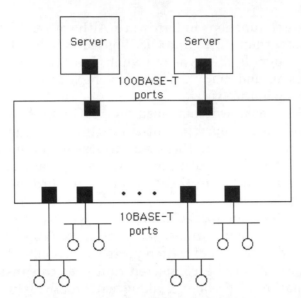

FIGURE 2.13 Using high-speed connections to servers.

response times through a switch. In examining Figure 2.13 let's assume a small query results in the server responding by transmitting the contents of a large file back to the client. If data flows into the switch at 100 Mbps and flows from the switch to the client at 10 Mbps, any buffer area in the switch used to provide temporary storage for speed incompatibilities between ports will rapidly be filled and eventually overflow, resulting in the loss of frames which, when compensated for by retransmission, compounds the problem. Thus, a mechanism is required to regulate the flow of data into and out of switch ports. That mechanism is known as *flow control,* and specific methods used to implement flow control will be covered in succeeding chapters when we examine the operation of specific types of LAN switches.

For now we can note that the intelligent switching hub or LAN switch is a highly versatile device that may support single or multiple devices per port and whose operation can vary based upon its architecture. By providing the capability for supporting multiple simultaneous cross-connections, the LAN switch can significantly increase network bandwidth, and its ability to support high-speed network connections enhances its versatility. Now that we have a basic appreciation for the operational characteristics of generic LAN switches, we can use that information as a base and focus our attention upon specific types of switches in succeeding chapters.

Ethernet Switches

3

Building upon the previous chapter, which introduced us to the general operation and utilization of LAN switches, we will now begin to focus our attention upon specific types of switches. In this chapter we will examine Ethernet switches in terms of their use in supporting both 10- and 100-Mbps Ethernet standards as well as the emerging gigabit Ethernet standard. Since an appreciation of the operation of different types of Ethernet switches requires knowledge of the format and composition of Ethernet frames, we will first turn our attention to that topic. Once we have an appreciation for the composition of Ethernet frames we will then examine the operation and utilization of Ethernet switches. In doing so we will examine Ethernet switch features as well as the use of switches in constructing tiered networks and their use in constructing server farms.

ETHERNET FRAME COMPOSITION

In this section we will first look at the composition of various types of Ethernet frames. In actuality, there is only one Ethernet frame, whereas the CSMA/CD frame format standardized by the

IEEE is technically referred to as an 802.3 frame. However, in this book we will collectively refer to CSMA/CD operations as *Ethernet* and, when appropriate, indicate differences between Ethernet and the IEEE 802.3 Ethernet-based CSMA/CD standard by a comparison of the two. One such area worthy of a comparison is the frame format, which differs between Ethernet and the IEEE 802.3 Ethernet-based CSMA/CD standard. Once we understand the composition of Ethernet and IEEE 802.3 frames, we will examine the function of fields within each frame and then discuss the overhead of the frame with respect to its information transfer capability.

Frame Fields

Figure 3.1 illustrates the fields that, grouped as an entity, result in general frame composition of Ethernet and IEEE 802.3 frames. A third type of frame that I would be remiss if I did not mention is the Fast Ethernet, 100BASE-TX frame. That frame differs from the IEEE 802.3 frame through the addition of a byte at each end to mark the beginning and end of the frame. Because those bytes do not alter the composition of the frame I will focus on the fields within Ethernet and IEEE 802.3 frames, and then describe the bytes unique to Fast Ethernet. In comparing the format of Ethernet and IEEE 802.3 frames, you will note

Ethernet

Preamble	Destination Address	Source Address	Type	Data	Frame Check Sequence
8 bytes	6 bytes	6 bytes	2 bytes	46–1500 bytes	4 bytes

IEEE 802.3

Preamble	Start of Frame Delimiter	Destination Address	Source Address	Length	Data	Frame Check Sequence
7 bytes	1 byte	2/6 bytes	2/6 bytes	2 bytes	46–1500 bytes	4 bytes

FIGURE 3.1 Ethernet and IEEE 802.3 frame formats.

that they differ slightly. An Ethernet frame contains an eight-byte preamble, whereas the IEEE 802.3 frame contains a seven-byte preamble followed by a one-byte start-of-frame delimiter field. A second difference between the composition of Ethernet and IEEE 802.3 frames concerns the two-byte Ethernet type field. That field is used by Ethernet to specify the protocol carried in the frame, enabling several protocols to be carried independently of one another. Under the IEEE 802.3 frame format, the type field was replaced by a two-byte length field which specifies the number of bytes that follow that field as data.

The differences between Ethernet and IEEE 802.3 frames, while minor, make the two incompatible with one another. This means that your network must contain all Ethernet-compatible network interface cards (NICs), all IEEE 802.3–compatible NICs, or adapter cards that can examine the frame and automatically determine its type, a process described later in this chapter. Fortunately, the fact that the IEEE 802.3 frame format represents a standard means that most vendors now market 802.3-compliant hardware and software. Although a few vendors continue to manufacture Ethernet or dual functioning Ethernet/IEEE 802.3 hardware, such products are primarily used to provide organizations with the ability to expand previously developed networks without requiring the wholesale replacement of NICs. Although the IEEE 802.3 standard has essentially replaced Ethernet, because of their similarities and the fact that 802.3 was based upon Ethernet we will consider both to be Ethernet. Now that we have an overview of the structure of Ethernet and 802.3 frames, let's probe deeper and examine the composition of each frame field. In doing so we will take advantage of the similarity between Ethernet and IEEE 802.3 frames to examine the fields of each frame on a composite basis, noting the differences between the two when appropriate.

Preamble Field

The preamble field consists of eight (Ethernet) or seven (IEEE 802.3) bytes of alternating 1 and 0 bits. The purpose of this field is to announce the frame and to enable all receivers on the network to synchronize themselves to the incoming frame. In addition, this field by itself under Ethernet or in conjunction with the start-of-frame delimiter field under the IEEE 802.3 standard ensures there is a minimum spacing period of 9.6 ms between frames for error detection and recovery operations.

Start-of-Frame Delimiter Field

This field is applicable only to the IEEE 802.3 standard, and can be viewed as a continuation of the preamble. In fact, the composition of this field continues in the same manner as the format of the preamble, with alternating 1 and 0 bits used for the first six bit positions of this one-byte field. The last two bit positions of this field are 11, which breaks the synchronization pattern and alerts the receiver that frame data follows.

Both the preamble field and the start-of-frame delimiter field are removed by the Ethernet chip set or controller when it places a received frame in its buffer. Similarly, when a controller transmits a frame, it prefixes the frame with those two fields if it is transmitting an IEEE 802.3 frame or a preamble field if it is transmitting a true Ethernet frame.

Destination Address Field

The destination address identifies the recipient of the frame. Although this may appear to be a simple field, in actuality this field can vary between IEEE 802.3 and Ethernet frames with respect to field length. In addition, each field can consist of two or more subfields, whose settings govern such network operations as the type of addressing used on the LAN, and whether the frame is addressed to a specific station or to more than one station. To obtain an appreciation for the use of this field, let's examine how it is used under the IEEE 802.3 standard as one of the two field formats applicable to Ethernet.

Figure 3.2 illustrates the composition of the source and destination address fields. As indicated, the two-byte source and destination address fields are applicable only to IEEE 802.3 networks, whereas the six-byte source and destination address fields are applicable to both Ethernet and IEEE 802.3 networks.

Although you can select either a two- or six-byte destination address field, when working with IEEE 802.3 equipment, all stations on the LAN must use the same addressing structure. Today, almost all 802.3 networks use six-byte addressing because

A. Two-byte field (IEEE 802.3)

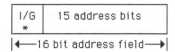

B. Six-byte field (Ethernet and IEEE 802.3)

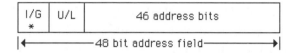

I/G bit subfield   '0' = individual address
                   '1' = group address
U/L bit subfield   '0' = universally administered addressing
                   '1' = locally administered addressing

* Set to '0' in source address field

FIGURE 3.2   Source and destination address field formats.

the inclusion of a two-byte field option was designed primarily to accommodate early LANs that use 16-bit address fields. Both destination and source addresses are normally displayed by network monitors in hexadecimal, with the first three bytes separated from the last three by a colon (:) when six-byte addressing is used. For example, the source address 02608C876543 would be displayed as 02608C:876543. As we will shortly note, the first three bytes identify the manufacturer of the adapter card, while the following three bytes identify a specific adapter manufactured by the vendor identified by the first three bytes or six hex digits.

I/G Subfield.   The one-bit I/G subfield is set to a 0 to indicate that the frame is destined to an individual station, and a setting of 1 indicates that the frame is addressed to more than one station. Here the latter situation indicates a group address.

One special example of a group address is the assignment of all 1s to the address field. Here the address, hex FF-FF-FF-FF-FF-FF, is recognized as a broadcast address and each station on the network will receive and accept frames with that destination address.

An example of the use of a broadcast destination address is the Service Advertising Packet (SAP) transmitted every 60 seconds by NetWare servers. The SAP is used to inform other servers and workstations on the network of the presence of that server. Since the SAP uses a destination address of FF-FF-FF-FF-FF-FF, it is recognized by every node on the network.

When a destination address specifies a single station, the address is referred to as a *unicast* address. A group address that defines multiple stations is known as a *multicast* address, whereas a group address that specifies all stations on the network is, as previously mentioned, referred to as a *broadcast* address.

U/L Subfield. The U/L subfield is applicable only to the six-byte destination address field. The setting of this field's bit position indicates whether the destination address was assigned by the IEEE (universally administered) or assigned by the organization via software (locally administered).

Universal versus Locally Administered Addressing. Each Ethernet Network Interface Card (NIC) contains a unique address burned into its read-only memory (ROM) at the time of manufacture. To ensure this universally administered address is not duplicated, the IEEE assigns blocks of addresses to each manufacturer. Those addresses normally include a three-byte prefix which identifies the manufacturer and is assigned by the IEEE, as well as a three-byte suffix which is assigned by the adapter manufacturer to its NIC. For example, the prefix hex 02-60-8C identifies a NIC manufactured by Digital Equipment Corporation.

Although the use of universally administered addressing eliminates the potential for duplicate network addresses, it does not provide the flexibility obtainable from locally administered addressing. For example, under locally administered addressing, you can configure mainframe software to work with a predefined group of addresses via a gateway PC. Then, as you add new stations to your LAN, you simply use your installation program to assign a locally administered address to the NIC instead of using its universally administered address. As long as your mainframe computer has a pool of locally administered addresses that includes your recent assignment, you do not have to modify your mainframe communications software configuration. Because the modification of mainframe communications software typically requires recompile and reload activity to be performed, doing so requires the attached network to become inoperative for a short period of time. As a large mainframe may service hundreds or thousands of users, such changes are normally performed late in the evening or on a weekend, making the changes for the use of locally administered addressing more responsive to users than the changes required when universally administered addressing is used.

Source Address Field

The source address field identifies the station that transmitted the frame. Similar to the destination address field, the source address can be either two or six bytes in length.

The two-byte source address is supported only under the IEEE 802.3 standard and requires the use of a two-byte destination address, with all stations on the network required to be set to two-byte addressing field use. The six-byte source address field is supported by both Ethernet and the IEEE 802.3 standard. When a six-byte address is used, the first three bytes represent the address assigned by the IEEE to the manufacturer for incorporation into each NIC's ROM. The vendor then normally assigns the last three bytes for each of its NICs.

Table 3.1 lists the NIC identifiers for 30 Ethernet card manufacturers. Note that MIPS, Ungermann-Bass, and Data General were assigned two blocks of addresses by the IEEE, resulting in Table 3.1 containing 33 distinct three-byte identifiers. The entries in Table 3.1 represent a portion of three-byte identifiers assigned by the IEEE over the past decade and does not include obsolete identifiers or identifiers currently assigned to all vendors. For a comprehensive list of currently assigned three-byte identifiers, readers should contact the IEEE.

TABLE 3.1 Ethernet NIC Manufacturer IDs

NIC Manufacturer	Three-Byte Identifier
Cisco	00-00-0C
Cabletron	00-00-1D
TRW	00-00-2A
Network General	00-00-65
MIPS	00-00-6B
MIPS	00-00-77
Proteon	00-00-93
Wellfleet	00-00-A2
Xerox	00-00-AA
Western Digital	00-00-C0
Emulex	00-00-C9
Shiva	00-80-D3
Intel	00-AA-00
Ungermann-Bass	00-DD-00
Ungermann-Bass	00-DD-01
Racal Interlan	02-07-01
3Com	02-60-8C
BBN	08-00-08
Hewlett-Packard	08-00-09
Unisys	08-00-0B
Tektronix	08-00-11
Data General	08-00-A
Data General	08-00-1B
Sun	08-00-20
DEC	08-00-2B
Bull	08-00-38
Sony	08-00-46
Sequent	08-00-47
IBM	08-00-5A
Silicon Graphics	08-00-69
Excelan	08-00-6E
Danish Data Elektronix	08-00-75
AT&T	80-00-10

Many software and hardware-based network analyzers as well as network management stations include the capability to identify each station on a LAN, count the number of frames transmitted by the station and destined to the station, and identify the manufacturer of the NIC used in the station. Concerning the latter capability, this is accomplished by the network analyzer or network manager containing a table of three-byte identifiers assigned by the IEEE to each NIC manufacturer along with the name of the manufacturer. Then the device compares the three-byte identifier read from frames flowing on the network and compares each identifier to the identifiers stored in its identifier table. By providing information concerning network statistics, network errors, and the vendor identifier for the NIC in each station, you may be able to isolate problems faster or more thoroughly consider future options concerning the acquisition of additional NICs.

Type Field

The two-byte type field is applicable only to the Ethernet frame. This field identifies the higher-level protocol contained in the data field. Thus, this field tells the receiving device how to interpret the data field.

Under Ethernet, multiple protocols can exist on the LAN at the same time. Xerox served as the custodian of Ethernet address ranges licensed to NIC manufacturers and defined the protocols supported by the assignment of type field values.

Table 3.2 lists 18 of the more common Ethernet type field assignments. To illustrate the ability of Ethernet to transport multiple protocols, assume a common LAN was used to connect stations to both Unix and NetWare servers. Frames with the hex value 0800 in the type field would identify the IP protocol, while frames with the hex value 8137 in the type field would identify the transport of IPX and SPX protocols. Thus, the placement of an appropriate hex value in the Ethernet type field provides a mechanism to support the transport of multiple protocols on the local area network. Under the IEEE 802.3 standard, the type field was replaced by a length field, which precludes compatibility between pure Ethernet and 802.3 frames.

TABLE 3.2 Ethernet Type Field Assignments

Protocol	Hex Value Assigned
IP	0800
X.75 Internet	0801
X.25 Level 3	0805
Address Resolution Protocol	0806
Banyan Systems	0BAD
BBN Simnet	5208
DEC MOP Dump/Load	6001
DEC MOP Remote Console	6002
DEC DECNET Phase IV Route	6003
DEC LAT	6004
DEC Diagnostic Protocol	6005
DEC LANBridge	8038
DEC Ethernet Encryption	803D
Appletalk	809B
IBM SNA Service on Ethernet	80D5
AppleTalk ARP	80F3
NetWare IPX/SPX	8137
SNMP	814C

Length Field

The two-byte length field, applicable to the IEEE 802.3 standard, defines the number of bytes contained in the data field. Under both Ethernet and IEEE 802.3 standards, the minimum size frame must be 64 bytes in length from preamble through frame check sequence (FCS) fields. This minimum size frame ensures that there is sufficient transmission time to enable Ethernet NICs to detect collisions accurately, based on the maximum Ethernet cable length specified for a network and the time required for a frame to propagate the length of the cable. The minimum frame length of 64 bytes and the possibility of using two-byte addressing fields mean that each data field must be a minimum of 46 bytes in length. If data being transported is less than 46 bytes, the data field is padded to obtain 46 bytes. However, the number of PAD characters is not included in the length field value. NICs that support both Ethernet and IEEE 802.3 frame formats use the value in this field to distinguish between the two frames. That is, since the maximum length of the data field is 1500 bytes, a value that exceeds hex 05DC indicates that instead of a length field (IEEE 802.3), the field is a type field (Ethernet).

Because the data field cannot exceed 1500 bytes, the length field's maximum value cannot exceed 1500 decimal. Concerning its minimum value, when the data field contains less than 46 bytes, the data field is padded to reach 46 bytes in length. However, the length field does not include padding and reflects the actual number of characters in the data field.

Data Field

As previously discussed, the data field must be a minimum of 46 bytes in length to ensure that the frame is at least 64 bytes in length. This means that the transmission of 1 byte of information must be carried within a 46-byte data field; if the information to be placed in the field is less than 46 bytes, the remainder of the field must be padded. Although some publications subdivide the data field to include a PAD subfield, the latter actually represents optional fill characters that are added to the information in the data field to ensure a length of 46 bytes. The maximum length of the data field is 1500 bytes, which results in the use of multiple frames to transport full screen images and almost all file transfers.

Frame Check Sequence Field

The frame check sequence (FCS) field is applicable to both Ethernet and the IEEE 802.3 standard and provides a mechanism for error detection. Each transmitter computes a cyclic redundancy check (CRC) which covers both address fields, the type/length field, and the data field. The transmitter then places the computed CRC in the four-byte FCS field.

The CRC is developed by treating the composition of the previously mentioned fields as one long binary number. The n bits to be covered by the CRC represent the coefficients of a polynomial M(X) of degree n − 1. Here, the first bit in the destination address field corresponds to the X^{n-1} term, while the last bit in the data field corresponds to the X^0 term. Next, M(X) is multiplied by X^{32} and the result of that multiplication process is divided by the following polynomial:

$$G(X) = X^{32}+X^{26}+X^{23}+X^{22}+X^{16}+X^{12}+X^{11}+X^{10}+X^8+X^7+X^5+X^4+X^3+X+1$$

Readers should note that the term X^n represents the setting of a bit to a 1 in position n. Thus, part of the generating polynomial $X^5+X^4+X^3+X^1$ represents the binary value 11011.

The result of the division produces a quotient and remainder. The quotient is discarded, and the remainder becomes the CRC value placed in the four-byte FCS field. This 32-bit CRC reduces the probability of an undetected error to 1 bit in every 4.3 billion, or approximately 1 bit in $2^{32} - 1$ bits.

Once a frame reaches its destination, the receiver uses the same polynomial to perform the same operation upon the received data. If the CRC computed by the receiver matches the CRC in the FCS field, the frame is accepted. Otherwise, the receiver discards the received frame, as it is considered to have one or more bits in error. The receiver will also consider a received frame to be invalid and discard it under two additional conditions. Those conditions occur when the frame does not contain an integral number of bytes, or when the length of the data field does not match the value contained in the length field. Obviously the latter condition applies only to the 802.3 standard because an Ethernet frame uses a type field instead of a length field.

Fast Ethernet

The frame format of Fast Ethernet duplicates the IEEE 802.3 frame with the exception of the use of prefix and suffix bytes that surround the frame. The prefix bit is known as the start-of-stream delimiter (SSD), while the suffix byte is known as the end-of-stream delimiter (ESD).

The SSD is used to align a received frame for subsequent decoding, whereas the ESD is used as an indicator that data transmission has terminated normally and a properly formed stream has been transmitted. Figure 3.3 illustrates how the SSD and ESD byes are used to "frame" the IEEE 802.3 frame. At the 100-Mbps operating rate of 100BASE-TX the frames are known as *streams,* which accounts for the names of the two delimiters.

In comparing the Fast Ethernet to Ethernet and IEEE 802.3 frame formats illustrated in Figure 3.1 you will note that, apart from the starting and ending stream delimiters, the Fast Ethernet frame duplicates the older frames. Another difference between the two is not shown, as it is not actually observable from a comparison of frames, since this difference is associated with the time between frames. Ethernet and IEEE 802.3 frames are Manchester encoded and have an interframe gap of 9.6 µs between frames. In comparison, the Fast Ethernet 100BASE-TX frame is transmitted using 4B5B encoding, and idle codes are used to mark a 0.96-µs interframe gap. Both the SSD and ESD fields can be considered to fall within the interframe gap of Fast Ethernet frames. Thus, computation between Ethernet/IEEE 802.3 and Fast Ethernet becomes simplified, as the latter has an operating rate 10 times the former and an interframe gap one-tenth of the former.

SSD 1 byte	Preamble 7 bytes	SFD 1 byte	Destination Address 6 bytes	Source Address 6 bytes	L/T 2 bytes	Data 45 to 1500 bytes	FCS 1 byte	ESD

Legend:
SSD = start-of-stream delimiter
SFD = start-of-frame delimiter
L/T = length (IEEE 802.3)/type (Ethernet)
ESD = end-of-stream delimiter

FIGURE 3.3 Fast Ethernet frame. The 100BASE-TX frame differs from the IEEE 802.3 frame through the addition of a byte at each end to mark the beginning and ending of the stream delimiter.

ETHERNET LOGICAL LINK CONTROL

The logical link control (LLC) sublayer was defined under the IEEE 802.2 standard to make the method of link control independent of a specific access method. Thus, the 802.2 method of link control spans Ethernet (IEEE 802.3), Token Bus (IEEE 802.4), and Token-Ring (IEEE 802.5) local area networks. Functions performed by the LLC include generating and interpreting commands which control the flow of data, including recovery operations when a transmission error is detected.

Link control information is carried within the data field of an IEEE 802.3 frame as an LLC Protocol Data Unit. Figure 3.4 illustrates the relationship between the IEEE 802.3 frame and the LLC Protocol Data Unit.

Since the LLC layer is bounded below the MAC sublayer and bounded above by the network layer, service access points (SAPs) provide a mechanism for exchanging information between the LLC layer and the MAC and network layers. Thus, they can be considered to function similar to a mailbox. For example, from the network layer perspective a SAP represents the place to leave messages concerning the services requested by an application.

The destination services access point (DSAP) is one byte in length and is used to specify the receiving network layer process. Since an IEEE 802.3 frame does not include type field, the DSAP

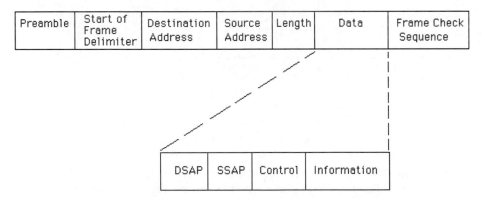

FIGURE 3.4 Formation of LLC protocol data unit. Control information is carried within a MAC frame.

field is used to denote the destination upper-layer protocol carried within the frame. For example, the DSAP hex value EQ indicates that the data field contains NetWare data. The source service access point (SSAP) is also one byte in length. The SSAP specifies the sending network layer process. Since the destination and source protocols must be the same, the value of the SSAP field will always match the value of the DSAP field. Both DSAP and SSAP addresses are assigned by the IEEE. For example, hex address FF represents a DSAP broadcast address. The control field contains information concerning the type and class of service being used for transporting LLC data. For example, a hex value of 03 when NetWare is being transported indicates that the frame is using an unnumbered format for connectionless services.

Types and Classes of Service

Under the 802.2 standard there are three types of service available for sending and receiving LLC data. These types are discussed in the next three paragraphs. Figure 3.5 provides a visual summary of the operation of each LLC service type.

Type 1

Type 1 is an unacknowledged connectionless service. The term *connectionless* refers to the fact that transmission does not occur between two devices as if a logical connection was established. Instead, transmission flows on the channel to all stations; however, only the destination address acts upon the data. As the name of this service implies, there is no provision for the acknowledgment of frames. Neither is there a provision for flow control to regulate transmission or for error recovery. Therefore, this is an unreliable service.

Despite those shortcomings, Type 1 is the most commonly used service, since most protocol suites use a reliable transport mechanism at the transport layer which eliminates the need for reliability at the link layer. In addition, by eliminating the time to establish a virtual link and the overhead of acknowledgments a Type 1 service can provide a greater throughput than other LLC types of services.

Type 2 Connection-oriented service

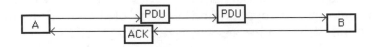

Type 3 Acknowledged connectionless source

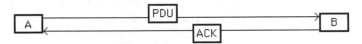

Legend:
PDU = protocol data unit
ACK = acknowledgment
A,B = stations on the network

FIGURE 3.5 Local link control service types.

Type 2

The Type 2 connection-oriented service requires a logical link to be established between the sender and the receiver prior to information transfer. Once the logical connection is established data will flow between the sender and receiver until either party terminates the connection. During data transfer a Type 2 LLC service provides all of the functions lacking in a Type 1 service, with a sliding window used for flow control. When IBM's SNA data is transported on a LAN, it uses connection-oriented services. Type 2 LLC is also commonly referred to as LLC 2.

Type 3

The Type 3 acknowledged connectionless service contains provision for the setup and disconnection of transmission. However, Type 3 service acknowledges individual frames using the stop-

and-wait flow control method. Type 3 service is primarily used in an automated factory process-control environment, where one central computer communicates with many remote devices that typically have a limited storage capacity.

Classes of Service

All logical link control stations support Type 1 operations. This level of support is known as Class I service. The classes of service supported by LLC indicate the combinations of the three types of LLC service types supported by a station. Class I supports Type 1 service, Class II supports both Type 1 and Type 2, Class III supports Type 1 and Type 3 service, while Class IV supports all three service types. Since service Type 1 is supported by all classes, its use can be considered a least common denominator which enables all stations to communicate using a common form of service.

Other Ethernet Frame Types

Two additional frame types that warrant discussion are Ethernet-802.3 and Ethernet-SNAP. In actuality, both types of frames represent a logical variation of the IEEE 802.3 frame in which the composition of the data field varies from the composition of the LLC protocol data unit illustrated in Figure 3.4.

Ethernet-802.3

The Ethernet-802.3 frame represents a proprietary subdivision of the IEEE 802.3 data field to transport NetWare. Ethernet-802.3 is one of several types of frames that can be used to transport NetWare. The actual frame type used is defined at system setup by binding NetWare to a specific type of frame.

Figure 3.6 illustrates the format of the Ethernet-802.3 frame. Due to the absence of LLC fields, this frame is often referred to as raw 802.3.

For those using or thinking of using NetWare, a word of caution is in order concerning frame types. Novell uses the term Ethernet-802.2 to refer to the IEEE 802.3 frame. Thus, if you set up NetWare for Ethernet-802.2 frames, in effect your network is IEEE 802.3 compliant.

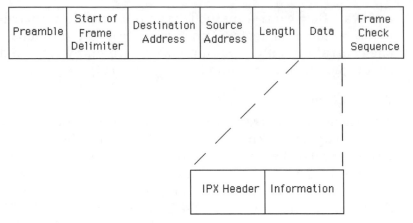

FIGURE 3.6 Novell's NetWare Ethernet-802.3 frame. An Ethernet-802.3 frame subdivides the data field into an IPX header field and an information field.

Ethernet-SNAP

The Ethernet Subnetwork Access Protocol (Ethernet-SNAP) frame, unlike the Ethernet-802.3 frame, can be used to transport several protocols. AppleTalk Phase II, NetWare, and TCP/IP protocols can be transported due to the inclusion of an Ethernet type field in the Ethernet-SNAP frame. Thus, SNAP can be considered as an extension which permits vendors to create their own Ethernet protocol transports. Ethernet-SNAP was defined by the IEEE 802.1 committee to facilitate interoperability between IEEE 802.3 LANs and Ethernet LANs. This was accomplished, as we will soon note, by the inclusion of a type field in the Ethernet-SNAP frame.

Figure 3.7 illustrates the format of an Ethernet-SNAP frame. Although the format of this frame is based upon the IEEE 802.3 frame format, it does not use DSAP and SSAP mailbox facilities and the control field. Instead, it places specific values in those fields to indicate that the frame is a SNAP frame.

The value hex AA is placed into the DSAP and SSAP fields, while hex 03 is placed into the control field to indicate that a SNAP frame is being transported. The hex 03 value in the control field defines the use of an unnumbered format which is the only format supported by a SNAP frame.

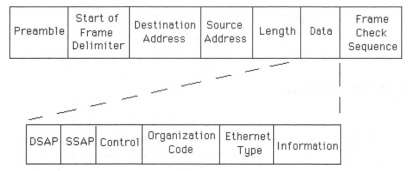

FIGURE 3.7 Ethernet-SNAP frame format.

The organization code field references the organizational body that assigned the value placed in the following field, the Ethernet type field. A hex value of 00-00-00 in the organization code field indicates that Xerox assigned the value in the Ethernet type field. Through the use of the Ethernet-SNAP frame, you obtain the ability to transport multiple protocols in a manner similar to the original Ethernet frame that used the type field for this purpose. Here the hex value of 00-00-00 in the organization code field enables the values previously listed in Table 3.2 to represent different protocols carried by the SNAP frame.

Frame Determination

Through software, a receiving station can determine the type of frame and correctly interpret the data carried in the frame. To accomplish this, the value of the two bytes that follows the source address is first examined. If the value is greater than 1500, this indicates the occurrence of an Ethernet frame. If the value is less than or equal to 1500, the frame can be either a pure IEEE 802.3 frame or a variation of that frame. Thus, more bytes must be examined.

If the next two bytes have the hex value FF:FF, the frame is a NetWare Ethernet-802.3 frame. This is because the IPX header has hex FF:FF in the checksum field which is contained in the first two bytes in the IPX header. If the two bytes contain the hex value AA:AA, this indicates that it is an Ethernet-SNAP frame. Any other value determined to reside in those two bytes then indicates that the frame must be an Ethernet-802.3 frame.

SWITCH OPERATIONS

Although features incorporated into Ethernet switches considerably differ among vendors as well as within vendor product lines, upon occasion we can categorize these communications devices by the operating rate of the ports they support. Doing so results in five basic types of Ethernet switches, which are listed in Table 3.3. Switches that are restricted to operating at one data rate are commonly used for departmental operations, while switches that support a mixed data rate are commonly used in a tiered-network structure at a higher layer in the tier than switches that operate at a uniform data rate. Concerning the latter, when used in a tiered-network structure the lower uniform operating rate switch is commonly used at the lower level in the tier.

Multi-Tier Network Construction

Figure 3.8 illustrates the generic use of a two-tiered Ethernet switch-based network, with the switch at the higher tier functioning as a backbone connectivity mechanism which enables access to shared servers commonly known as global servers by users across departmental boundaries, while switches in the lower tier facilitate access to servers shared within a specific department. This hierarchical networking structure is commonly used with other types of backbone switches, such as

TABLE 3.3 Types of Ethernet Switches Based on Port Operating Rates

All ports operate at 10 Mbps

Mixed 10/100 Mbps port operation

All ports operate at 100 Mbps

Mixed 10/100/1000 Mbps port operation

All ports operate at 1000 Mbps

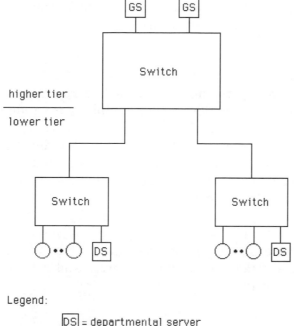

FIGURE 3.8 Generic construction of a two-tiered Ethernet switch-based network.

FDDI and ATM, as well as with other types of lower-tier switches. One common variation associated with the use of a tiered switch-based network is the placement of both departmental and global servers on an upper-tier switch. This placement allows all servers to be colocated in a common area for ease of access and control and is commonly referred to as a *server farm*. However, if an upper-tier switch should fail, access to all servers could be affected, representing a significant disadvantage of this design. A second major disadvantage is the fact that all traffic has to be routed through at least two switches when a server farm is constructed. In comparison, when servers primarily used by departmental employees are connected to a switch serving departmental users, most traffic remains local to the local switch at the bottom of the tier.

Basic Architecture

Regardless of the operating rate of each port on an Ethernet switch, most devices are designed in a similar manner. That is, most switches consist of a chassis into which a variety of cards are inserted, similar in many respects to the installation of cards into the system expansion slots of personal computers. Modular Ethernet switches that are scalable commonly support CPU, Logic, matrix, and port cards.

CPU Card

The CPU card commonly manages the switch, identifies the types of LANs attached to switch ports, and performs self-directed switch tests.

Logic Module

The logic module is commonly responsible for comparing the destination address of frames read on a port against a table of addresses it is responsible for maintaining, and instructing the matrix module to initiate a cross-bar switch once a comparison of addresses results in the selection of a destination port address.

Matrix Module

The matrix module of a switch can be considered to represent a cross-bar of wires from each port to each port as illustrated in Figure 3.9. Upon receipt of an instruction from a logic module the matrix module initiates a cross-connection between the source and destination port for the duration of the frame.

Port Module

The port module can be considered to represent a cluster of physical interfaces to which either individual stations or network segments are connected based upon whether the switch supports single or multiple MAC addresses per port. Some port modules permit a mixture of port cards to be inserted, resulting

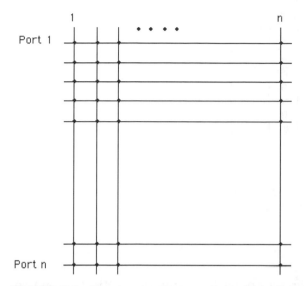

FIGURE 3.9 The key to the operation of a switch is a matrix module which enables each port to be cross-connected to other ports. The matrix of a switch with n ports can be considered to represent an n × n star-wired backplane.

in, as an example, 10- and 100-Mbps as well as full-duplex connections to be supported. In comparison, other port modules are capable of supporting only one type of LAN connection. In addition, there are significant differences among vendor port modules concerning the number of ports supported. Some modules are limited to supporting 2 or 4 ports, while other modules may support 6, 8, or 10 ports. Although we are focusing our attention upon Ethernet switches in this chapter, it should be noted that many switches support other types of LAN port modules whose use will be discussed later in this chapter and in succeeding chapters.

Redundancy

In addition to the previously mentioned modules, most switches also support single and redundant power supply modules and may also support redundant matrix and logic modules. Figure 3.10 illustrates a typical Ethernet modular switch chassis showing the installation of 11 modules, including five 8-port modules, to form a 40-port switch.

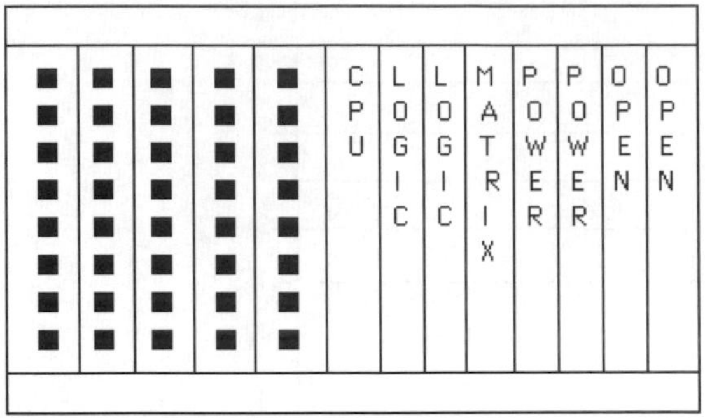

FIGURE 3.10 A typical Ethernet modular switch chassis containing a mixture of port, CPU, logic, matrix, and power cards.

Switch Features

There are literally an ever-expanding number of features being incorporated into Ethernet switches. Those features range from providing such basic functions as port and segment switching (discussed in Chapter 2) to methods developed by some vendors to prevent erroneous frames from being transferred through the switch in a cut-through mode of operation. In this section we will review 18 distinct switch features, which are summarized in alphabetical order in Table 3.4.

The table of features presented was constructed not only to list features you should note, but, in addition, as a mechanism to facilitate the evaluation of switches. That is, you can indicate your requirement for a particular feature and then note whether or not that requirement can be satisfied by the various vendor products by replacing "Vendor A" and "Vendor B" with the names of switches you are evaluating. By duplicating this table you can extend the two rightmost columns to evaluate more than two products. As we examine each feature listed in Table 3.4, our degree of exploration will be based upon whether or not the feature was described in Chapter 2, and on its use in an Ethernet environment. If the feature was described in Chapter 2, we will limit our discussion to a brief review of the feature. However, if the feature is implemented in a unique manner for an Ethernet switch, we will then discuss its operation in considerable detail.

TABLE 3.4 Ethernet Switch Features

Feature	Requirement	Vendor A	Vendor B
Address table size support			
Addresses/port	_____	_____	_____
Addresses/switch	_____	_____	_____
Architecture			
ASIC based	_____	_____	_____
CISC based	_____	_____	_____
RISC based	_____	_____	_____
Autonegotiation ports	_____	_____	_____
Backplane transfer capacity	_____	_____	_____
Error prevention	_____	_____	_____
Fat pipe	_____	_____	_____
Filtering/forwarding rate support			
Filtering rate	_____	_____	_____
Forwarding rate	_____	_____	_____
Flow control			
Backpressure	_____	_____	_____
Software drivers	_____	_____	_____
No control	_____	_____	_____
Full-duplex port operation	_____	_____	_____
Jabber control	_____	_____	_____
Latency	_____	_____	_____
Management	_____	_____	_____
Module insertion	_____	_____	_____
Port buffer size	_____	_____	_____
Port module support	_____	_____	_____
Spanning tree support	_____	_____	_____
Switch type			
Port-based switch	_____	_____	_____
Segment-based switch	_____	_____	_____
Switching mode			
Cut-through	_____	_____	_____
Store-and-forward	_____	_____	_____
Hybrid	_____	_____	_____
Virtual LAN support	_____	_____	_____

Address Table Size Support

The ability of a switch to correctly forward packets to their intended direction depends upon the use of address tables. Similarly, the capability of a switch to support a defined number of workstations depends upon the number of entries that can be placed in its address table. Thus, the address table size can be viewed as a constraint which affects the ability of a switch to support network devices.

There are two address table sizes you may have to consider—the number of addresses supported per port and the number of addresses supported per switch. The first address table constraint is applicable only for ports that support the connection of network segments. In comparison, the total number of addresses recognized per switch represents a constraint which affects the entire switch. Many Ethernet switches support up to 1024 addresses per port for segment-based support. Such switches may only support a total of 8192 addresses per switch. This means that a 16-port switch with eight fully populated segments could not support the use of the eight remaining ports as the switch would run out of address table entries. Thus, it is important to consider the number of addresses supported per port and per switch and match such data against your anticipated requirements.

Architecture

There are three basic methods used to construct LAN switches. Those methods include the use of Application Specific Integrated Circuits (ASICs), Complex or Conventional Instruction Set Computers (CISCs), and Reduced Instruction Set Computers (RISCs). Although the use of a ASIC-based architecture commonly results in a very low latency and high level of performance, upgrades are difficult to accomplish as such circuits must be replaced. In comparison, both conventional microprocessor and RISC-based switches use instructions in replaceable ROM. Although the differences may appear trivial, if an ASIC-based switch, for example, requires an upgrade to comply with a pending vLAN standard you would probably require a technician to visit your site to perform the upgrade. In comparison, you might be able to simply download a new software release from the vendor's World Wide Web site or electronic bulletin board to update a RISC- or CISC-based switch.

Autonegotiation Ports

To provide a mechanism to migrate from 10 Mbps to 100 Mbps, National Semiconductor developed a chip set known as Nway, which provides an automatic data rate sensing capability as part of an autonegotiation function. This capability enables a switch port to support either a 10- or 100-Mbps Ethernet attachment to the port; however, this feature works only when cabled to a 10/100-Mbps network adapter card. You may otherwise have to use the switch console to configure the operating rate of the port or the port may be fixed to a predefined operating rate.

Backplane Transfer Capacity

The backplane transfer capacity of a switch provides you with the ability to determine how well the device can support a large number of simultaneous cross-connections, as well as its ability to perform flooding. For example, consider a 64-port 10BASE-T switch with a backplane transfer capacity of 400 Mbps. Since the switch can support a maximum of 64/2 or 32 cross-connects, the switch's backplane must provide at least a 32×10 Mbps or a 320 Mbps transfer capacity. However, when it encounters an unknown destination address on one port, the switch will output or flood the packet onto all ports other than the port the frame was received on. Thus, to operate in a nonblocked mode the switch must have a buffer transfer capacity of 64×10 Mbps or 640 Mbps.

Error Prevention

Some switch designers recognize that the majority of runt frames (frames improperly terminated) result from a collision occurring during the time it takes to read the first 64 bytes of the frame. On a 10-Mbps Ethernet LAN this is equivalent to a time of 51.2 µs. In a cut-through switch environment when latency is minimized it becomes possible to pass runt frames to the destination. To prevent this from happening, some switch designers permit the user to introduce a 51.2-µs delay, which provides sufficient time for the switch to verify that the frame is of sufficient length to have a high degree of probability that it is not a runt frame. Other switches that operate in the cut-through mode may simply impose a 51.2-μs delay to enable this error prevention feature. Regardless of the method used, the delay is applicable only to cut-through switches that support LAN segments, as single-user ports do not generate collisions.

Fat Pipe

A *fat pipe* is a term used to reference a high-speed port. When 10BASE-T switches were first introduced, the term actually referred to a group of two or more ports operating as an entity. Today a fat pipe can reference a 100-Mbps port on a switch primarily consisting of 10-Mbps operating ports or a 155-Mbps ATM port on a 10/100 or 100-Mbps switch. In addition, some vendors retain the term fat pipe as a reference to a group of ports operating as an entity.

Filtering and Forwarding Rate Support

The ability of a switch to interpret a number of frame destination addresses during a defined time interval is referred to as its *filtering rate*. In comparison, the number of frames that must be routed through a switch during a predefined period of time is referred to as the *forwarding rate*. Both the filtering and forwarding rates govern the performance level of a switch with respect to its ability to interpret and route frames. When considering these two metrics, it is important to understand the maximum frame rate on an Ethernet LAN, so let's turn our attention to that topic prior to discussing these metrics in additional detail.

On a 10-Mbps Ethernet network there is a gap or "dead time" of 9.6 μs between frames. Since the longest Ethernet frame is 1526 bytes and each bit has a pulse duration of 100 ns, we can compute the time per frame as follows:

$$9.6 \text{ μs} + 1526 \text{ bytes} \times 8 \text{ bits/byte}$$
or $\quad 9.6 \text{ μs} + 12208 \text{ bits} \times 100 \text{ ns/bit}$
or $\quad 1.23 \text{ ms}$

Thus, in one second there can be a maximum of 1/1.23 ms or 812 maximum-size frames. For a minimum length frame of 72 bytes the time per frame is computed as follows:

$$9.6 \ \mu s + 72 \ \text{bytes} \times 8 \ \text{bits/byte} \times 100 \ \text{ns/bit}$$
$$\text{or} \quad 67.2 \times 10^{-6} \ \text{second}$$

Thus, in one second there can be a maximum of $1/67.2 \times 10^{-6}$ or 14880 minimum-size 72-byte frames on a 10-Mbps Ethernet network.

If we are using a 100-Mbps Ethernet network, the minimum and maximum frame rates are ten times those associated with a 10-Mbps network. Table 3.5 summarizes the frame rates for Ethernet and Fast Ethernet networks.

In examining the frame rates listed in Table 3.5, it is important to note that when applied to a switch they represent the rate per Ethernet or Fast Ethernet port on the switch. Some switch vendors specify an aggregate filtering and forwarding rate, forcing potential users to compute the per-port rate. This computation is not actually necessary, since you can easily compute the aggregate filtering and forwarding rates the switch should support under different loading conditions prior to frames being dropped. For example, consider a 64-port switch limited to 10BASE-10 connections. The maximum number of cross-connections the switch can support when forwarding frames is 32. Thus, the switch should be capable of forwarding 14880×32 or 476,160 minimum-length frames per second. Concerning its filtering rate, since each port can receive up to 14,880 frames per second, the switch should be capable of filtering $14,880 \times 64$ or 952,320 frames per second. Although filtering

TABLE 3.5 Ethernet/Fast Ethernet Frame Rates

	Maximum Length Frames	*Minimum Length Frames*
Ethernet	812	14,880
Fast Ethernet	8,120	148,800

and forwarding rates beyond those computed guarantee a switch will not drop or be unable to forward frames, a lesser capability does not necessarily mean the device is ill-suited for use. This is because the probability of all ports bursting at a maximum frame rate is very low. Similarly, the probability of n/2 cross-connections being required at one point in time is also very low. Thus, the filtering and forwarding rates, while important when evaluating switches, must also be analyzed in conjunction with other features.

Flow Control

Flow control represents the orderly regulation of transmission. In a switched network environment there are a number of situations for which flow control can be used to prevent the loss of data and subsequent retransmissions, which can create a cycle of lost data followed by retransmissions. The most common cause of lost data results from a data rate mismatch between source and destination ports. For example, consider a server connected to a switch via a Fast Ethernet 100-Mbps connection which responds to a client query when the client is connected to a switch port at 10 Mbps. Without the use of a buffer within the switch, this speed mismatch would always result in the loss of data. Through the use of a buffer, data can be transferred into the switch at 100 Mbps and transferred out at 10 Mbps. However, since the input rate is ten times the output rate, the buffer will rapidly fill. In addition, if the server is transferring a large quantity of data the buffer could overflow, resulting in subsequent data sent to the switch being lost. Thus, unless the length of the buffer is infinite, an impossible situation, there would always be some probability that data could be lost.

Another common cause of lost data is when multiple source port inputs are contending for access to the same destination port. If each source and destination port operates at the same data rate, then only two source ports contending for access to the same destination port can result in the loss of data. Thus, a mechanism is required to regulate the flow of data through a switch. That mechanism is flow control.

All Ethernet switches I am familiar with have either buffers in each port, or centralized memory that functions as a buffer.

The key difference between switch buffers is in the amount of memory used. Some switches have 128 K, 256 Kbytes, or even 1 or 2 Mbytes per port, whereas other switches may support the temporary storage of 10 or 20 full-length Ethernet frames. To prevent buffer overflow three common techniques are used—backpressure, software, and no control. Let's examine each technique.

Backpressure. Backpressure represents a technique by which a switch generates a false collision signal. In actuality, the switch port operates as if it detected a collision and initiates the transmission of a jam pattern. The jam pattern consists of 32 to 48 bits that can have any value other than the CRC value that corresponds to any partial frame transmitted before the jam.

The transmission of the jam pattern ensures that the collision lasts long enough to be detected by all stations on the network. In addition, the jam signal serves as a mechanism to cause nontransmitting stations to wait until the jam signal ends prior to attempting to transmit, preventing additional potential collisions from occurring. Although the jam signal temporarily stops transmission, enabling the contents of buffers to be output, the signal also adversely affects all stations connected to the port. Thus, a network segment consisting of a number of stations connected to a switch port would result in all stations having their transmission capability suspended even when just one station was directing traffic to the switch.

Backpressure is commonly implemented based upon the level of buffer memory used. When buffer memory is filled to a predefined level, that level serves as a threshold for the switch to generate jam signals. Then, once the buffer is emptied beyond another lower level, that level serves as a threshold to disable backpressure operations.

Software Drivers. Software drivers enable a switch to directly communicate with an attached device. This enables the switch to enable and disable the stations' transmission capability. Currently, software drivers are available as a NetWare Loadable Module (NLM) for NetWare servers, and may be available for Windows NT by the time you read this book.

No Control. Many switch vendors rely upon the fact that the previously described traffic patterns that can result in buffers overflowing and the loss of data have a relatively low probability of occurrence for any significant length of time. In addition, upper layers of the OSI Reference Model will retransmit lost packets. Thus, many switch vendors rely upon the use of memory buffers and do not incorporate flow control into their products. Whether or not this is an appropriate solution will depend upon the traffic you anticipate flowing through the switch.

Full-Duplex Port Operation

If a switch port supports the connection of only one station, a collision can never occur. Recognizing this fact, most Ethernet switch vendors now support full-duplex (FDX) or bidirectional traffic flow by using two of the four wire connections for transmission in the opposite direction. Full-duplex support is available for 10BASE-T and Fast Ethernet connections, and for most (but not all) port-switching switches. Since collisions can occur on a segment, switch ports used for segment-based switching cannot support full-duplex transmission.

In addition to providing a simultaneous bidirectional data flow capability, the use of full duplex permits an extension of cabling distances. For example, at 100 Mbps the use of a fiber cable for full-duplex operations can support a distance of 2,000 meters while only 412 meters is supported using half-duplex transmission via fiber.

Due to the higher cost of full-duplex ports and adapter cards, you should carefully evaluate the potential use of FDX prior to using this capability. For example, most client workstations will obtain a minimal gain through the use of a full-duplex capability since humans operating computers rarely perform simultaneous two-way operations. Thus, other than speeding acknowledgments associated with the transfer of data, the use of an FDX connection for workstations represents an excessive capacity that should only be considered when vendors are competing for sales and as such they provide this capability as a standard. In comparison, the use of an FDX transmission capability to connect servers to switch ports enables a server to respond to one request while receiving a subsequent request.

Thus, the ability to utilize the capability of FDX transmission is enhanced by using this capability on server to switch port connections.

Although vendors would like you to believe that FDX doubles your transmission capability, in actuality you will obtain only a fraction of this advertised throughput. This is because most network devices, including servers that are provided with an FDX transmission capability, use that capability only a fraction of the time.

Jabber Control

A jabber is an Ethernet frame whose length exceeds 1518 bytes. Jabbers are commonly caused by defective hardware or collisions, and can adversely affect a receiving device by its misinterpretation of data in the frame. A switch operating in the cut-through mode with jabber control will truncate the frame to an appropriate length. In comparison, a store-and-forward switch will normally automatically drop a jabbered frame.

Latency

When examining vendor specifications the best word of advice is to be suspicious of latency notations, especially those concerning store-and-forward switches. Many vendors do not denote the length of the frame used for latency measurements, while some vendors use what might be referred to as creative accounting when computing latency. Let's review the formal definition of latency. *Latency* can be defined as the difference in time (t) from the first bit arriving at a source port to the first bit output on the destination port. Modern cut-through switches have a latency of approximately 40 µs, while store-and-forward switches have a latency between 80 to 90 µs for a 72-byte frame, and 1250 to 1300 µs for a maximum length 1500-byte frame.

Latency functions as a break on the two-way exchange of information through a switch, such as a client/server session. Thus, the minimum waiting time through a switch is twice the switch latency for each data exchange, which lowers the effective throughput of the switch.

A cross-point or cut-through switch minimizes latency, which can be an important consideration when transferring video or audio information. From an examination of the composition of an Ethernet frame you can determine the minimum amount of time required by a switch to recognize the destination address and initiate a cross-connection. That is, the first two fields of an Ethernet frame are the 8-byte preamble and 6-byte destination address. Thus, a switch must read 14 bytes prior to being able to determine the destination address of a frame. At a 10-Mbps operating rate this means that any Ethernet switch has a minimum latency of:

$$\frac{14 \text{ bytes} \times 8 \text{ bits/byte}}{10 \text{ Mbps}} \quad \text{or } 11.2 \text{ μs}$$

For a store-and-forward Ethernet switch an entire frame is first stored. Since the maximum length of an Ethernet frame is 1526 bytes, this means that the maximum latency for a store-and-forward 10-Mbps Ethernet switch is:

$$\frac{1526 \text{ bytes} \times 8 \text{ bits/byte}}{10 \text{ Mbps}} \quad \text{or } 1.2208 \text{ ms}$$

plus the time required to perform a table look-up and cross-connection between source and destination ports. Since a 10-Mbps Ethernet LAN has a 9.6-μs gap between frames, this means that the minimum delay time between frames flowing through a cut-through switch is 20.8 μs. Figure 3.11 illustrates the composi-

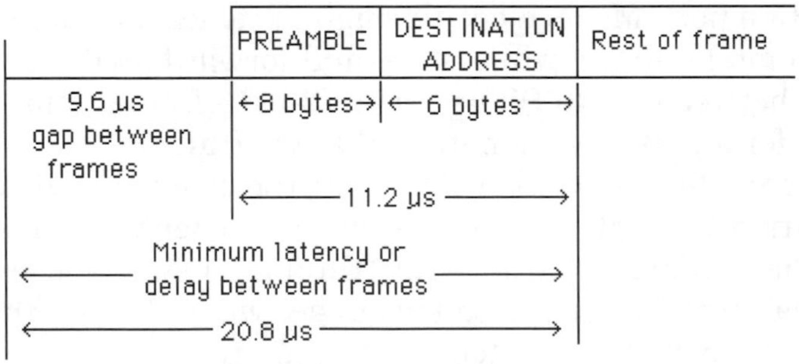

FIGURE 3.11   Switch latency includes a built-in delay resulting from the structure of the Ethernet frame.

tion of this delay at a 10-Mbps operating rate. For a store-and-forward switch, considering the 9.6-μs gap between frames results in a maximum latency of 1230.4 μs plus the time required to perform a table look-up and initiate a cross-connection between source and destination ports.

Management

The most common method used to provide switch management involves the integration of RMON support for each switch port. This enables an SNMP console to obtain statistics from the RMON group or groups supported by each switch. Since the retrieval of statistics on a port-by-port basis can be time consuming, most switches that support RMON also create a database of statistics to facilitate their retrieval.

Module Insertion

Modular switches support two different methods of module insertion—switch power down and hot. As their names imply, a switch power down method requires you to first deactivate the switch and literally bring it down. In comparison, the ability to perform hot insertions enables you to add modules to an operating switch without adversely affecting users.

Port Buffer Size

Switch designers incorporate buffer memory into port cards as a mechanism to compensate for the difference between the internal speed of the switch and the operating rate of an endstation or segment connected to the port. Some switch designers increase the amount of buffer memory incorporated into port cards to use in conjunction with a flow control mechanism, while other switch designers may use port buffer memory as a substitute for flow control. If used only as a mechanism for speed compensation, the size of port buffers may be limited to a few thousand bytes of storage. When used in conjunction with a flow control mechanism or as a flow control mechanism, the amount of buffer memory per port may be up to 64, 128, or 256 Kbytes, perhaps even up to 1 or 2 Mbytes. Although you might expect more buffer memory to provide better results this may not necessarily be true. For example, assume a workstation on a segment is connected to a port that has a large buffer with just enough free memory to accept one frame. When the workstation transmits a sequence of frames only the first is able to be placed into the buffer. If the switch then initiates flow control as the contents of its port buffer is emptied, subsequent frames are barred from moving through the switch. When the switch disables flow control it is possible that another station with data to transmit is able to gain access to the port prior to the station that sent frame one in a sequence of frames. Due to the delay in emptying the contents of a large buffer, it becomes possible that subsequent frames are sufficiently delayed as they move through a switch to a mainframe via a gateway that a time-dependent session could time out. Thus, you should consider your network structure in conjunction with the operating rate of switch ports and the amount of buffer storage per port to determine if an extremely large amount of buffer storage could potentially result in session timeouts. Fortunately, most switch manufacturers limit port buffer memory to 128 Kbytes, which at 10 Mbps results in a maximum delay of

$$\frac{128 \times 1024 \times 8 \text{ bits/byte}}{10 \text{ Mbps}}$$

or .10 seconds.

Port Module Support

Although many Ethernet switches are limited to supporting only Ethernet networks, the type of networks supported can considerably differ between vendor products as well as within a specific vendor product line. Thus, you may wish to examine the support of port modules for connecting 10BASE-2, 10BASE-5, 10BASE-T, and 100BASE-T LANs. In addition, if your organization supports various types of LANs or is considering the use of switches to form a tier-structured network using a different type of high-speed backbone, you should examine port support for FDDI, full-duplex Token-Ring, and ATM connectivity. Many modular Ethernet switches include the ability to add translating bridge modules, enabling support for several different types of networks through a common chassis.

Spanning Tree Support

Ethernet networks use the spanning tree algorithm to prevent loops that, if enabled, could result in the continuous replication of frames. In a bridged network, spanning tree support is accomplished by the use of Bridge Protocol Data Units (BPDUs) which, as explained in Chapter 2, enable bridges to select a root bridge and agree upon a network topology that prevents loops from occurring. Since a switch in effect represents a sophisticated bridge, we would want to prevent the use of multiple switches from forming a loop. For example, consider Figure 3.12, which illustrates the use of two switches to interconnect two LANs. If both switches were active, a frame from the client connected on LAN A destined to the server on LAN B would be placed back onto LAN A by switch S1, causing a packet loop and the replication of the packet, a situation we want to avoid. By incorporating spanning tree support into each switch, they can communicate with one another to construct a topology that does not contain loops. For example, one switch in Figure 3.12 would place a port in a blocking mode while the other switch would have both ports in a forwarding mode of operation.

Switch Type

As discussed in Chapter 2, a switch will either support one or multiple addresses per port. If it supports one address per port it is a port-based switch. In comparison, if it supports multiple addresses per switch, it is considered to be a segment-based

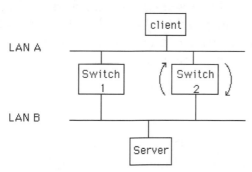

FIGURE 3.12 The need for loop control.

switch even if only one endstation is connected to some or all ports on the switch.

Switching Mode

Ethernet switches can be obtained to operate in a cut-through, store-and-forward, or hybrid operating mode. As discussed in Chapter 2, the hybrid mode of operation represents toggling between cut-through and store-and-forward based on a frame error rate threshold. That is, a hybrid switch might initially be set to operate in a cut-through mode and compute the CRC for each frame on the fly, comparing its computed values to the CRCs appended to each frame. When a predefined frame error threshold is reached the switch would change its operating mode to store-and-forward, enabling erroneous frames to be discarded. Some switch vendors reference a hybrid switch mode as an error-free cut-through operating mode.

Virtual LAN Support

A virtual LAN can be considered to represent a broadcast domain created through the association of switch ports, MAC addresses, or a network layer parameter. Thus, there are three basic types of vLAN creation methods you can evaluate when examining the functionality of an Ethernet switch. In addition, some vendors now offer a rules-based vLAN creation capability which enables users to have an almost infinite number of vLAN creation methods with the ability to go down to the bit level within a frame as a mechanism for vLAN associations.

The primary advantages associated with the use of vLANs include responding to ad-hoc working group formations, limiting broadcast traffic, and providing an enhanced level of security. Since vLANs are covered as an entity later in this book, we will defer a detailed examination of their creation method and utilization until Chapter 6.

Networking

Since there is really no typical Ethernet network, a discussion of the use of switches in a networking environment is best served by focusing on workgroup or departmental and organizational switch configurations. By examining the variety of methods by which switches can be used, we can then tailor their use to specific organizational requirements. Thus, our examination of Ethernet switching configurations can be considered to represent a discussion of the use of building blocks which, when joined together, can be used to create various structures.

Basic Switching

For most desktop applications a 10-Mbps capability will be sufficient for many years to come. This means that the typical department or workgroup can use a basic 10-Mbps Ethernet switch with a few 100-Mbps ports or a fat pipe capability to provide a connection to one or more local file servers. Figure 3.13 illustrates the use of a 10/100-Mbps Ethernet switch to support a small department or workgroup.

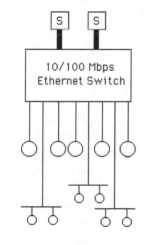

Legend:

〇 〇 = segment

S = server

◯ = workstation

▮ = 100 Mbps connection

FIGURE 3.13 Supporting a small department or workgroup.

In examining the use of the switch shown in Figure 3.13, the segments shown might be used to support a few workstations grouped in close proximity to one another, or they could be replaced by directly connected workstations, with the configuration dependent upon the type of switch used and the ability to configure several stations onto conventional hubs if it makes sense to do so based upon station activity and their proximity to one another. Concerning the switch-to-server connections, unless you have a number of servers which are configured to allow distributed access, which may not result in bottlenecks when connected at 10 Mbps, you should consider using 100-Mbps connections. This is because most file servers, especially modern Pentium Pro and Alpha-based servers, can easily generate 40 to 60 Mbps or more of data. When such platforms include multiple processors, servers can easily deliver 100 Mbps of data. Thus, the use of 100-Mbps connections with an appropriate amount of port buffer memory can considerably enhance client/server operations at the workgroup level.

Expanding the Workgroup

As a workgroup expands or several workgroups are grouped together to form a department, most organizations will want to consider the use of a two-tiered switching network. The first or lower-level tier would represent switches dedicated to supporting a specific workgroup including local servers. The upper tier would include one or more switches used to interconnect workgroup switches as well as to provide workgroup users with access to departmental servers whose access crosses workgroup boundaries. Since the upper-tier switch or switches are used to interconnect workgroup switches, the upper-tier switches are commonly referred to as *backbone* switches. Figure 3.14 illustrates a possible use of one backbone switch to interconnect two workgroup switches.

Since the backbone switch provides an interconnection between workgroup switches as well as access to departmental servers, the failure of a backbone switch would have a much more significant effect upon communications than the failure of a workgroup switch. Thus, you should consider using a backbone switch with redundant power supplies, common logic, and other key modules. Then, the failure of one module at worst would make only one or a few port connections inoperative. If you acquire one or a few additional port modules you would then have the ability to re-cable around a port failure without having to wait for a replacement module to be shipped to your location.

When using one or more backbone switches it is important to note that these switches directly affect the throughput between workgroups as well as the transfer of information to and from departmental servers. Due to this, most organizations will use dedicated 100-Mbps Ethernet switches for backbone operations. If this type of switch is not available at an economical cost, an alternative is to use a 10/100-Mbps switch with enough 100-Mbps ports to provide connections from workgroup switches as well as to departmental servers.

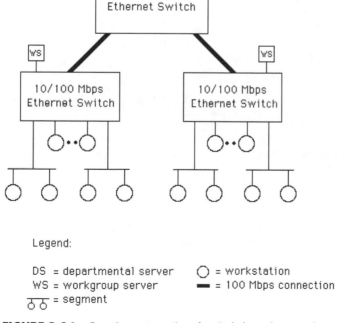

FIGURE 3.14 Creating a two-tiered switch-based network.

Although the use of a 100-Mbps backbone Ethernet switch can provide sufficient bandwidth for most applications, it cannot provide what is referred to as a Quality of Service (QoS) in which bandwidth is reserved for the use of high-priority communications that require a dedicated path through a switch whenever communication occurs. Examples of data streams requiring a QoS include videoconferencing, audio/telephone communica-

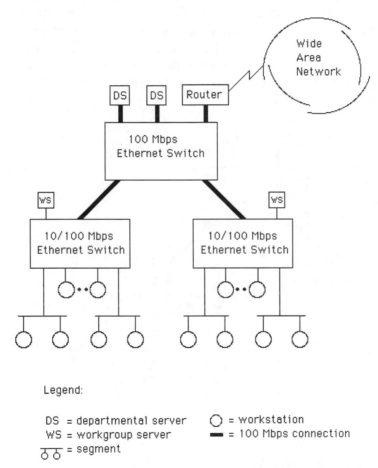

Legend:

DS = departmental server   ◯ = workstation
WS = workgroup server   ▬ = 100 Mbps connection
⟔ = segment

FIGURE 3.15 Interconnecting geographically dispersed switch-based networks.

tions, and other types of time-dependent transmissions usually lumped under the term *multimedia*. Although the use of Ethernet switches may provide an acceptable level of performance under light switching loads, as traffic increases file transfers and interactive query-responses could adversely affect multimedia applications. In such situations the use of ATM switches should be considered. The operation and utilization of ATM switches are described in Chapter 5.

Organizational Switching

Building upon the departmental switching illustrated in Figure 3.14, you can use routers to interconnect geographically dispersed departments. Doing so can result in an organizational Ethernet switching network that could span different locations in the same city, different cities, one or more states, a country, or the entire globe. Figure 3.15 illustrates the attachment of one router to a backbone switch, connecting the backbone at one location to a Wide Area Network. Although the actual use of one or more routers will be governed by our specific networking requirements, Figure 3.15 illustrates how you can connect one switch-based network to other switch-based networks.

As you design your network infrastructure you should consider the use of one or more Ethernet switch features previously discussed in this chapter to enhance the performance of your network. For example, you may wish to use full-duplex ports for local and departmental server connections. In addition, by the time you read this book Gigabit switches should be available; their use could provide you with another option to consider when constructing a tiered-network structure.

Token-Ring and FDDI Switching

4

Although Token-Ring has historically been more expensive to implement than Ethernet, it represents a more sophisticated networking environment which provides a more orderly form of communications. The order is provided by the circulation of a token which must be acquired for a station to transmit data as well as priority and reservation fields which, when considered as an entity, result in network utilization levels that can exceed 90 percent without resulting in session timeouts or other types of delays. In comparison, Ethernet's CSMA/CD access protocol permits multiple stations to simultaneously attempt to gain access to a network. Due to the effect of collisions, the transmission of jam patterns when collisions occur, and the delay associated with the random exponential backoff algorithm, Ethernet networks become saturated when utilization exceeds 50 percent. Based upon the preceding, Token-Ring continues to be used by organizations that require consistent response times associated with transaction processing and other mission-critical applications. Thus, most organizations that initially installed Token-Ring LANs will more than likely focus their attention upon the use of Token-Ring and FDDI switches instead of migrating to Fast Ethernet and the use of Ethernet switches.

In this chapter we turn our attention to the operation and utilization of Token-Ring and FDDI switches and the use of FDDI LANs as a backbone networking option. Since the operation of Token-Ring and FDDI switches are based upon frames transported on those networks, the first portion of this chapter will provide a review of the structure of Token-Ring and FDDI frames. In doing so we will also examine Token-Ring's media access control (MAC) and logical link control (LLC) since certain MAC and LLC operations directly affect the functionality and operation of Token-Ring switches. Once the preceding is accomplished, we will turn to the operation and utilization of switches designed to support the transmission of Token-Ring and FDDI traffic and how such switches can be used with other types of LAN switches. We will also examine the use of FDDI as a backbone network as well as discuss why the use of this type of network can provide an enhanced capability for backbone operations in comparison to the use of Fast Ethernet switches.

TOKEN-RING TRANSMISSION FORMATS

Three types of transmission formats are supported on a Token-Ring network—token, abort, and frame. In this section we will examine each format, with special emphasis on the format of the Token-Ring frame.

The Token Format

The token format as illustrated in Figure 4.1a is the mechanism by which access to the ring is passed from one computer attached to the network to another device connected to the network. Here the token format consists of three bytes, of which the starting and ending delimiters are used to indicate the beginning and end of a token frame. The middle byte of a token frame is an access control byte. Three bits are used as a priority indicator, three bits are used as a reservation indicator, while one

a. Token format

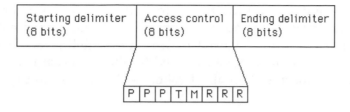

b. Abort token format

Starting delimiter	Ending delimiter

c. Frame format

Starting delimiter (8 bits)	Access control (8 bits)	Frame control (8 bits)	Destination address (48 bits)	Source address (48 bits)	Routing information (optional)

Information variable	Frame check sequence (32 bits)	Ending delimiter (8 bits)	Frame status (8 bits)

Legend:

P = priority bit
T = token bit
M = monitor bit
R = reservation bit

FIGURE 4.1   Token, abort, and frame formats.

bit is used for the token bit, and another bit position functions as the monitor bit.

When the token bit is set to a binary 0 it indicates that the transmission is a token. When it is set to a binary 1 it indicates that data in the form of a frame is being transmitted.

The Abort Token

The second Token-Ring frame format signifies an abort token. In actuality there is no token, since this format is indicated by a starting delimiter followed by an ending delimiter. The transmission of an abort token is used to abort a previous transmission. The format of an abort token is illustrated in Figure 4.1b.

The Token Frame

The third type of Token-Ring frame format occurs when a station seizes a free token. At that time the token format is converted into a frame which includes the addition of frame control, addressing data, an error detection field, and a frame status field. The format of a Token-Ring frame is illustrated in Figure 4.1c. By examining each of the fields in the frame we will also examine the token and token abort frames due to the commonality of fields between each frame.

Starting/Ending Delimiters

The starting and ending delimiters mark the beginning and ending of a token or frame. Each delimiter consists of a unique code pattern which identifies it to the network. To understand the composition of the starting and ending delimiter fields requires us to review the method by which data is represented on a Token-Ring network using Differential Manchester encoding.

Differential Manchester Encoding.   Figure 4.2 illustrates the use of Differential Manchester encoding, comparing its operation to non-return to zero (NRZ) and conventional Manchester encoding.

In Figure 4.2a, NRZ coding illustrates the representation of data by holding a voltage low (–V) to represent a binary 0 and high (+V) to represent a binary 1. This method of signaling is called non-return to zero since there is no return to a 0 V position after each data bit is coded.

One problem associated with NRZ encoding is the fact that a long string of 0 or 1 bits does not result in a voltage change. Thus, to determine that bit m in a string of n bits of 0's or 1's is

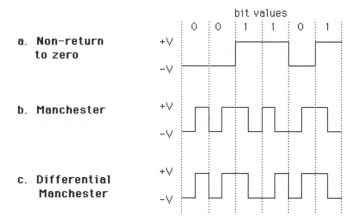

FIGURE 4.2 Differential Manchester encoding. In Differential Manchester encoding the direction of the signal's voltage transmission changes whenever a binary 1 is transmitted but remains the same for a binary 0.

set to a 0 or 1 requires sampling at predefined bit times. This in turn requires each device on a network using NRZ encoding to have its own clocking circuitry.

To avoid the necessity of building clocking circuitry into devices requires a mechanism for encoded data to carry clocking information. One method by which encoded data carries clocking information is obtained from the use of Manchester encoding, which is illustrated in Figure 4.2b. In Manchester encoding, each data bit consists of a half-bit time signal at a low voltage (−V) and another half-bit time signal at the opposite positive voltage (+V). Every binary 0 is represented by a half-bit time at a low voltage and the remaining bit time at a high voltage. Every binary 1 is represented by a half-bit time at a high voltage followed by a half bit time at a low voltage. By changing the voltage for every binary digit, Manchester encoding ensures that the signal carries self-clocking information.

In Figure 4.2c, Differential Manchester encoding is illustrated. The difference between Manchester encoding and Differential Manchester encoding occurs in the method by which binary 1's are encoded. In Differential Manchester encoding, the direction of the signal's voltage transition changes whenever a binary 1 is transmitted, but remains the same for a binary 0. The

IEEE 802.5 standard specifies the use of Differential Manchester encoding and this encoding technique is used on Token-Ring networks at the physical layer to transmit and detect four distinct symbols—a binary 0, a binary 1, and two nondata symbols.

Nondata Symbols. Under Manchester and Differential Manchester encoding there are two possible code violations that can occur. Each code violation produces what is known as a nondata symbol and is used in the Token-Ring frame to denote starting and ending delimiters, similar to the use of the flag in an HDLC frame. However, unlike the flag whose bit composition 01111110 is uniquely maintained by inserting a 0 bit after every sequence of five set bits and removing a 0 following every sequence of five set bits, Differential Manchester encoding maintains the uniqueness of frames by the use of nondata J and nondata K symbols. This eliminates the bit-stuffing operations required by HDLC.

The two nondata symbols each consist of two half-bit times without a voltage change. The J symbol occurs when the voltage is the same as that of the last signal, while the K symbol occurs when the voltage becomes opposite of that of the last signal. Figure 4.3 illustrates the occurrence of the J and K nondata symbols based upon different last bit voltages. Readers will note in comparing Figure 4.3 to Figure 4.2c that the J and K nondata

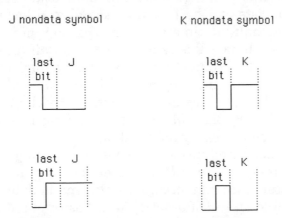

FIGURE 4.3 J and K nondata symbol composition. J and K nondata symbols are distinct code violations that cannot be mistaken for data.

symbols are distinct code violations that cannot be mistaken for either a binary 0 or a binary 1.

Now that we understand the operation of Differential Manchester encoding and the composition of the J and K nondata symbols, we can focus our attention upon the actual format of each frame delimiter.

The start delimiter field marks the beginning of a frame. The composition of this field is the bits and nondata symbols JK0JK000. The end delimiter field marks the end of a frame as well as denotes whether the frame is the last frame of a multiple frame sequence using a single token or if there are additional frames following this frame. The format of the end delimiter field is JK1JK1IE, where I is the intermediate frame bit. If I is set to 0, this indicates it is the last frame transmitted by a station. If I is set to 1, this indicates that additional frames follow this frame. E is an *error-detected* bit. The E bit is initially set to 0 by the station transmitting a frame, token, or abort sequence. As the frame circulates the ring, each station checks the transmission for errors. Upon detection of a frame check sequence (FCS) error, inappropriate nondata symbol, illegal framing, or another type of error, the first station detecting the error will set the E bit to a value of 1. Since stations keep track of the number of times they set the E bit to a value of 1, it becomes possible to use this information as a guide to locating possible cable errors. For example, if one workstation accounted for a very large percentage of E bit settings in a 72-station network, there is a high degree of probability that there is a problem with the lobe cable to that workstation. The problem could be a crimped cable or a loose connector and represents a logical place to commence an investigation in an attempt to reduce E bit errors.

Access Control Field

The second field in both token and frame formats is the access control byte. As illustrated in Figure 4.1a, this byte consists of four subfields and serves as the controlling mechanism for gaining access to the network. When a free token circulates the network the access control field represents one-third of the length of the frame since it is prefixed by the start delimiter and suffixed by the end delimiter.

TABLE 4.1 Priority Bit Settings

Priority Bits	Priority
000	Normal user priority, MAC frames that do not require a token and response type MAC frames
001	Normal user priority
010	Normal user priority
011	Normal user priority and MAC frames that require tokens
100	Bridge
101	Reserved
110	Reserved
111	Specialized station management

The lowest priority that can be specified by the priority bits in the access control byte is 0 (000), while the highest is seven (111), providing eight levels of priority. Table 4.1 lists the normal use of the priority bits in the access control field. Workstations have a default priority of three, while bridges have a default priority of four.

To reserve a token, a workstation inserts its priority level in the priority reservation subfield. Unless another station with a higher priority bumps the requesting station, the reservation will be honored and the requesting station will obtain the token. If the token bit is set to 1, this serves as an indication that a frame follows instead of the ending delimiter.

A station that needs to transmit a frame at a given priority can use any available token that has a priority level equal to or less than the priority level of the frame to be transmitted. When a token of equal or lower priority is not available, the ring station can reserve a token of the required priority through the use of the reservation bits. In doing so the station must follow two rules. First, if a passing token has a higher priority reservation than the reservation level desired by the workstation, the station will not alter the reservation field contents. Second, if the reservation bits have not been set or indicate a lower priority than that desired by the station, the station can now set the reservation bits to the required priority level.

Once a frame is removed by its originating station, the reservation bits in the header will be checked. If those bits have a nonzero value, the station must release a nonzero priority token, with the actual priority assigned based upon the priority used by the station for the recently transmitted frame, the reservation bit settings received upon the return of the frame, and any stored priority.

On occasion, the Token-Ring protocol will result in the transmission of a new token by a station prior to that station having the ability to verify the settings of the access control field in a returned frame. When this situation arises, the token will be issued according to the priority and reservation bit settings in the access control field of the transmitted frame.

Figure 4.4 illustrates the operation of the priority (P) and reservation (R) bit fields in the access control field. In this example, the prevention of a high-priority station from monopolizing the network is illustrated by station A entering a Priority-Hold state. This occurs when a station originates a token at a higher priority than the last token it generated. Once in a Priority-Hold state, the station will issue tokens that will bring the priority level eventually down to zero as a mechanism to prevent a high-priority station from monopolizing the network.

The Monitor Bit.   The monitor bit is used to prevent a token with a priority exceeding zero or a frame from continuously circulating on the Token-Ring. This bit is transmitted as a 0 in all tokens and frames, except for a device on the network which functions as an active monitor and thus obtains the capability to inspect and modify that bit. When a token or frame is examined by the active monitor it will set the monitor bit to a 1 if it was previously found to be set to 0. If a token or frame is found to have the monitor bit already set to 1, this indicates that the token or frame has already made at least one revolution around the ring and an error condition has occurred, usually caused by the failure of a station to remove its transmission from the ring or the failure of a high-priority station to seize a token. When the active monitor finds a monitor bit set to 1 it assumes an

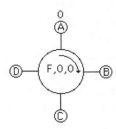

a. Station A generates a frame
    using a non-priority token P,R=0,0.

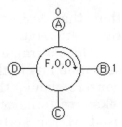

b. Station B reserves a priority
    1 in the reservation bits in
    the frame P,R=0,1; Station A
    enters a priority-hold state.

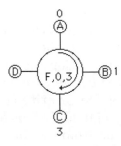

c. Station C reserves a priority of 3,
    overriding B's reservation of 1; P,R=0,3.

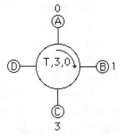

d. Station A removes its frame and
    generates a token at reserved
    priority level 3; P,R=3,0.

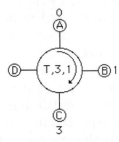

e. Station B repeats priority token and
   makes a new reservation of priority
   level 1; P,R=3,1

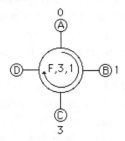

f. Station C grabs token and
   transmits a frame with a priority
   of 3; P,R=3,1.

FIGURE 4.4 Priority and reservation field utilization.

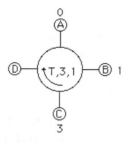

g. Upon return of frame to Station C it's removed. Station C generates a token at the priority just used; P,R=3,1

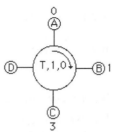

h. Station A in a priority-hold state grabs token and changes its priority to 1; P,R=1,0. Station A stays in priority-hold state until priority reduced to 0.

Legend:

(A), (B), (C), (D) = stations

Numeric outside station identifier indicates priority level.

FIGURE 4.4   *(continued)*

error condition has occurred. The active monitor then purges the token or frame and releases a new token onto the ring. Now that we understand the role of the monitor bit in the access control field and the operation of the active monitor on that bit, let's consider the active monitor.

Active Monitor.   The active monitor is the device that has the highest address on the network. All other stations on the network are considered as standby monitors and watch the active monitor.

As previously explained, the function of the active monitor is to determine if a token or frame is continuously circulating the ring in error. To accomplish this the active monitor sets the monitor count bit as a token or frame goes by. If a destination workstation fails or has its power turned off the frame will circulate back to the active monitor, where it is then removed from the network. In the event the active monitor should fail or be turned off, the standby monitors watch the active monitor by looking for an active monitor frame. If one does not appear within seven seconds, the standby monitor that has the highest network address then takes over as the active monitor.

Frame Control Field

The frame control field informs a receiving device on the network of the type of frame that was transmitted and how it should be interpreted. Frames can be either logical link control (LLC) or reference physical link functions according to the IEEE 802.5 media access control (MAC) standard. A media access control frame carries network control information and responses, while a logical link control frame carries data.

The eight-bit frame control field has the format FFZZZZZZ, where FF are frame definition bits. The top of Table 4.2 indicates the possible settings of the frame bits and the assignment of those settings. The ZZZZZZ bits convey media access control buffering information when the FF bits are set to 00. When the

TABLE 4.2 Frame Control Field Subfields

F bit settings	Assignment
00	MAC frame
01	LLC frame
10	Undefined (reserved for future use)
11	Undefined (reserved for future use)

Z bit settings	Assignment*
000	Normal buffering
001	Remove ring station
010	Beacon
011	Claim token
100	Ring purge
101	Active monitor present
110	Standby monitor present

*When F bits set to 00, Z bits are used to notify an adapter that the frame is to be expressed buffered.

FF bits are set to 01 to indicate an LLC frame, the ZZZZZZ bits are split into two fields, designated rrrYYY. Currently, the rrr bits are reserved for future use and are set to 000. The YYY bits indicate the priority of the logical link control data. The lower portion of Table 4.2 indicates the value of the Z bits when used in MAC frames to notify a Token-Ring adapter that the frame is to be expressed buffered.

Destination Address Field

Although the IEEE 802.5 standard supports both 16-bit and 48-bit address fields, IBM's implementation, as well as that of most other vendors, requires the use of 48-bit address fields. IBM's destination address field is made up of five subfields as illustrated in Figure 4.5. The first bit in the destination address identifies the destination as an individual station (bit set to 0) or as a group (bit set to 1) of one or more stations. The latter provides the capability for a message to be broadcast to a group of stations.

Universally Administered Address. The universally administered address is a unique address permanently encoded into an adapter's ROM. Because it is placed into ROM, it is also known as a burned-in address. The IEEE assigns blocks of addresses to each vendor manufacturing Token-Ring equipment, which ensures that Token-Ring adapter cards manufactured by different vendors are uniquely defined. Some Token-Ring adapter manufacturers are assigned universal addresses that

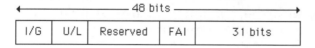

Legend:

    I/G = individual or group bit address identifier
    U/L = universally or locally administered bit identifier
    FAI = functional address indicator

FIGURE 4.5 Destination address subfields. The reserved field contains the manufacturer's identification in 22 bits represented by 6 hex digits.

contain an organizationally unique identifier. This identifier consists of the first six hex digits of the adapter card address and is also referred to as the manufacturer identification. For example, cards manufactured by IBM will begin with the address X08005A or X10005A, whereas adapter cards manufactured by Texas Instruments will begin with the address X400014.

Locally Administered Address.   A key problem with the use of universally administered addresses is the requirement to change software coding in a mainframe computer whenever a workstation connected to the mainframe via a gateway is added or removed from the network. To avoid constant software changes, locally administrated addressing can be used. This type of addressing temporarily overrides universally administrated addressing; however, the user is now responsible for ensuring the uniqueness of each address.

Functional Address Indicator.   The functional address indicator subfield in the destination address identifies the function associated with the destination address, such as a bridge, active monitor, or configuration report server.

The functional address indicator indicates a functional address when set to 0 and the I/G bit position is set to a 1—the latter indicating a group address. This condition can occur only when the U/L bit position is also set to a 1 and results in the ability to generate locally administered group addresses that are called functional addresses. Table 4.3 lists the functional addresses defined by the IEEE. Currently, 14 functional addresses have been defined out of a total of 31 that are available for use, with the remaining addresses available for user definitions or reserved for future use.

Address Values.   The range of addresses that can be used on a Token Ring primarily depends upon the settings of the I/G, U/L, and FAI bit positions. When the I/G and U/L bit positions are set to 00, the manufacturer's universal address is used. When the I/G and U/L bits are set to 01, individual locally administered addresses are used in the defined range listed in Table 4.3. When all three bit positions are set, this situation indicates a group address within the range contained in Table 4.4. If the I/G

TABLE 4.3 IEEE Functional Addresses

Active Monitor	XC000 0000 0001
Ring Parameter Server	XC000 0000 0002
Network Server Heartbeat	XC000 0000 0004
Ring Error Monitor	XC000 0000 0008
Configuration Report Server	XC000 0000 0010
Synchronous Bandwidth Manager	XC000 0000 0020
Locate—Directory Server	XC000 0000 0040
NETBIOS	XC000 0000 0080
Bridge	XC000 0000 0100
IMPL Server	XC000 0000 0200
Ring Authorization Server	XC000 0000 0400
LAN Gateway	XC000 0000 0800
Ring Wiring Concentrator	XC000 0000 1000
LAN Manager	XC000 0000 2000
User-defined	XC000 0000 8000 through XC000 4000 0000

TABLE 4.4 Token-Ring Addresses

	Bit Settings			
	I/G	*U/L*	*FAI*	*Address/Address Range*
Individual, universally administered	0	0	0/1	Manufacturer's serial no.
Individual, locally administered	0	1	0	X4000 0000 0000 – X4000 7FFF FFFF
Group address	1	1	1	XC000 8000 0000 – XC000 FFFF FFFF
Functional address	1	1	0	XC000 0000 0001 – XC000 0000 2000 (bit-sensitive)
All-stations broadcast	1	1	1	XFFFF FFFF FFFF
Null address	0	0	0	X0000 0000 0000

and U/L bits are set to 11 but the FAI bit is set to 0, this indicates that the address is a functional address. In this situation the range of addresses is bit-sensitive, permitting only those functional addresses listed in Table 4.3.

In addition to the previously mentioned addresses, there are two special destination address values that are defined. An address of all 1's (FFFFFFFFFFFF) identifies all stations as destination stations. If a null address is used in which all bits are set to 0 (X000000000000), the frame is not addressed to any workstation. In this situation it can only be transmitted but not received, enabling you to test the ability of the active monitor to purge this type of frame from the network.

Source Address Field

The source address field always represents an individual address which specifies the adapter card responsible for the transmission. The source address field consists of three major subfields as illustrated in Figure 4.6. When locally administered addressing occurs, only 24 bits in the address field are used since the 22 manufacturer identification bit positions are not used.

The routing information bit identifier identifies the fact that routing information is contained in an optional routing information field. This bit is set when a frame will be routed across a bridge using IBM's source routing technique.

Routing Information Field

The routing information field is optional and is included in a frame when the RI bit of the source address field is set. Figure 4.7 illustrates the format of the optional routing information

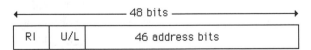

FIGURE 4.6 Source address field (RI: routing information bit identifier, U/L: universally or locally administered bit identifier). The 46 address bits consist of 22 manufacturer identification bits and 24 universally administered bits when the U/L bit is set to 0. If set to 1, a 31-bit locally administered address is used with the manufacturer's identification bits set to 0.

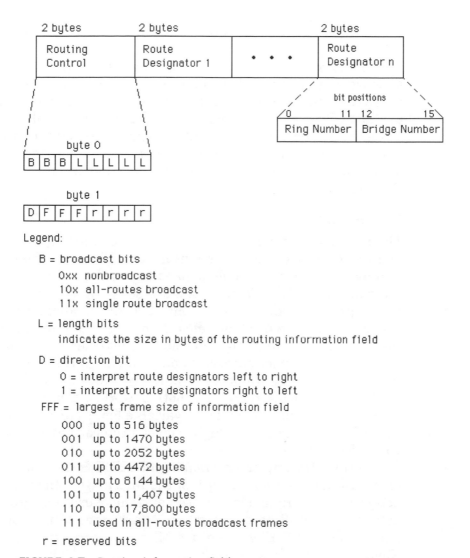

FIGURE 4.7 Routing information field.

field. If this field is omitted, the frame cannot leave the ring it was originated on under IBM's source routing bridging method. Under transparent bridging, the frame can be transmitted onto another ring. The routing information field is of variable length and contains a control subfield and one or more two-byte route designator fields when included in a frame as the latter are required to control the flow of frames across one or more bridges.

The maximum length of the routing information field (RIF) supported by IBM is 18 bytes. Since each RIF field must contain a 2-byte routing control field, this leaves a maximum of 16 bytes available for use by up to eight route designators. As illustrated in Figure 4.7, each two-byte route designator consists of a 12-bit ring number and a 4-bit bridge number. Thus, a maximum total of 16 bridges can be used to join any two rings in an Enterprise Token-Ring network.

Information Field

The information field is used to contain Token-Ring commands and responses as well as carry user data. The type of data carried by the information field depends upon the F bit settings in the frame type field. If the F bits are set to 00 the information field carries media access control (MAC) commands and responses that are used for network management operations. If the F bits are set to 01 the information field carries logical link control (LLC) or user data. Such data can be in the form of portions of a file being transferred on the network or an electronic mail message being routed to another workstation on the network. The information field is of variable length and can be considered to represent the higher-level protocol enveloped in a Token-Ring frame.

In the IBM implementation of the IEEE 802.5 Token-Ring standard the maximum length of the information field depends upon the Token-Ring adapter used and the operating rate of the network. Token-Ring adapters with 64 Kbytes of memory can handle up to 4.5 Kbytes on a 4-Mbps network and up to 18 Kbytes on a 16-Mbps network.

Frame Check Sequence Field

The frame check sequence field contains four bytes which provide the mechanism for checking the accuracy of frames flowing on the network. The cyclic redundancy check data included in the frame check sequence field covers the frame control, destination address, source address, routing information, and information fields. If an adapter computes a cyclic redundancy check that does not match the data contained in the frame check sequence field of a frame, the destination adapter discards the frame information and sets an error bit (E bit) indicator. This error bit indicator, as previously discussed, actually represents a ninth bit position of the ending delimiter and serves to inform the transmitting station that the data was received in error.

Frame Status Field

The frame status field serves as a mechanism to indicate the results of a frame's circulation around a ring to the station that initiated the frame. Figure 4.8 indicates the format of the frame status field. The frame status field contains three subfields that are duplicated for accuracy purposes since they reside outside of CRC checking. One field (A) is used to denote if an address was recognized, while a second field (C) indicates if the frame was copied at its destination. Each of these fields is one bit in length. The third field, which is two bit positions in length (rr), is currently reserved for future use.

TOKEN-RING MEDIA ACCESS CONTROL

As previously discussed, a MAC frame is used to transport network commands and responses. As such, the MAC layer controls the routing of information between the LLC and the physical

| A | C | r | r | A | C | r | r |

A = address-recognized bits
B = frame-copied bits
r = reserved bits

FIGURE 4.8 The frame status field denotes whether the destination address was recognized and whether the frame was copied. Since this field is outside of CRC checking, its subfields are duplicated for accuracy.

network. Examples of MAC protocol functions include the recognition of adapter addresses, physical media access management, and message verification and status generation. A MAC frame is indicated by the setting of the first two bits in the frame control field to 00. When this situation occurs, the contents of the information field which carries MAC data is known as a *vector*.

Vectors and Subvectors

Only one vector is permitted per MAC frame. That vector consists of a major vector length (VL), a major vector identifier (VI), and zero or more subvectors.

As indicated in Figure 4.9, there can be multiple subvectors within a vector. The vector length (VL) is a 16-bit number that gives the length of the vector, including the VL subfield in bytes. VL can vary between decimal 4 and 65 535 in value. The minimum value VL can be assigned results from the fact that the smallest information field must contain both VL and VI subfields. Since each subfield is two bytes in length, the minimum value of VL is 4.

When one or more subvectors is contained in a MAC information field, each subvector contains three fields. The subvector length (SVL) is an eight-bit number which indicates the length of the subvector. Since an eight-bit number has a maximum value of 255 and cannot indicate a length exceeding 256 bytes (0–255), a method was required to accommodate subvector values (SVV) longer than 254 bytes. The method used is the placement of XFF in the SVL field to indicate that SVV exceeds 254 bytes. Then, the actual length is placed in the first two bytes following SVL. Finally, each SVV contains the data to be transmitted. The command field within the major vector identifier contains bit values referred to as code points which uniquely identify the type of MAC frame. Figure 4.9 illustrates the format of the MAC frame information field, while Table 4.5 lists currently defined vector identifier codes for six MAC control frames defined under the IEEE 802.5 standard.

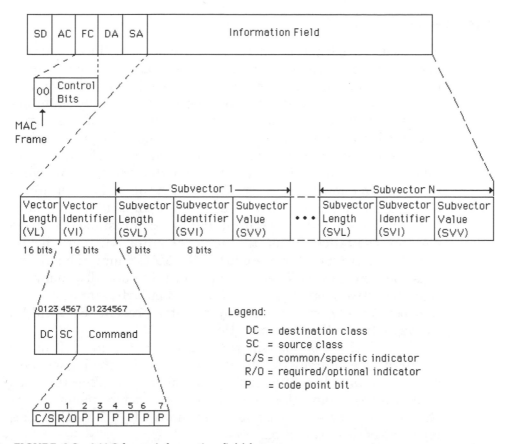

FIGURE 4.9 MAC frame information field format.

TABLE 4.5 Vector Identifier Codes

Code Value	MAC Frame Meaning
010	Beacon (BCN)
011	Claim token (CL_TK)
100	Purge MAC frame (PRG)
101	Active monitor present (AMP)
110	Standby monitor present (SMP)
111	Duplicate address test (DAT)

MAC Control

As discussed earlier in this chapter, each ring has a station known as the active monitor which is responsible for monitoring tokens and taking action to prevent the endless circulation of a token on a ring. Other stations function as standby monitors and one such station will assume the functions of the active monitor if that device should fail or is removed from the ring. For the standby monitor with the highest network address to take over the functions of the active monitor, the standby monitor needs to know there is a problem with the active monitor. If no frames are circulating on the ring but the active monitor is operating, the standby monitor might falsely presume the active monitor has failed. Thus, the active monitor will periodically issue an active monitor present (AMP) MAC frame. This frame must be issued every 7 seconds to inform the standby monitors that the active monitor is operational. Similarly, standby monitors periodically issue a standby monitor present (SMP) MAC frame to denote they are operational.

If an active monitor fails to send an AMP frame within the required time interval, the standby monitor with the highest network address will continuously transmit claim token (CL_TK) MAC frames in an attempt to become the active monitor. The standby monitor will continue to transmit CL_TK MAC frames until one of three conditions occurs:

- A MAC CL_TK frame is received and the sender's address exceeds the standby monitor's station address.
- A MAC beacon (BCN) frame is received.
- A MAC purge (PRG) frame is received.

If one of the preceding conditions occurs, the standby monitor will cease its transmission of CL_TK frames and resume its standby function.

Purge Frame

If a CL_TK frame issued by a standby monitor is received back without modification and neither a beacon nor purge frame is received in response to the CL_TK frame, the standby monitor becomes the active monitor and transmits a purge MAC frame. The purge frame is also transmitted by the active monitor each time a ring is initialized or if a token is lost. Once a purge frame is transmitted, the transmitting device will place a token back on the ring.

Beacon Frame

In the event of a major ring failure, such as a cable break or the continuous transmission by one station (known as jabbering), a beacon frame will be transmitted. The transmission of BCN frames can be used to isolate ring faults. For an example of the use of a beacon frame, consider Figure 4.10, in which a cable fault results in a ring break. When a station detects a serious problem with the ring, such as the failure to receive a frame or token, it transmits a beacon frame. That frame defines a failure domain which consists of the station reporting the failure via the transmission of a beacon and its nearest active upstream neighbor (NAUN), as well as everything between the two.

If a beacon frame makes its way back to the issuing station, that station will remove itself from the ring and perform a series of diagnostic tests to determine if it should attempt to reinsert

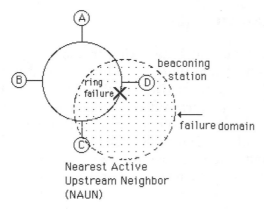

FIGURE 4.10 Beaconing. A beaconing frame indicates a failure occurring between the beaconing station and its nearest active upstream neighbor—an area referred to as a failure domain.

itself into the ring. This procedure ensures that a ring error caused by a beaconing station can be compensated for by having that station remove itself from the ring. Since beacon frames indicate a general area where a failure occurred, they also initiate a process known as autoreconfiguration. The first step in the autoreconfiguration process is the diagnostic testing of the beaconing station's adapter. Other steps in the autoreconfiguration process include diagnostic tests performed by other nodes located in the failure domain in an attempt to reconfigure a ring around a failed area.

Duplicate Address Test Frame

The last type of MAC command frame is the duplicate address test (DAT) frame. This frame is transmitted during a station initialization process when a station joins a ring. The station joining the ring transmits a MAC DAT frame with its own address in the frame's destination address field. If the frame returns to the originating station with its address-recognized (A) bit in the frame control field set to 1, this means that another station on the ring is assigned that address. The station attempting to join the ring will send a message to the ring network manager concerning this situation and will not join the network.

TOKEN-RING LOGICAL LINK CONTROL

In concluding our overview of Token-Ring frame operations, we will examine the flow of information within a Token-Ring network at the logical link control (LLC) sublayer. The LLC sublayer is responsible for performing routing, error control, and flow control. In addition, this sublayer is responsible for providing a consistent view of a LAN to upper OSI layers, regardless of the type of media and protocols used on the network.

Figure 4.11 illustrates the format of an LLC frame which is carried within the information field of the Token-Ring frame. As previously discussed in this chapter, the setting of the first two

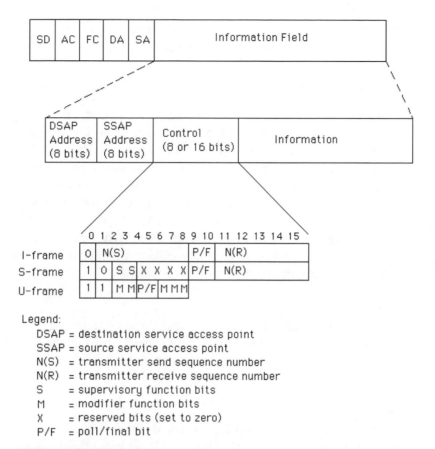

Legend:
    DSAP = destination service access point
    SSAP = source service access point
    N(S) = transmitter send sequence number
    N(R) = transmitter receive sequence number
    S   = supervisory function bits
    M   = modifier function bits
    X   = reserved bits (set to zero)
    P/F   = poll/final bit

FIGURE 4.11   Logical link control frame format.

bits in the frame control field of a Token-Ring frame to 01 indicates that the information field should be interpreted as an LLC frame. The portion of the Token-Ring frame which carries LLC information is known as a protocol data unit and consists of either three or four fields, depending upon the inclusion or omission of an optical information field. The control field is similar to the control field used in the HDLC protocol and defines three types of frames—information (I-frames) are used for sequenced messages, supervisory (S-frames) are used for status and flow

control, while unnumbered (U-frames) are used for unse-
quenced, unacknowledged messages.

Service Access Points

Service access points can be considered interfaces to the upper
layers of the OSI Reference Model, such as the network layer
protocols. A station can have one or more SAPs associated with
it for a specific layer and can have one or more active sessions
initiated through a single SAP. Thus, we can consider a SAP to
function similarly in scope to a mailbox, containing an address
which enables many types of mailings to reach the box. However, instead of mail, SAP addresses identify different network
layer processes and function as locations where messages can be
left concerning desired network services.

DSAP

The first field in the LLC protocol data unit is the destination
services access point (DSAP). The DSAP address field identifies
one or more service access points for which information is to be
delivered.

SSAP

The second field in the LLC protocol data unit is the source services access point (SSAP). The SSAP address field identifies the
service access point which transmitted the frame. Both DSAP
and SSAP addresses are assigned to vendors by the IEEE to
ensure that each is unique.

Both DSAPs and SSAPs are eight-bit fields; however, only
seven bits are used for addressing, which results in a maximum
of 128 distinct addresses available for each service access point.
The eighth DSAP bit indicates whether the destination is an
individual or a group address, while the eighth SSAP bit indicates whether the PDU contains a request or a response.

The control field contains information which defines how
the LLC frame will be handled. U-frames are used for what is
known as connectionless service in which frames are not

acknowledged, while I-frames are used for connection-oriented services in which frames are acknowledged.

Connectionless Service

Unacknowledged connectionless service is also known as a Type 1 operation. In this mode of operation there is no data link connection establishment between SAPs of the end stations prior to the transmission of information. Thus, this service can provide rapid data transfer since there is no connection overhead. Since there is no provision for acknowledgment or confirmation of data transfers, Type 1 service is not reliable and higher layer services must be used to provide error recovery operations.

Connection-oriented Service

Connection-oriented or Type 2 service requires a logical link layer connection to be established between a transmitting and receiving station prior to the flow of information occurring. Once a connection is established, each frame is acknowledged. Thus, a connection-oriented service provides frame acknowledgment and does not require the use of higher-layer services to provide for error recovery.

Acknowledged Connectionless Service

Acknowledged connectionless service, which is known as Type 3 service, has been proposed as an enhancement to current standards. Under a Type 3 service there is no connection establishment prior to the occurrence of the exchange of data. However, during data transfer individual frames are acknowledged.

Flow Control

Two techniques are used at the link layer to control the flow of data in an orderly manner and prevent transmitting stations from overwhelming receivers with data. The first technique is known as a sliding window and is employed by Type 2 LLC operations. Under the sliding window flow control method, up to 127 frames may be outstanding prior to requiring an acknowledgment from a destination station. This method is full duplex and permits data to be simultaneously transmitted in each direction.

A second flow control method known as *stop and wait* is used in Type 3 services. Under the stop-and-wait method of flow control, the originating station cannot send more data until the destination station returns a positive acknowledgment.

In comparison to the sliding window method the stop-and-wait method of flow control is inefficient. This is because a receiver can acknowledge multiple PDUs in a single acknowledgment when using a sliding window protocol as well as transmit up to 127 frames without requiring an acknowledgment.

FDDI

Work on the Fiber Distributed Data Interface (FDDI) dates back to 1982, during which time vendors and standards bodies recognized the need for higher-speed LAN products and standards to govern the operation of those products. FDDI was standardized by the American National Standards Institute (ANSI) X3T9.5 Task Group and its use provides advantages over Ethernet and Token-Ring with respect to its operating rate, reliability, and immunity to electromagnetic interference.

Operating at 100 Mbps, FDDI is five to twenty times faster than Token-Ring and ten times faster than 10BASE-T. This makes it suitable for use as a mechanism to interconnect lower-speed LANs, in effect resulting in many FDDI networks functioning as a backbone network. In the area of reliability, the FDDI standard specifies dual fiber-optic counter-rotating rings. This provides built-in redundancy which can compensate for the effect of a network failure. The third major advantage associated with the use of FDDI relates to its use of optical media. Those advantages include the ability to install optical cable without the use of a conduit, the extended transmission distance of an optical system, and its immunity to electrical interference. Since the topology of an FDDI differs from a Token-Ring LAN, a short discussion of the topology and flow of tokens on FDDI is warranted to obtain an appreciation for the operation of this LAN.

General Operation

FDDI uses two rings which are formed in a ring-star topology. One ring is known as the primary, while the other ring is known as the secondary ring. The primary ring is similar to the main ring path in a Token-Ring network, while the secondary ring acts like a Token-Ring backup ring path. However, the FDDI backup ring, unlike the Token-Ring backup path, can automatically be placed into operation as a "self-healing" mechanism. When this occurs, data flow is counter to the flow of data that occurred on the primary ring and results in many persons referring to FDDI as a counter-rotating ring topology.

Token Use

Similar to the IEEE 802.5 Token-Ring standard, a rotating token is used to provide stations with permission to transmit data. When an FDDI station wants to transmit information it waits until it detects the token and captures or absorbs it. Once the station controls the token it can transmit information until it either has no more data to send or until a token-holding timer expires. When either situation occurs, the station then releases the token onto the ring so it can be used by the next station that has data to transmit. This token-passing technique is more formally known as a timed-token-passing technique and uses bandwidth more efficiently than the 802.5 token-passing method. This is because only one token and one frame can be present on a Token-Ring network. In comparison, although only one token is present on an FDDI network at any time, multiple frames from one or more stations can be traversing an FDDI network.

Network Access

Access to an FDDI network is accomplished through the use of three types of stations—a single attached station (SAS) and two types of dual attached stations (DAS).

Dual Attached Station. A dual attached station connects to both counter rotating rings used to form an FDDI ring. Each DAS contains two defined optical connection pairs. One pair, called the A interface or port, contains one primary ring input and the secondary ring output. The second pair, called the B interface or port, contains the primary ring output and the secondary ring input. Through the use of two optical transceivers each DAS can transmit and receive data on each ring.

A second type of DAS is known as a concentrator. In addition to the previously described A and B interfaces, a DAS concentrator contains a series of extra ports that are called M, or master ports. The M ports on a DAS concentrator provide connectivity to single attached stations (SASs), a DAS, or another concentrator. Thus, the concentrator provides additional ports which extends the ability to access the primary ring to other stations.

The connection between DAS nodes occurs through the use of two cable sheaths, each containing two fiber optic cables. One pair of cables functions as the primary ring, while the second pair of cables functions as a counter-rotating secondary ring used for backup operations. To ensure the correct cabling to form a dual ring, a main ring cable used to interconnect two dual attached stations or a DAS to a concentrator contains a type A connector on one end and a type B connector on the other end of the cable.

Single Attached Station. In comparison to dual attached stations that provide a connection to the dual FDDI rings, a single attached station can only be connected to a single ring. The connection of single attached stations to a DAS concentrator can resemble a star topology, even though the interconnection of DAS and DAS concentrators forms a ring. The connection between SAS nodes is accomplished through the use of a single cable sheath containing two fiber optic cables. Since a single attached station contains only a single optical transceiver, its cost is less than a dual attached station. However, its inability to connect to the dual ring lowers its reliability in comparison to the connection of workstations to an FDDI network through a dual attached station.

One of the functions performed by the concentrator includes sensing when an attached SAS is not powered on. When this situation occurs, the concentrator electronically reroutes data to the next sequentially located station. This permits cable faults or a malfunctioning SAS to be electronically bypassed.

Figure 4.12 illustrates the major components of an FDDI network as well as how a ring can be reconfigured in the event of a cable fault or DAS failure. In this example, it was assumed that a cable fault occurred between the upper-right and extreme-right dual attached stations. Each of those stations has the capability to monitor light levels and recognize a cable failure. By two adjacent stations wrapping away from the failure, the dual ring becomes converted into a single ring and connectivity is restored. When the failure condition is corrected the restoration of an appropriate light level causes each DAS to

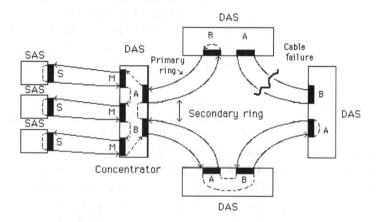

Legend:
A = A interface contains primary ring input and secondary ring input
B = B interface contains primary ring output and secondary ring input
M = master port
S = slave port
DAS = dual attached station
SAS = single attached station

FIGURE 4.12 FDDI ring operation during cable fault failure. Two dual attached stations can perform a wrap operation to convert a dual ring into a single ring which bypasses a cable or device failure.

remove the previously implemented wrap and restores the network to its dual ring operation.

Data Encoding

The transmission of data on fiber optic cable is accomplished through the use of intensity modulation. That is, a binary 1 is represented by a pulse of light, while a binary 0 is represented by the absence of an optical signal.

One of the key problems associated with any signaling technique that uses the presence or absence of voltage, current, or light to denote binary digits is the potential lack of synchronization from the coding method. Intensity modulation is no exception to this problem, since long strings of 1's or 0's produced by simply turning a light signal on and off will result in a situation where a receiver must either have clocking circuitry or it will lose synchronization with the transmitter. Since clocking circuitry can be costly, a more economical alternative to obtain synchronization between transmitters and receivers is to encode binary data in such a manner that it guarantees the presence of signal transitions even when there are few transitions in the data being transmitted.

As previously explained, Token-Ring networks use Differential Manchester encoding to obtain signal transitions that enable clocking to be derived from an incoming data stream. Although intensity modulation could be performed to encode data according to Differential Manchester encoding, doing so would result in a baud rate of 200 M signals per second to obtain a 100-Mbps operating rate. This high signaling rate would be expensive to implement, thus, designers looked for another method to encode data and obtain the required level of signal transitions for receivers to derive clocking from a transmitted signal. That encoding and signaling method is first obtained by placing each group of four bits into a five-bit code (4B/5B encoding). Then, the five-bit group is transmitted using a non-return to zero inverted (NRZI) signaling method.

NRZI Signaling. NRZI signaling results in a change of state used to represent a 0 bit, while no change of state represents a binary 1. NRZI is a form of differential signaling in that the polarity of different signal elements can change when their state changes. This enables the signal to be decoded by comparing the polarity of adjacent signal elements instead of the absolute value of the signal element. However, by itself NRZI signaling will not ensure a level of transitions necessary to keep a receiver in synchronization with a transmitter. This is because a long string of 0's or 1's will not have transitions. Thus, data must be encoded using the 4B/5B encoding technique, which enables NRZI signaling to produce the required signal transitions.

4B/5B Encoding.   Under 4B/5B encoding, each group of four bits is encoded into a five-bit symbol. In addition to permitting signaling to be achieved at a 125-Mbps signal rate in comparison to a 200-M baud rate that would be required under Differential Manchester encoding, the use of 4B/5B encoding permits the design of the resulting 5B codes to ensure that a transition occurs at least twice for each five-bit code.

Table 4.6 lists the FDDI 4B/5B codes. The use of the 5B code permits patterns beyond the 16 combinations available from a four-bit code to be used to represent special network-related functions. For example, the J and K bits used in Differential Manchester encoding for the Token-Ring starting delimiter are developed as special 5B codes in FDDI to prefix tokens and frames. When we examine the FDDI frame formats we will also examine the use of certain 5B code functions.

In examining Table 4.6, you will note that only twenty-four 5B codes are defined, even though thirty-two could be defined. The remaining eight 5B code combinations are either invalid, since under NRZI signaling no more than three zeros in a row are allowed, or represent a "Halt" code.

Frame Formats

Similar to Token-Ring networks, there are distinct frames and frame formats that are used on FDDI networks for information transfer. Figure 4.13 illustrates two FDDI frame formats used to transfer information. Like Token-Ring networks, the basic FDDI frame can convey MAC control data and LLC information. In addition, a station management frame permits management infor-

TABLE 4.6 FDDI 4B/5B Codes

Function/4-Bit Group	5B Code	Symbol
Starting delimiter		
First symbol of sequential SD pair	11000	J
Second symbol of sequential SD pair	10001	K
Ending delimiter	01101	T
Data symbols		
0000	11110	0
0001	01001	1
0010	10100	2
0011	10101	3
0100	01010	4
0101	01011	5
0110	01110	6
0111	01111	7
1000	10010	8
1001	10011	9
1010	10110	10
1011	10111	11
1100	11010	12
1101	11011	13
1110	11100	14
1111	11101	15
Control indicators		
Logical ZERO (reset)	00111	R
Logical ONE (set)	11001	S
Line status symbols		
Quiet	00000	Q
Idle	11111	I
Halt	00100	H

mation to be transported between stations and higher-level processes. As defined by ANSI, the station management (SMT) standard is used to control the FDDI PMD, PHY, and MAC layers. Services provided by SMT include fault detection, fault isolation, and ring reconfiguration. Data carried by SMT frames can be used by such higher-level processes as Simple Network Management Protocol (SNMP) services to permit network administrators to monitor and control each FDDI network node from a central console. In addition to collecting data, SMT provides network administrators with the ability to dynamically alter the network by adding or removing predefined stations. Thus, SMT frames carry both monitoring and control information.

FDDI Token.   As illustrated in the top portion of Figure 4.13, the FDDI token consists of five fields. The preamble field is variable in length and is formed by 16 or more 5B I symbols. The

a. FDDI token

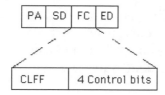

b. FDDI frame

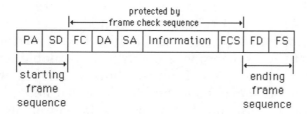

PA = preamble
SD = starting delimiter
FC = frame control
ED = ending delimiter
DA = destination address
SA = source address
FCS = frame check sequence
FS = frame status
C   = class bit
L   = length of address fields
FF = format
Control bits = depend upon frame type

FIGURE 4.13   FDDI frame formats.

starting delimiter field consists of the 5B J symbol followed by the 5B K symbol. That field is followed by the frame control field, which identifies the type of frame.

The frame control field is eight bits in length, with the class and length of address fields bit positions used to indicate one of two possible settings per bit position. When the class bit is set to 0, this indicates an asynchronous class of transmission, while setting the class bit to 1 indicates a synchronous class of transmission. The length of address fields bit indicates the use of 48-bit addressing fields when set to 0 and the use of 16-bit addressing fields when set to 1. The two format bits are used to indicate a MAC or SMT frame when set to 00 or an LLC frame when set to 01. A setting of 10 is implementation dependent, while a setting of 11 is currently reserved for future use. The second half of the frame control field consists of four control bits whose values are dependent upon the type of frame defined by the format bits.

There are two special values that can be assigned to the frame control field—hex 80 and hex C0. If the frame control field is set to hex 80 it indicates an unrestricted token, while a value of hex C0 in this eight-bit field indicates a restricted token. The restricted token is generated by a station on an FDDI network that wishes to communicate with another station using all of the asynchronous bandwidth available on the network. Readers are referred to the following section, which discusses the allocation of bandwidth on an FDDI network and the two classes of traffic on that network—asynchronous and synchronous.

When the frame control field is directly followed by the ending delimiter an FDDI token is formed. Here the ending delimiter is the 5B T symbol.

FDDI Frame.   As indicated in Figure 4.13, the first three fields of the FDDI token and frame are the same. Thereafter, the frame contains destination and source address fields which identify the frame recipient and frame originator, respectively. Each address field can be either 16 or 48 bits in length but must be of similar length.

The source address field is followed by a variable information field that can range in length from 0 to 4472 bytes. That field is followed by a frame check sequence (FCS) field 32 bits in length which protects all data from the frame control field through the information field. The ending delimiter and frame status fields function as the ending FDDI frame sequence, with the ending delimiter formed by the use of the 5B T symbol which consists of the bit pattern 01101.

Bandwidth Allocation

In a Token-Ring network, access is obtained by the setting of priority and reservation bits which enables a station to acquire a token. Once a token is acquired, it is converted into a single frame to transport a unit of information. In comparison, a token flowing on an FDDI network is removed from the network by a station that has data to transmit—a process referred to as *absorption*. Once a token is absorbed, the absorbing station can transmit one or more frames prior to returning the token onto the network, with the number of frames that can be transmitted based upon the frame size and the setting of timers within the station. Thus, any discussion of FDDI bandwidth allocation must consider the timers supported by each station in an FDDI network. Since those timers, as well as the frame control field of an FDDI token, govern the two classes of traffic that can be carried by an FDDI network, a logical place to initiate an explanation of FDDI bandwidth allocation is by explaining the two classes of traffic supported by this network. Once we do this we will then examine the timers supported by each FDDI station and then use the preceding to discuss how an FDDI network allocates bandwidth capacity.

Classes of Traffic. FDDI defines two classes of traffic—asynchronous and synchronous. These classes of transmission should not be confused with an asynchronous and synchronous mode of transmission. The asynchronous class of transmission is transmission that occurs when the token holding rules of an FDDI network permit transmission. In comparison, the synchronous class of transmission results in a guaranteed percentage of the ring's bandwidth allocated for a particular transmission. Once synchronous bandwidth is allocated, the remaining bandwidth becomes available for asynchronously transmitted frames. That bandwidth is shared by all stations in a fair and equitable manner based upon the use of timers.

Timers. The control of the amount of asynchronous and synchronous traffic that can be transmitted by a station is governed by FDDI's timed token access protocol. This protocol is based upon the use of timers used by each station to regulate their operation. These timers include a token rotation timer (TRT), token holding timer (THT), and valid transmission timer (TVX).

Token Rotation Timer. The TRT is used to time the period between the receipt of tokens. Under the timed token access protocol, stations expect to see a token within a specified period of time, referred to as the target token rotation time (TTRT). The value for the TTRT is set when a station initializes itself on the ring and is the same for all stations on the ring.

When a token passes a station, the station sets its TRT to the value of the TTRT and then decrements its TRT. If the TRT expires prior to the token returning to the station, a counter known as the late counter is incremented. The decision on whether a station can transmit a synchronous or asynchronous class of traffic depends upon the value of the TRT and the value of a counter known as the late counter.

When a token arrives at a station three events occur which govern the allocation of bandwidth. First, upon receiving a token a station can initiate the transmission of synchronous frames. Whether or not it does so and the number of frames it can transmit depend upon several factors that will be discussed shortly.

Token Holding Timer. If the token was received earlier than expected, the token rotation timer (TRT) will be positive and the station will store that value in its token holding timer (THT). Thus, the value of the THT represents the amount of time by which the token was received earlier than expected. Finally, the station resets the TRT to the value assigned to the target token rotation timer (TTRT) and begins to decrement that timer.

Synchronous Transmission. As previously mentioned, the receipt of a token enables a station to initiate the transmission of synchronous frames. The ability of a station to transmit synchronous frames depends upon whether or not the station was enabled by an application for synchronous transmission. If enabled, the number of synchronous frames the station can transmit is based upon the size of each frame to be transmitted and the time allocated for synchronous transmission. The frame size governs the amount of time required to place a frame on the ring, while the total time the station can transmit synchronously is based upon the value of the station's synchronous allocation timer. That timer is set to zero when a station is not enabled by an application for synchronous transmission. When enabled for synchronous transmission, the value of the synchronous allocation timer can be different for each station on the ring; however, the sum of all synchronous allocation timers on the active stations on the ring must always be less than the target token rotation time.

If enabled for synchronous transmission, a station will either transmit all the frames it has synchronously or only those frames that can be transmitted within the allocated synchronous allocation timer value. When that timer expires or all synchronous frames are transmitted and the timer has not expired, the station may then be able to transmit asynchronous frames.

Asynchronous Transmission. The decision whether or not a station can transmit asynchronous frames is based upon the value of the late counter. If the value of the late counter is zero, which means that the TRT did not expire, asynchronous frames can be transmitted for the length of time stored in the token holding timer (THT). When the value of that timer reaches zero the token must then be placed back onto the ring.

During both synchronous and asynchronous transmission, the token rotation timer (TRT) continues to decrement. If both synchronous and asynchronous transmissions were stopped due to the expiration of the synchronous allocation timer and the token holding timer and other stations have data to send, the TRT can be expected to expire prior to the token reappearing at the station. When this occurs, the token will be late, the TRT will be zero, and the THT will also be set to zero. With a value of zero in the token holding timer the station cannot transmit any asynchronous frames the next time it receives a token. Thus, the timed token access protocol penalizes a station that transmitted its fully allocated amount of traffic; however, the penalty only applies to asynchronous traffic and a station can always transmit synchronous traffic when it receives a token.

If the station is penalized, the next token will arrive early and the station's late counter will be decremented. Once the value of the late counter reaches zero, the station can again begin to transmit asynchronous traffic.

The preceding bandwidth allocation method guarantees an amount of ring capacity to synchronous traffic. Asynchronous traffic is transmitted only when there is spare capacity on the ring and the use of the previously described counters and timers provides a level of fairness for asynchronous transmission.

In discussing the composition of the frame control field, we indicated a setting of hex 80 indicates a restricted token. The use of this type of token provides another mechanism for allocating asynchronous transmission by permitting two stations to use all of the asynchronous bandwidth available on the ring. When one station wishes to communicate with another station using all of the available asynchronous bandwidth, it transmits its asynchronous frames and then releases a restricted token. Due to FDDI rules, only the last station that receives an asynchronous frame can use a restricted token for asynchronous transmission; this enables two stations to continue transmitting to one another. Since the restricted token is applicable only to asynchronous transmission, any station that has synchronous traffic can use that token, ensuring that the guaranteed level of synchronous bandwidth remains available to all stations on the ring.

Transmission Example. To illustrate the FDDI capacity allocation algorithm, let us assume that the target token rotation timer was set to 100 milliseconds for all stations, while the synchronous allocation timer was set to 10 milliseconds for our station. Table 4.7 lists the settings of the different station timers and the occurrence of various events during the capacity alloca-

TABLE 4.7 FDDI Capacity Allocation Process Example

1. Token arrives at station.
2. TRT is set to value of TTRT (100 ms).
3. Token absorbed by station.
4. Synchronous traffic transmitted for 10 ms (synchronous allocation timer value).
5. Token released onto ring.
6. Token reappears 50 ms later.
7. Token absorbed.
8. TRT now 40 ms due to 10 ms transmission of synchronous traffic and 50 ms on ring.
9. Token holding timer set to TRT value (40 ms).
10. TRT reset to 100 and begins to decrement.
11. Synchronous traffic again sent for 10 ms.
12. Asynchronous traffic sent for 40 ms (THT value).
13. TRT now has a value of 50 (100–10–40).
14. Token released.
15. Assume other stations transmit data and token reappears after 70 ms.
16. TRT expires and late counter incremented to a value of 1.
17. THT set to a value of 0.
18. Assume no synchronous traffic to be sent. Asynchronous traffic cannot be sent since TRT expired and THT now has a value of 0.
19. TRT reset to 100.
20. Assume token reappears in 30 ms.
21. TRT now set to 70 ms. Although token is early the late count has a value of 1. Thus, token considered to be late and the station can only transmit synchronous traffic.
22. Token absorbed.
23. Station transmits synchronous traffic for 10 ms (synchronous allocation timer value).
24. Late count value decremented to 0.
25. Token placed back on ring.
26. Assume token reappears 40 ms later.
27. TRT now set to 70–40, or 30 ms. Since late count is 0, station can transmit asynchronous traffic for up to 30 ms.

tion process for a station on an FDDI network, based upon several predefined events occurring on the ring. By examining the entries in Table 4.7, you can appreciate the method by which timers and the late counter govern the ability of stations to transmit asynchronous and synchronous traffic.

RING SWITCHING AND FDDI NETWORKING

Now that we have an appreciation for the operation of Token-Ring and FDDI networks, we can use that information as a base for examining the operation and utilization of switches designed to support each type of LAN. In this section we will focus our attention upon Token-Ring and FDDI switches. We'll also look at the use of FDDI as a backbone mechanism to interconnect Token-Ring and other types of LANs.

Token-Ring Switches

Similar to our discussion of Ethernet switches, Token-Ring switches can be categorized by the type of switching performed as well as the number of addresses supported per port. However, due to differences in the architecture between Token-Ring and Ethernet LANs, the architecture supported by each type of switch can differ even when they support similar features.

Types of Switching

There are two Token-Ring switching methods—port switching and segment switching. When a port-switching method is employed only one end-station can be connected to a switch port. In comparison, when segment switching is employed a ring containing two or more stations can be connected to a switch port. For both situations the switch port can be considered as a participant on a Token Ring. Thus, the passing of a token governs the ability of the port and other stations on the ring to transmit, functioning as a built-in flow control mechanism. This is an important advantage associated with Token-Ring switches in comparison to Ethernet switches as the token can be used as a mechanism to regulate traffic routed between ports, providing a built-in flow control mechanism.

Switching Methods

Token-Ring switches support source route, transparent, and source route transparent bridging protocols. A Token-Ring switch is similar to an Ethernet switch in that it begins its operation by flooding frames until it learns the output port associated with different MAC addresses and, when available, routing information field (RIF) data. The switch constructs a forwarding table in memory and initiates frame forwarding decisions based upon table look-up results or a set of rules when certain destination ring operations are noted, such as a beaconing condition that precludes the direct placement of a frame onto a beaconing ring. Later in this section we will examine Token-Ring switching methods in additional detail.

Primary Operation

Although similar to an Ethernet switch with respect to supporting multiple simultaneous cross connections, a Token-Ring switch also provides network managers and administrators with a significant tool to reduce problems associated with the use of backbone rings. To illustrate this concept, consider Figure 4.14, which shows the use of a backbone ring to provide connec-

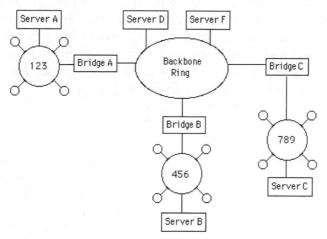

FIGURE 4.14   Using a backbone ring.

tivity between stations located on three separate Token-Ring networks. In this example, each numbered ring has its own local server while departmental or organizational servers that are accessed by users from different rings are placed on the backbone ring. Thus, servers A, B, and C can be considered to represent workgroup servers, while servers D and E can be considered to represent departmental servers.

In examining the backbone ring network configuration illustrated in Figure 4.14, you can note a variety of problems that provide a firm rationale for the use of Token-Ring switches. For example, let's assume a user on ring 123 requires access to either server D or E connected to the backbone ring. First, the user's adapter card on ring 123 must acquire a free token. If a frame was received from bridge A, it automatically obtains a priority of 4 and commonly overrides a station's reservation priority of 1. This means a sequence of frames from one of the other rings flowing through bridge A onto ring 123 would require a station on that ring to wait for three token or frame rotations until it could acquire a token and convert it into a frame. Then, the frame must compete with any priority 4 frames from bridges B and C that require access to the backbone ring. Thus, the flow of data between rings can result in a degree of unpredictable delays.

The solution to the previously discussed problem can be obtained via the use of routers or switches to form a collapsed backbone. Routers operate at the network layer of the OSI Reference Model, resulting in a latency delay of 1000 μs or higher. In addition, on a per-port basis they are considerably more expensive than switches. Since the backplane of a Token-Ring switch considerably exceeds n×16 Mbps where n represents the number of ports on the switch, such switches can support multiple simultaneous connections from rings to servers. This permits stations to communicate with servers as if the servers were directly connected to each ring. In addition, since bridges are eliminated, a cross-connection between a station on a ring and a global server cannot be delayed by bridge traffic, such as Bridge Protocol Data Units (BPDUs) as bridges are eliminated from the network.

We can replace the backbone ring previously illustrated in Figure 4.14 with a segment-switching Token-Ring switch. Figure 4.15 illustrates the use of this type of switch to connect

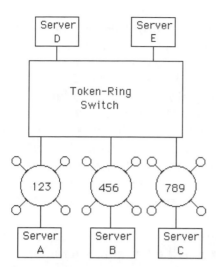

FIGURE 4.15 Using a segment-switching Token-Ring switch. A common use of Token-Ring switches is to replace backbone rings, resulting in a "collapsed backbone."

users on three rings and two departmental servers. This network can be considered to represent a collapsed backbone and represents one of the most common uses for a Token-Ring switch.

By adjusting the connections to a Token-Ring switch you may be able to obtain additional performance benefits. For example, some local servers when moved to a separate port from a ring can provide a higher level of performance if the servers are connected to full-duplex ports. Since the full-duplex Token-Ring operation is standardized, let's examine that standard prior to discussing the range of features that can be incorporated into Token-Ring switches.

The IEEE 802.5r Standard

Under the IEEE 802.5r standard a Token-Ring switch is referred to as a dedicated Token-Ring (DTR) concentrator. The DTR concentrator consists of a backplane, referred to as a data transfer unit (DTU); classic ports, referred to as C-Ports; and a Transmit Immediate (TXI) protocol, which defines full-duplex operations required to obtain simultaneous bidirectional 16-Mbps data flow. C-Ports can support either individual stations or a ring. Concerning the latter, since a ring is formed by the use of one or more multistation access units (MAUs) that are referred to as classic concentrators, a typical DTR concentrator schematic commonly shows a C-Port connected to a "classic concentrator" to denote the connection of the port to a ring. Figure 4.16 illustrates a schematic diagram showing the potential connections to a DTR concentrator. The TXI protocol can only be used with a single station on a port. This is because the use of a single station eliminates the necessity to acquire a token prior to being able to transmit data.

Support for full-duplex Token-Ring operation is accomplished through the use of modified Token-Ring adapter cards. Such modified adapters do not include a repeater path, which is normally used to allow a frame appearing on the receive path of a lobe to be placed on its transmit path. Figure 4.17 compares the operation of conventional and full-duplex operating Token-Ring adapter cards.

In examining the illustration in the left portion of Figure 4.17 note that although the title is "conventional," in reality a

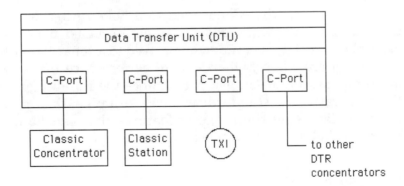

Note: Transmit Immediate (TXI) protocol defines full-duplex operations, enabling a simultaneous bidirectional 16-Mbps data flow.

FIGURE 4.16 Connecting to a dedicated Token-Ring (DTR) concentrator.

conventional Token-Ring adapter permits both reception and transmission of data to occur at the same time. Although this is indeed a full-duplex operation, only received data can be simultaneously placed onto the lobe's transmit path. If a workstation is receiving a frame and has data to send, the frame must circulate back to the originator and be converted into a token. Then, upon receipt of the token the workstation can transmit data. In comparison, when one Token-Ring station is connected to a port on a Token-Ring switch, as a frame is received the port can generate a new frame in the opposite direction, providing a true full-duplex operation in which different frames are simultaneously transmitted and received.

Although many vendors imply that the support of full-duplex transmission doubles the throughput of a Token-Ring port to 36 Mbps, in actuality your ability to increase the throughput through a port depends upon the type of traffic supported by the port. For example, connecting a workstation to a full-duplex port would more than likely provide a negligible gain in throughput since most client/server communications are essentially half-duplex. However, the attachment of a server via

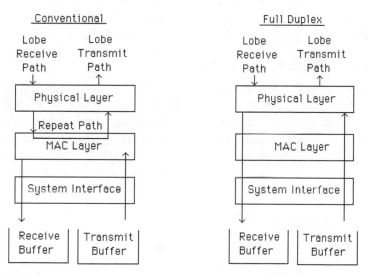

FIGURE 4.17 Comparing conventional and full-duplex Token-Ring adapter card operators.

a full-duplex port would enable the server to process query N while transmitting response N − 1 to query N − 1. Thus, you can obtain a degree of overlap of operations by using a server on a full-duplex switching port.

Features to Note

Although Token-Ring switches have many features in common with Ethernet devices, they also have some unique features due to the use of the access protocol they are designed to support. In this section we will turn our attention to obtaining an understanding of key Token-Ring switch features we will more than likely wish to evaluate when comparing products from different vendors. Similar to our discussion concerning Ethernet switch features covered in Chapter 3, you can use a list of features as a mechanism to compare Token-Ring switches manufactured by various vendors as well as for comparing a variety of products manufactured by the same vendor. Table 4.8 lists 11 categories of Token-Ring features; however, certain features, such as addresses supported, which are evaluated in the same manner, are not described in this section since they were previously described when we focused our attention upon Ethernet switches. Token-Ring switch features that differ to a degree from Ethernet switch features follow in alphabetical order.

Bridging Support

In an Ethernet environment, bridging is transparent with the spanning tree algorithm used to prevent loops from occurring. In a Token-Ring environment, bridging can occur via source routing, source routing transparent (SRT), or transparent bridging. Thus, support for all three bridging methods may be required based upon your organization's current and proposed network configuration.

Broadcast Control

Certain network devices, such as Novell servers, periodically broadcast Server Advertising Protocol (SAP) messages to announce their presence and type of service. If the server is located on its own ring, those broadcasts only affect devices on

TABLE 4.8 Token-Ring Switch Features to Note

Feature	Requirement	Vendor A	Vendor B
Address support			
Per port	_____	_____	_____
Per switch	_____	_____	_____
Bridging support			
Source routing	_____	_____	_____
Source routing transparent	_____	_____	_____
Transparent	_____	_____	_____
Broadcast control	_____	_____	_____
Fat pipe	_____	_____	_____
Frame processing	_____	_____	_____
Full-duplex	_____	_____	_____
High-speed ports	_____	_____	_____
Latency			
Cut-through	_____	_____	_____
Store-and-forward	_____	_____	_____
Module replacement			
Power down	_____	_____	_____
Hot-swapable	_____	_____	_____
Switching method			
Port switching	_____	_____	_____
Segment switching	_____	_____	_____
Switching techniques			
Cut-through	_____	_____	_____
Store-and-forward	_____	_____	_____
Hybrid	_____	_____	_____
Contents of RIF	_____	_____	_____
Virtual LAN support	_____	_____	_____

its ring. However, if you move a server to a dedicated switch port this action will periodically flood all switch ports unless the switch has a broadcast suppression feature.

Fat Pipe

In a switched Token-Ring environment, a fat pipe capability is offered by some vendors. This capability references the grouping of two to four connections between the switch and another switch or server. One vendor currently provides the capability to operate four connections as one logical link between a Token-Ring switch and one or more servers and two connections between switches. When full-duplex connections are used to develop such logical links, this provides a maximum throughput of 128 Mbps between the switch and connected servers and 64 Mbps between switches. Figure 4.18 illustrates the use of "token pipes" to obtain additional Token-Ring switch bandwidth.

Frame Processing Priority

Since Token-Ring frames include a priority field it becomes possible for a Token-Ring switch to prioritize traffic through the device without having to modify the frame. For example, since priority ranges between 0 and 7, some vendors route frames into

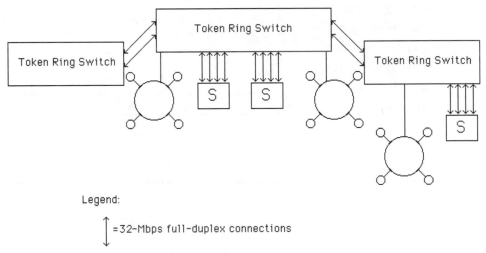

Legend:

↕ =32-Mbps full-duplex connections

FIGURE 4.18 Using token pipes to obtain additional bandwidth.

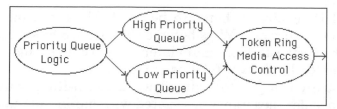

FIGURE 4.19 Incorporating priority into a Token-Ring switch.

high- and low-priority queues similar to the frame processing queues illustrated in Figure 4.19. Since station software can be used to set a higher priority for voice, image, and other types of transported data, it becomes possible to prioritize multimedia traffic through a Token-Ring switch if it includes a priority mechanism.

Full-Duplex Ports

A full-duplex port provides a bidirectional 16-Mbps transmission capacity to one station. To effectively use this capability, you should consider attaching servers and gateways to such ports.

High-Speed Ports

Some Token-Ring switches are limited to supporting only Token-Ring connections. A high-speed port on such switches may then be limited to those that support a full-duplex mode of operation. In comparison, other switches may support the connection of a 100BASE-T, FDDI, or an ATM network. Thus, you should consider both the number and type of high-speed ports supported by a Token-Ring switch if you want to consider networking those switches together via a tiered switch-based network. As an alternative, you can consider the installation of an FDDI ring to serve as the upper tier and connect each Token-Ring switch directly to the FDDI ring. Both networking scenarios will be examined later in this chapter.

Latency

For both cut-through and store-and-forward switching there is a minimum amount of latency you must consider. For cut-through switching the reading of the destination address in a frame (see

Figure 4.1) requires 9 bytes to be read. Thus, the minimum amount of latency at 4 Mbps becomes 9 bytes × 8 bits/4 Mbps or 18 μs. At 16 Mbps the minimum latency for a cut-through switch is (9 bytes × 8 bits/byte)/16 Mbps or 4.5 μs.

If you are using a store-and-forward Token-Ring switch you should consider the latency associated with minimum- and maximum-length frames. At 4 Mbps an information field of 1 byte requires 21 bytes of overhead, resulting in a frame length of 22 bytes. The maximum length of the information field, which is 4500 bytes at an operating rate of 4 Mbps, also requires 21 bytes of overhead, resulting in a maximum frame length of 4521 bytes. Thus, the minimum latency for a store-and-forward switch at 4 Mbps becomes (22 bytes × 8 bits/bytes)/4 Mbps or 44 μs. The minimum latency when a full-length frame is transported becomes (4521 bytes × 8 bits/byte)/4 Mbps or 9.042 ms. At 16 Mbps the minimum-length frame remains at 22 bytes that includes frame overhead while the maximum-length frame expands to 18,000 bytes. Thus, the minimum latency associated with store-and-forward Token-Ring switches connected to 16 Mbps devices becomes (22 bytes × 8 bits/byte)/16 Mbps or 11 μs and (18021 bytes × 8 bits/byte)/16 Mbps or 9.01 ms. Table 4.9 summarizes the preceding computations.

In examining the entries in Table 4.9 it is important to note that they represent the overhead associated with the physical

TABLE 4.9 Minimum Latency Due to Frame Length

Type of Switch/Operating Rate	Latency
Cut-through	
4 Mbps	18 μs
16 Mbps	4.5 μs
Store-and-forward	
Minimum-length frame	
4 Mbps	44 μs
16 Mbps	11 μs
Maximum-length frame	
4 Mbps	9.042 ms
16 Mbps	9.010 ms

structure of Token-Ring frames. All switches will have a latency beyond those figures summarized in the table; however, since those figures indicate the delays attributable to the physical structure of Token-Ring frames, they provide a better reference for comparing latency between switches than if you based your comparisons from zero.

Module Replacement

Since Token-Ring switches are key networking devices their failure can adversely affect a significant number of users beyond a single ring failure. Due to this, it is extremely important to be able to fix a partial switch failure while adversely affecting as few users as possible. To do so requires the ability to have hot-swappable components as well as dual power supplies and common logic modules that automatically replace failing modules.

Switching Method

As previously discussed, Token-Ring switches can be obtained to support port or segment switching. A port-switching switch supports a single ring station per port. In comparison, a segment-switching switch supports a ring with multiple stations. Similar to Ethernet, the address table capacity of a segment-switching Token-Ring switch is an important feature to consider. The number of addresses supported per port defines the maximum size of a ring in terms of workstations on the network that can be supported by a switch port. In comparison, the total number of addresses per switch governs the size of multiple rings as well as the number of individual stations that can be connected to a switch.

Switching Techniques

Similar to Ethernet switches, Token-Ring switches can support one of three switching methods common to Ethernet switches as well as a unique method based upon the contents of the Token-Ring frames routing information field (RIF). Some Token-Ring switches support cross-point or cut-through switching. Other switches employ store-and-forward switching, while a few switches support both methods. Concerning the latter, like their Ethernet relatives, they are commonly referred to as adaptive or hybrid switches. The fourth method, which is based upon the contents of the RIF, is unique to Token-Ring switches. One of the key differences between Ethernet and Token-Ring switching techniques results from the fact that a Token-Ring network can be in a beaconing condition which precludes the ability of a cut-through switch to immediately place a frame onto a beaconing network. In addition, due to the inclusion of a routing informa-tion field within the Token-Ring standard it becomes possible for switches to use the contents of a RIF as a mechanism to for-ward frames.

There are three types of frames a Token-Ring switch must consider—all-routes broadcast, single-route broadcast, and non-broadcast. An all-routes broadcast frame is copied onto all switch ports similar to the manner by which an Ethernet switch handles broadcast frames. A single-route broadcast frame is commonly handled in the same manner as an all-routes broad-cast. Doing so enables the manual configuration of the switch to be avoided. The third type of Token-Ring frame is a nonbroad-cast frame. This type of frame is directly forwarded onto the appropriate output port based upon the results of comparing the destination address against the contents of the address-port table. The only exception to this is when no match occurs, resulting in a flooding operation being performed.

Due to the preceding, let's examine the methods by which Token-Ring switches can be designed to perform their switching operations.

Cut-through Switch. A Token-Ring cut-through switch must be capable of supporting both partial and full buffering. Full buffering results in a store-and-forward mode of operation and is required when a destination ring is in a beaconing condition which temporarily precludes the ability to place a frame on the ring. When partial buffering occurs, the switch will analyze the frame header until it recognizes the destination address so it can perform a search of its address-port table to obtain the des-tination port to initiate a cross-connect. If the destination port is a segment represented by a ring the switch will normally want to obtain a degree of priority to enable it to place the frame on the ring with a minimum of delay. To do so the switch will prob-ably use a priority of 4 to mimic the priority of a bridge.

Store-and-Forward.   There are three conditions that necessitate a cut-through switch moving into a store-and-forward mode of operation. First, if a destination ring is beaconing the switch cannot directly output a frame and must store it until the beaconing condition terminates. Second, if the switch connects dissimilar operating rate stations or segments it must also operate as a store-and-forward switch. A third condition which necessitates the operation of a store-and-forward mode of operation is when a frame to be switched follows a frame being buffered. Of course, if the switch is limited to a port sharing mode of operation, all three conditions previously mentioned will not occur and the switch can function as a pure cut-through switch.

Hybrid.   A hybrid switch uses the frame error rate as a decision criterion for switching between cut-through and store-and-forward modes of operation. Although this is similar to the manner by which Ethernet hybrid switches operate, there are differences between the two when segment switching is supported. When a Token-Ring switch supports segment switching and a hybrid switching mode, it must switch from cut-through to a store-and-forward mode of operation whenever one of the three previously described conditions occur. In comparison, an Ethernet switch does not have to worry about those conditions occurring.

Source Routing.   As previously mentioned, the ring and bridge addresses contained in a Token-Ring routing information field can be used as a mechanism to forward frames through a switch. When source routing is used, the switch must be capable of understanding the contents of the Token-Ring RIF.

Networking

Similar to the use of Ethernet switches the use of Token-Ring switches depends upon the networking requirements of your organization. Since those requirements can differ from organization to organization, the best method to illustrate the use of Token-Ring switches is by focusing on their generic use at the workgroup and departmental level within an organization.

Workgroup Utilization

When used at the workgroup level a Token-Ring switch is most effective for increasing bandwidth availability to servers and power users, such as engineers operating computer-aided design (CAD) workstations on heavily used ring segments. Since the typical workgroup use of a Token-Ring switch involves moving one or more servers off a ring and onto a dedicated switch port, a popular name used to reference this network configuration is *server segmentation.*

Figure 4.20 illustrates an example of the use of a Token-Ring switch to provide both a workstation and server segmentation function. In the top portion of Figure 4.20 two servers are shown located on the same ring with n users. Thus, the average bandwidth per station if the ring operates at 16 Mbps becomes $16/(n + 2)$ Mbps. The lower portion of Figure 4.20 illustrates the use of a Token-Ring segment switch to perform both a workstation and server segmentation function. In this example each server is connected to a port on the switch and the ring was evenly subdivided so that there are n/2 workstations on each

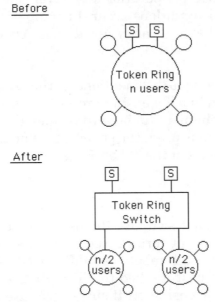

FIGURE 4.20 Using a Token-Ring switch for workstation and server segmentation.

ring connected to individual switch ports. If all connections occur at 16 Mbps, each server obtains a 16-Mbps capability while each workstation obtains an average bandwidth of $16/(n + 2)$ Mbps. In addition, due to each server having its own switch connection, both servers can be accessed at the same time, a condition not possible under the regular Token-Ring configuration illustrated at the top of Figure 4.20. In addition, through the use of a fat pipe or a full-duplex connection between each server and the switch client/server, communications can be additionally enhanced.

Backbone Switching

In a Token-Ring environment a common method used to link workgroups together into departments is through the use of a backbone ring. As previously discussed in this chapter the flow of frames between rings via a backbone ring results in a number of problems. Those problems include delays associated with a frame gaining access to multiple rings as it flows from source to destination, delays resulting from network problems such as a beaconing state on a ring the frame must traverse, delays due to the transmission of BPDUs, and the large amount of traffic backbone rings commonly sustain due to their use as a link between stations, servers, gateways, routers, and other devices transmitting frames on local rings that may require their transmission via a backbone ring. Thus, at the departmental level a common use of Token-Ring switches is as a replacement for a backbone ring.

To illustrate the potential afforded by the use of a Token-Ring switch to minimize delays when replacing a backbone ring, consider Figure 4.21. In the top portion of that illustration two global servers (GS) and a mainframe are shown connected to the backbone ring as a mechanism to enable users on three workgroup rings to access those facilities as well as access data on another ring's local server (LS), if the latter requirement should arise. If client/mainframe and/or client/global server activity is large, it becomes relatively easy for the backbone ring to become overloaded. This is because you have users on three local rings bidding for access to the backbone ring to initiate a connection for all nonlocal communications. In addition, all BPDU traffic is

Before

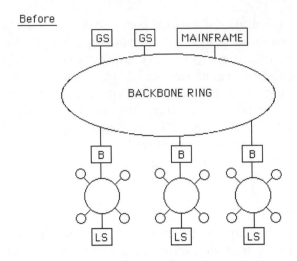

After

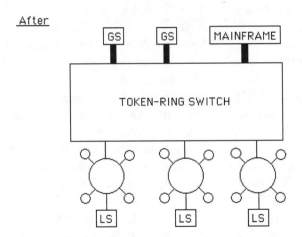

Legend:

▬▬ = full-duplex connection
LS = local server
GS = global server

FIGURE 4.21 Using a switch as a backbone ring replacement.

transported between bridges via the backbone ring, further adding to the traffic load on that ring.

The lower portion of Figure 4.21 illustrates the use of a Token-Ring switch to replace the backbone ring. Note that the connections to both global servers and the mainframe are shown as full-duplex connections since it is assumed that they are the most heavily accessed devices on the network as well as the probable source of a majority of network traffic. Although each local server is shown still connected to its local network, those connections could be modified based upon a traffic analysis of your existing network. For example, if one or more local servers is responsible for a high level of network utilization, you would probably want to consider connecting the server directly to a switch port. This would be especially true if access to a local server is on an interworkgroup basis and users from other rings commonly access a local server.

Interdepartmental Networking

A third common method associated with the use of Token-Ring switches is to connect two or more departments together. A frequent method used to provide this capability is through the use of a two-tiered switch-based network, with the lower tier consisting of Token-Ring switches while the upper tier is commonly a higher-speed switch, such as an ATM or FDDI switch.

Figure 4.22 illustrates an example of the creation of a two-tiered switch-based network, with the lower tier consisting of three departmental Token-Ring switches. Those switches in turn connect two or more workgroups into a departmental network. The second or topmost tier consists of a single FDDI switch operating at 100 Mbps per port. Through the use of one FDDI port on each Token-Ring switch access is obtained to the FDDI switch.

In addition to providing a collapsed backbone capability, a Token-Ring switch with a high-speed FDDI port can be used for interswitch networking. This can be accomplished by connecting a Token-Ring switch FDDI port to an FDDI ring that can be used as a transport mechanism between switches, as illustrated

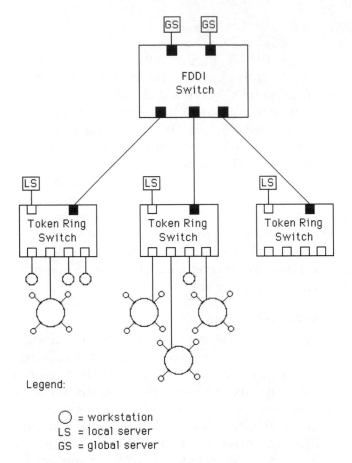

FIGURE 4.22 Creating a tiered network.

in Figure 4.23. The primary advantages associated with this networking structure include the ability to interconnect switches from various vendors as well as to access any devices, such as common servers, that might be connected to the FDDI ring. If switches were directly connected to one another you would then depend upon their intercommunications capability, which varies from vendor to vendor. If you link switches via a common backbone LAN, such as an FDDI ring, the switches can then transmit data between each device by a common frame format.

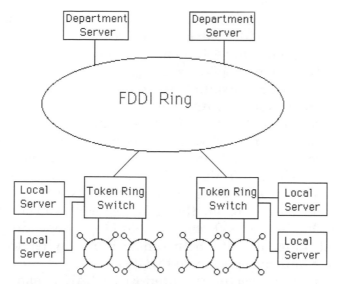

FIGURE 4.23 Communicating via an FDDI ring.

FDDI Switches and Networking

Although FDDI is a relatively old technology that dates to the 1980s, it represents a proven high-speed LAN technology that is currently installed in approximately half of the Fortune 500 companies. Since 155 Mbps ATM requires a recabling to category 5 copper twisted-pair, many organizations would prefer to protect their considerable investment in fiber as well as their FDDI adapters. In addition, FDDI is the only LAN with built-in redundancy due to its dual-ring topology. Recognizing the requirements of many organizations to enhance the performance of saturated FDDI networks, a number of vendors introduced FDDI switches. Similar to other types of LAN switches, FDDI switches enable network managers and administrators to subdivide their networks into switched segments.

When considering FDDI switches it is important to distinguish this type of communications device from Ethernet and Token-Ring switches that have one or possibly a few 100-Mbps FDDI ports. Those devices are designed to switch traffic from conventional Ethernet and Token-Ring LANs onto a high-speed port or ports that can represent a server of LAN connection. In comparison, an FDDI switch is designed to switch frames between two or more 100-Mbps backbone networks.

An FDDI switch subdivides a single ring into two or more, enabling available bandwidth to increase in a manner similar to the use of other types of LAN switches. Figure 4.24 illustrates the use of a four-port FDDI switch to segment a single FDDI LAN into four distinct networks. If each network has its own server it becomes possible for this topology to provide a maximum bandwidth of 400 Mbps when all client/server traffic is local. When interconnections are required between a client on one LAN and a server on another LAN segment, you can obtain a bandwidth of either 300 Mbps or 200 Mbps, depending upon local client/server activity, both considerably higher than the 100 Mbps obtainable on a single FDDI ring.

In Figure 4.24, each segmented FDDI LAN is shown with its own server. As an alternative, you could directly connect indi-

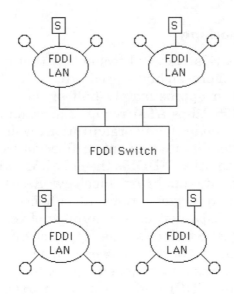

Legend:

S = server

◯ = workstation

FIGURE 4.24   Using an FDDI switch.

vidual servers to FDDI switch ports if a sufficient number of ports were available. Unlike Ethernet and Token-Ring switches, where some products can be obtained at a per-port cost considerably under $1,000, the typical cost of an FDDI switch on a per-port basis may be four to five times that amount. Thus, many network managers and administrators prefer to use FDDI switch ports to provide a connection to at least a small FDDI ring with multiple devices to economize on the use of relatively expensive FDDI switch ports.

Features to Consider

Although many FDDI switch features are similar to Ethernet and Token-Ring, a few deserve a degree of elaboration. Those features include IP fragmentation, header conversion, full-duplex capability, copper cable support, and the types of high-speed ports supported.

IP Frame Fragmentation.   Although the integration of Token-Ring and FDDI is a relatively simple process as both can support a common 4500-byte information field, the integration of Ethernet and FDDI requires an FDDI switch to support frame fragmentation so that longer FDDI frames can be broken into a series of shorter maximum 1500-byte-length frames supported by Ethernet. Since the Internet Protocol (IP) supports fragmentation, this means that an FDDI switch must also support IP fragmentation. Otherwise the FDDI LAN would have to be set to support a maximum frame length of 1500 bytes, which would degrade the performance of FDDI.

The ability of an FDDI switch to perform fragmentation requires it to operate at the network layer. In comparison, switches that operate only at the MAC layer cannot support fragmentation. If a switch supports fragmentation this means it implicitly has some routing features and may be able to be used to perform security filtering and other router functions that occur at the network layer.

Header Conversion.   The actual conversion of headers from Ethernet and Token-Ring to FDDI and vice versa is specified in the IEEE 802.1h standard for translational bridging. Thus, it is

TABLE 4.10 FDDI Switch Features to Note

Feature	Requirement	Vendor A	Vendor B
Backplane operating rate	_____	_____	_____
Full duplex	_____	_____	_____
IEEE 802.1h support	_____	_____	_____
IP fragmentation	_____	_____	_____
Latency	_____	_____	_____
Module replacement	_____	_____	_____
Ports			
FDDI			
Single attached station devices	_____	_____	_____
Dual attached station devices	_____	_____	_____
ATM	_____	_____	_____
Ethernet	_____	_____	_____
Token-Ring	_____	_____	_____
SONET	_____	_____	_____
DS3	_____	_____	_____
Routing features	_____	_____	_____
Switching method			
Port switching	_____	_____	_____
Segment switching	_____	_____	_____
Switching technique			
Cut-through	_____	_____	_____
Store-and-forward	_____	_____	_____
vLAN support	_____	_____	_____

quite common to see a notation in a vendor's FDDI switch specification sheet for support of that standard.

Full-Duplex Support. When used to connect individual stations on a point-to-point basis, a switch can be designed to support full-duplex transmission on the connected port by using one ring path in each direction. Thus, some switch vendors indicate a full-duplex 200-Mbps capability; however, you must note that this capability is limited to point-to-point connections to a switch port.

Copper Cable Support. Although FDDI was developed for use with multimode fiber, some vendors offer switch modules that support unshielded twisted-pair copper (UTP category 5) cable. This feature, which is sometimes referred to as *copper DDI* or *CDDI,* enables you to use existing category 5 cable or avoid the installation of more expensive fiber.

High-Speed Ports. Since FDDI operates at 100 Mbps, vendors that support tiered-switch networking do so via connections at higher operating rates. Such vendors commonly offer ATM or SONET port modules to either interconnect FDDI switches in a tiered-network environment or connect FDDI switches via a wide area network. Concerning the latter, many vendors also offer a T3 WAN connection operation which enables FDDI switches in geographically separated areas to be linked at an approximate 45-Mbps data rate.

To facilitate your evaluation of FDDI switches, Table 4.10 lists 12 categories of general FDDI switch features you may wish to consider. You can use this table to note your requirements for a particular switch feature and a mechanism to compare your requirements against a variety of vendor products.

ATM Switching

Until now we have focused our attention upon what many people refer to as legacy LANs. Similar to legacy mainframes, which many pundits predicted would suffer the same fate as the dodo bird, legacy LANs, to paraphrase Mark Twain, are being predicted to be obsolete prematurely. Although many network managers and LAN administrators have installed and will continue to install ATM networks as a mechanism to obtain a multimedia transmission capability, other persons will continue to maintain legacy LANs due to the cost associated with installing new adapters, switches, and cabling. However, since ATM can also function as a backbone switching mechanism, it can be used either as a replacement or supplement for existing legacy networks. Thus, the focus of this chapter will be upon both areas. In focusing upon ATM we will first review its operating characteristics, including ATM switching. Once we have an appreciation for how ATM operates, we will then turn our attention to how this relatively new technology is used as a backbone for connecting legacy switched-based networks. We will examine LAN emulation, a technology which enables legacy LAN addresses to be converted into the addressing used in ATM and which is essential for the use of ATM as a backbone network. Since ATM switches can include certain features that considerably differ from features incorporated into Ethernet and Token-Ring switches, we will conclude this chapter with a look at those features.

ATM OVERVIEW

Asynchronous Transfer Mode (ATM) represents a relatively new technology developed to transport both voice and data on a common network infrastructure.

Cell Size Rationale

Unlike packet-based technologies like X.25, Frame Relay, Ethernet, and Token Ring, which support variable-length frames, ATM transports all traffic in fixed-length 53-byte cells consisting of a 5-byte header and 48-byte payload, as illustrated in Figure 5.1.

The selection of a relatively short 53-byte ATM cell was based upon the necessity to minimize the effect of data transportation upon voice. For example, consider the use of Ethernet or Token-Ring as a data transport mechanism. Both types of LANs support variable-length information fields; a user could generate a burst of data which expands the frame length to a maximum value many times its minimum length. In doing so one user can effectively preclude other users gaining access to the network until the first frame is transmitted. While this is a

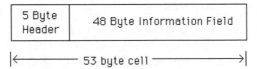

FIGURE 5.1 The ATM cell. The ATM cell is of fixed length, consisting of a 48-byte information field and five-byte header.

good design principle when all frames carry data, when digitized voice is transported the results can become awkward at the receiver. To illustrate this, assume your conversation is digitized and transported on a conventional Ethernet or Token-Ring network. As you say "Hello," "He" might be digitized and transported by a frame. Just prior to the letters "llo" leaving your mouth, assume a computer transmitted a burst of traffic that was transported by a long frame. Then, the digitization of "llo" would be stored temporarily until a succeeding frame could transport the data. At the receiver time gaps would appear, making the conversation sound awkward whenever bursts of data occurred. ATM is designed to eliminate this problem as cells are relatively short, resulting in cells transporting voice being able to arrive on a regular basis.

Another important advantage associated with the use of fixed-length cells concerns the design of switching equipment. This design enables processing to occur from firmware instead of requiring more expensive software if variable-length cells were supported.

In addition to its relatively short cell length facilitating the integration of voice and data, ATM provides three additional benefits. Those benefits are in the areas of scalability, transparency, and traffic classification.

Scalability

ATM cells can be transported on LANs and WANs at a variety of operating rates. This enables different hardware, such as LAN and WAN switches, to support a common cell format, a feature lacking with other communications technologies. An ATM cell generated on a 25-Mbps LAN is now capable of being transported from the LAN via a T-1 line at 1.544 Mbps to a central office where it might be switched onto a 2.4-Gbps SONET network for transmission on the communications carrier infrastructure, with the message maintained in the same series of 53-byte cells, with only the operating rate scaled for a particular transport mechanism.

Transparency

The ATM cell is application transparent, enabling it to transport voice, data, images, and video. Due to its application transparency, ATM enables networks to be constructed to support any type of application or application mix instead of requiring organizations to establish separate networks for different applications.

Traffic Classification

Five classes of traffic are supported by ATM to include one constant bit rate, three types of variable bit rates, and a user-definable class. By associating such metrics as cell transit delay, cell loss ratio, and cell delay variation to a traffic class, it becomes possible to provide a guaranteed quality of service on a demand basis. This enables a traffic management mechanism to adjust network performance during periods of unexpected congestion to favor traffic classes based upon the metrics associated with each class.

The ATM Protocol Stack

Similar to other networking architectures, ATM is a layered protocol. The ATM protocol stack is illustrated in Figure 5.2 and consists of three layers—the *ATM adaptation layer* (AAL), the *ATM layer,* and the *physical layer.* Both the AAL and physical layers are subdivided into two sublayers. Although the ATM

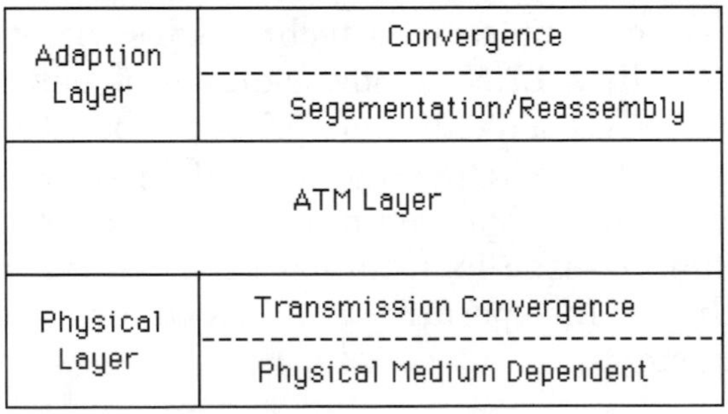

Adaption Layer	Convergence
	Segementation/Reassembly
ATM Layer	
Physical Layer	Transmission Convergence
	Physical Medium Dependent

FIGURE 5.2 The ATM protocol stack.

protocol stack consists of three layers, as we will shortly note, those layers are essentially equivalent to the first two layers of the ISO Reference Model.

ATM Adaptation Layer

As illustrated in Figure 5.2, the ATM adaptation layer consists of two sublayers—a convergence sublayer and a segmentation and reassembly sublayer. The function of the AAL is to adapt higher-level data into formats compatible with ATM layer requirements. To accomplish this task the ATM adaptation layer subdivides user information into segments suitable for encapsulation into the 48-byte information fields of cells. The actual adaptation process depends upon the type of traffic to be transmitted, although all traffic winds up in similar cells. Currently there are five different AALs defined, referred to as AAL classes, which are described later in this chapter.

When receiving information, the ATM adaptation layer performs a reverse process. That is, it takes cells received from the network and reassembles them into a format the higher layers in the protocol stack understand. This process is known as *reassembly*. Thus, the segmentation and reassembly processes result in the name of the sublayer that performs those processes.

The ATM Layer

As illustrated in Figure 5.2, the ATM layer provides the interface between the AAL and the physical layer. The ATM layer is responsible for relaying cells both from the AAL to the physical layer and to the AAL from the physical layer. The actual method by which the ATM layer performs this function depends upon its location within an ATM network. Since an ATM network consists of endpoints and switches, the ATM layer can reside at either location. Similarly, a physical layer is required at both ATM endpoints and ATM switches.

Since a switch examines the information within an ATM cell to make switching decisions, it does not perform any adaptation functions. Thus, the ATM switch operates at layers 1 and 2, while ATM endpoints operate at layers 1 through 3 of the ATM protocol stack as shown in Figure 5.3.

When the ATM layer resides at an endpoint, it will generate

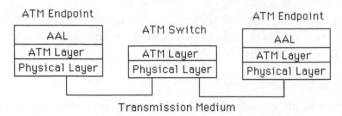

FIGURE 5.3   The ATM protocol stack within a network. The ATM adaption layer in only required at endpoints within an ATM network.

idle or "empty" cells whenever there is no data to send, a function not performed by a switch. Instead, in the switch the ATM layer is concerned with facilitating switching functions, examining cell header information which enables the switch to determine where each cell should be forwarded to. For both endpoints and switches, the ATM layer performs a variety of traffic management functions such as buffering incoming and outgoing cells as well as monitoring the transmission rate and conformance of transmission to service parameters that define a quality of service. At endpoints the ATM layer also indicates to the AAL whether or not there was congestion during transmission, permitting higher layers to initiate congestion control.

The Physical Layer

Although Figures 5.2 and 5.3 illustrate an ATM physical layer, a specific physical layer is not defined within the protocol stack. Instead, ATM uses the interfaces to existing physical layers defined in other protocols, which enables organizations to construct ATM networks on various types of physical interfaces which in turn connect to various types of media. Thus, the omission of a formal physical layer specification results in a significant degree of flexibility which enhances the capability of ATM to operate on LANs and WANs.

ATM Operation

As previously discussed, ATM represents a cell-switching technology that can operate at speeds ranging from T1's 1.544 Mbps to the gigabit-per-second rate of SONET. In doing so the lack of a specific physical layer definition means that ATM can be used on many types of physical layers, which makes it a very versatile technology.

Components

ATM networks are constructed upon the use of five main hardware components. Those components include ATM network interface cards, LAN switches, ATM routers, and ATM WAN switches.

ATM Network Interface Cards.   An ATM *network interface card* (NIC) is used to connect a LAN-based workstation to an ATM LAN switch. The NIC converts data generated by the workstation into cells that are transmitted to the ATM LAN switch and converts cells received from the switch into a data format recognizable by the workstation.

LAN Switch.   A *LAN switch* is a device used to provide interoperability between older LANs, such as Ethernet, Token-Ring, or FDDI and ATM. To do so the LAN switch supports a minimum of two types of interfaces, with one being an ATM interface which enables the switch to be connected to an ATM switch that forms the backbone of the ATM infrastructure. The other interface or interfaces represent connections to older types of LANs. Most LAN switches have one or at most two ATM interfaces as their primary design goal is to support the switching of legacy LAN traffic, such as Ethernet, Token-Ring, or FDDI. The ATM connection or connections permit ATM to be used as a backbone technology to interconnect legacy LANs and a mechanism to support the routing of data onto an ATM-based wide area network.

The LAN switch functions as both a switch and protocol converter. Data received on one port destined to the ATM network is converted from frames to cells and transferred to the switch port providing a connection to the ATM switch. Since one LAN switch port can be capable of servicing a LAN segment, the use of a switch can minimize an organization's investment in ATM NICs. This is illustrated in Figure 5.4, which illustrates the use of a LAN switch with a single ATM port to provide access to an ATM network for individual workstations connected directly to

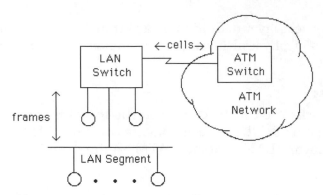

FIGURE 5.4 A LAN switch provides both a switching and protocol conversion function, allowing non-ATM devices to access an ATM network.

individual switch ports as well as a group of workstations on a LAN segment. Through the use of the LAN switch, an organization can selectively upgrade existing LANs to ATM while obtaining a connection to the ATM network.

The actual conversion of frames to cells requires an address translation process referred to as *LAN emulation* (LANE). This process, described later in this chapter, is required since ATM uses a different addressing technique than MAC addresses used by Ethernet, Token-Ring, and FDDI networks. LANE is required to enable ATM to link legacy LANs as a backbone network as well as when ATM is used as a wide area network to interconnect geographically separated non-ATM LANs.

ATM Router. An *ATM router* is a router containing one or more ATM NICs. As such, it can provide a direct or indirect capability for LAN workstations to access an ATM network or for two ATM networks to be interconnected. For example, a network segment or individual workstations could be connected to a router which in turn is connected to a LAN switch or directly to an ATM switch.

ATM WAN Switches. An *ATM switch* is a multiport device which forms the basic infrastructure for an ATM network. Unlike a conventional legacy LAN switch, an ATM switch per-

TABLE 5.1 ATM Communications Operating Rates

Operating Rate (Mbps)	Transmission Media
25–51	Unshielded twisted-pair category 5
100	Multimode fiber
155	Shielded twisted pair
622	Single-mode fiber

mits only a single end station to be connected to each switch port. By interconnecting ATM switches an ATM network can be constructed to span a building, city, country, or the globe.

The basic operation of an ATM switch is to route cells from an input port onto an appropriate output port. To accomplish this the switch examines fields within each cell header and uses that information in conjunction with table information maintained in the switch to route cells. Later in this chapter we will examine the composition of the ATM cell header in detail.

One of the key features of ATM switches reaching the market during the mid 1990s is their rate adaptation capability, which in general is a function of the transmission media used to connect endpoints and to connect switches to other switches. Table 5.1 lists some of the communications rates associated with various transmission media.

Network Interfaces

ATM supports two types of basic interfaces—*user-to-network interface* (UNI) and a *network-to-node interface* (NNI).

User-to-Network Interface. The UNI represents the interface between an ATM switch and an ATM endpoint. Since the connection of a private network to a public network is also known as a UNI, the terms *public* and *private UNI* are used to differentiate between the two types of user-to network interfaces. That is, a private UNI references the connection between an endpoint and switch on an internal, private ATM network, such as an organization's ATM-based LAN. In comparison, a public UNI would reference the interface between either a customer's endpoint or switch and a public ATM network.

Network-to-Node Interface. The connection between an endpoint and switch is simpler than the connection between two switches. This results from the fact that switches communicate information concerning the utilization of their facilities as well as pass setup information required to support endpoint network requests.

The interface between switches is known as a network-to-node or network-to-network Interface (NNI). Similar to the UNI, there are two types of NNIs. A Private NNI describes the switch-to-switch interface on an internal network such as an organization's LAN. In comparison, a public NNI describes the interface between public ATM switches, such as those used by communications carriers. Figure 5.5 illustrates the four previously described ATM network interfaces.

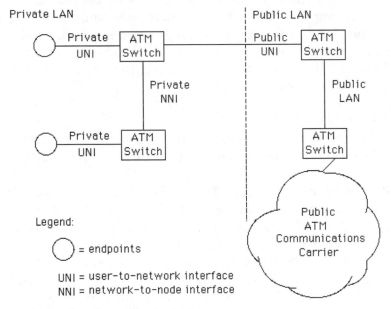

FIGURE 5.5 ATM network interfaces.

The ATM Cell Header

The structure of the ATM cell is identical in both public and private ATM networks, with Figure 5.6 illustrating the fields within the five-byte cell header. As we will soon note, although the cell header fields are identical throughout an ATM network, the use of certain fields depends upon the interface or the presence or absence of data being transmitted by an endpoint.

Generic Flow Control Field. The *generic flow control* (GFC) field consists of the first four bits of the first byte of the ATM cell header. This field is used to control the flow of traffic across the user-to-network interface (UNI) and is used only at the UNI. When cells are transmitted between switches, the four bits become an extension of the virtual path identifier (VPI) field, permitting a larger VPI value to be carried in the cell header.

Virtual Path Identifier Field. The *virtual path identifier* (VPI) identifies a path between two locations in an ATM network that provides transportation for a group of virtual channels, where a virtual channel represents a connection between two communicating ATM devices. When an endpoint has no data to transmit, the VPI field is set to all zeros to indicate an idle condition. As previously explained, when transmission occurs between

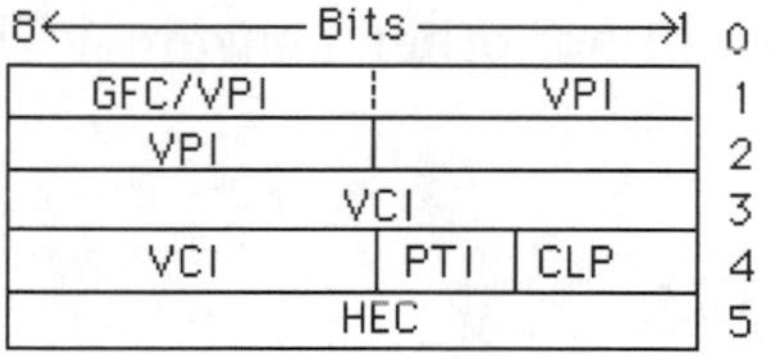

```
8 ←——————— Bits ——————→| 0
 ┌──────────────┬───┬──────────┐
 │  GFC/VPI     ┊       VPI    │ 1
 ├──────────────┴───┴──────────┤
 │  VPI         │              │ 2
 ├──────────────┴──────────────┤
 │           VCI               │ 3
 ├──────────────┬─────┬────────┤
 │   VCI        │ PTI │ CLP    │ 4
 ├──────────────┴─────┴────────┤
 │           HEC               │ 5
 └─────────────────────────────┘
```

Legend:

    GFC = generic flow control
    VPI = virtual path identifier
    VCI = virtual circuit indentifier
    PTI = payload type identifier
    CLP = cell loss priority
    HEC = header error check

FIGURE 5.6 The ATM cell header.

switches, the GFC field is used to support an extended VPI value.

Virtual Channel Identifier Field. The *virtual channel identifier* (VCI) represents the second part of the two-level routing hierarchy used by ATM, where a group of virtual channels are used to form a virtual path.

Figure 5.7 illustrates the relationship between virtual paths and virtual channels. Here the virtual channel represents a connection between two communicating ATM entities, such as an endpoint to a central office switch, or between two switches. The virtual channel can represent a single ATM link or a concatenation of two or more links, with communications on the channel occurring in cell sequence order at a predefined quality of service. In comparison, each virtual path (VP) represents a group of VCs transported between two points that can flow over one or more ATM links. Although VCs are associated with a VP, they are not unbundled or processed. Thus, the purpose of a virtual path is to provide a mechanism for bundling traffic routed toward the same destination. This technique enables switches to examine the VPI field within the cell header to make a decision concerning the relaying of the cell instead of having to examine the entire three-byte address formed by the VPI and the VCI. When an endpoint is in an idle condition, the VPI field is set to all zeros. Although the VCI field will also be set to all zeros to indicate the idle condition, other nonzero VCI values

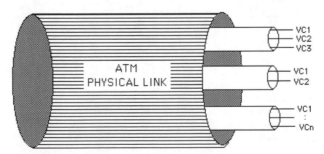

FIGURE 5.7 Relationship between virtual paths and virtual channels.

are reserved for use with a VPI zero value to indicate certain predefined conditions. For example, the VPI field value of zero when a VCI field value of 5 is used to transmit a signaling/connection request.

Payload Type Identifier Field. The *payload type identifier* (PTI) field consists of three bits in the fourth byte of the cell header. This field is used to identify the type of information carried by the cell. Values 0–3 are reserved to identify various types of user data, 4 and 5 denote management information, and 6 and 7 are reserved for future use.

Cell Loss Priority Field. The last bit in the fourth byte of the cell header represents the *cell loss priority* (CLP) field. This bit is set by the AAL layer and used by the ATM layer throughout an ATM network as an indicator of the importance of the cell. If the CLP is set to 1, it indicates the cell can be discarded by a switch experiencing congestion. If the cell should not be discarded due to the necessity to support a predefined quality of service, the AAL layer will set the CLP bit to 0. The CLP bit can also be set by the ATM layer if a connection exceeds the quality of service level agreed to during the initial communications handshaking process when setup information is exchanged.

Header Error Check Field. The last byte in the ATM cell header is the *header error check* (HEC). The purpose of the HEC is to provide protection for the first four bytes of the cell header against the misdelivery of cells due to errors affecting the addresses within the header. To accomplish this the HEC functions as an error detecting and correcting code. The HEC is capable of detecting all single- and certain multiple-bit errors as well as correcting single-bit errors.

ATM Connections and Cell Switching

Now that we have a basic understanding of the ATM cell header and the virtual path and virtual channel identifiers, we can turn our attention to the methods used to establish connections between endpoints as well as how connection identifiers are used for cell switching to route cells to their destination.

Connections

In comparison to most LANs that are connectionless, ATM is a connection-oriented communications technology. This means that a connection has to be established between two ATM endpoints prior to actual data being transmitted between the endpoints. The actual ATM connection can be established as a *permanent virtual circuit* (PVC) or as a *switched virtual circuit* (SVC).

A PVC can be considered as being similar to a leased line, with routing established for long-term use. Once a PVC is established, no further network intervention is required any time a user wishes to transfer data between endpoints connected via a PVC. In comparison, an SVC is similar to a telephone call made on the switched telephone network. That is, the SVC requires network intervention to establish the path linking endpoints each time a SVC occurs.

The "V" in PVC and SVC expresses *virtual* rather than permanent or dedicated connections. This means that through statistical multiplexing, an endpoint can receive calls from one or more distant endpoints.

Cell Switching

The VPI and VCI fields within a cell header can be used individually or collectively by a switch to determine the output port for relaying or transferring a cell. To determine the output port, the ATM switch first reads the incoming VPI, VCI, or both fields with the field read dependent upon the location of the switch in the network. Next, the switch will use the connection identifier information to perform a table look-up operation. That operation uses the current connection identifier as a match criterion to determine the output port the cell will be routed onto as well as a new connection identifier to be placed into the cell header. The new connection identifier is then used for routing between the next pair of switches or from a switch to an endpoint.

Types of Switches

There are two types of ATM switches, with the differences between each related to the type of header fields read for establishing cross-connections through the switch. A switch limited to reading and substituting VPI values is commonly referred to as a VP switch. This switch operates relatively fast. A switch that reads and substitutes both VPI and VCI values is commonly referred to as a *virtual channel* switch (VC switch). A VC switch generally has a lower cell operating rate than a VP switch as it must examine additional information in each cell header. You can consider a VP switch as being similar to a central office switch, while a VC switch would be similar to end office switches.

Using Connection Identifiers

To illustrate the use of connection identifiers in cell switching, consider Figure 5.8, which illustrates a three-switch ATM network with four endpoints. When switch 1 receives a cell on port 2 with VPI = 0, VCI = 10, it uses the VPI and VCI values to perform a table look-up, assigning VPI = 1, VCI = 12 for the cell header and switching the cell onto port 1. Similarly, when switch 1 receives a cell on port 3 with VPI = 0, VCI = 18 its table

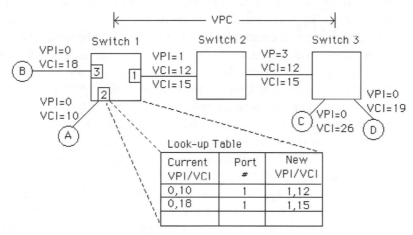

FIGURE 5.8 Cell switching example.

look-up operation results in the assignment of VPI = 1, VCI = 15 to the cell's header and the forwarding of the cell onto port 1. If we assume switch 2 is a VP switch, it only reads and modifies the VP, thus, the VCIs are shown exiting the switch with the same values they had upon entering the switch. At switch 3, the VC is broken down, with virtual channels assigned to route cells to endpoints C and D that were carried in a common virtual path from switch 1 to switch 3.

The assignment of VPI and VCI values is an arbitrary process which considers those already in use, with the look-up tables being created when a connection is established through the network. Concerning that connection, it results from an ATM endpoint requesting a connection setup via the user-to-network interface through the use of a signaling protocol which contains an address within the cell. That address can be in one of three formats. One (known as E.164) is the same used in public telephone networks, while the other two address formats include domain identifiers that allow address fields to be assigned by different organizations. The actual signaling method is based upon the signaling protocol used in ISDN and enables a quality of service to be negotiated and agreed to during the connection setup process. The quality of service is based upon metrics assigned to different traffic classes, permitting an endpoint to establish several virtual connections where each connection transports different types of data with different performance characteristics assigned to each connection. To obtain a better understanding of this important concept, let's first focus our attention upon the traffic classes supported by ATM which are listed in Table 5.2. By using different qualities of service for different traffic classes, an ATM endpoint could prioritize Class B so as to correctly receive time-sensitive frames for a videoconference while allowing relatively time-insensitive traffic, such as Class C, to be delayed or for cells to even be dropped during periods of congestion.

ATM is a complex evolving technology which provides the potential to integrate voice, data, and video across LANs and WANs. Although it is still in a state of infancy, several communications carriers have gone on record to commit the expenditure of a considerable amount of money to implement the technology into their infrastructure for WAN operations. A simi-

TABLE 5.2 ATM Traffic Classes

Class	Name	Description
A	Constant bit rate (CBR)	Connection-oriented voice or video, such as DS0s
B	Variable bit rate (VBR)	Connection-oriented data services, such as packet video, requiring the transfer of timing information between endpoints.
C	Connection-oriented (VBR)	Used for bursty data transfer for connection-oriented asynchronous traffic, such as IPX, X.25, Frame Relay.
D	Connectionless VBR	Used for transmitting VBR data without requiring a previously established connection, i.e., SMDS.
X	Simple and efficient adaptation layer (SEAL)	Similar to C but assumes higer-layer process provides error recovery.

lar commitment is not possible with respect to LANs as each organization is the ultimate controller of its destiny. However, unlike the use of ATM in a WAN environment which is beyond your control, you can directly control the use of ATM as a replacement or supplement for your organization's legacy LANs. Since an understanding of the use of ATM switches as a backbone to interconnect legacy networks requires an understanding of the LAN emulation process, we will examine both topics in the next section.

LAN EMULATION AND BACKBONE OPERATIONS

As previously noted in our examination of the operation of ATM, it can be categorized as a connection-oriented technology that uses dynamically assigned VPs and VCs for addressing. In comparison, legacy LANs are primarily connectionless and use MAC addresses. A third key difference between ATM and legacy LANs concerns the manner by which broadcast traffic is supported.

On a legacy LAN, the setting of bits within the address field of a frame will indicate that a frame is a broadcast frame. Then, this setting informs all other stations that they should copy the frame when it is encountered on the network. Since ATM uses a connection-oriented technology, a different method is required to support broadcast traffic. Table 5.3 summarizes the key differences between ATM and legacy LANs.

Recognizing the differences between ATM and legacy LANs that could preclude interoperability, the Technical Committee of the ATM Forum developed the LAN Emulation User-to-Network Interface (LUNI). The LUNI consists of a series of protocols that operate in a client/server environment and enable ATM attached end systems, as well as legacy LAN-to-ATM conversion devices, to emulate the connectionless operation of legacy LANs, including address conversion and broadcast operations. The emulation process is referred to as LAN emulation (LANE), and provides the mechanism for legacy LANs to be supported by an ATM backbone as well as for LAN traffic to be transported by ATM-based wide area networks. The actual network being emulated is a single segment or ring and the LAN emulation process enables different stations on different segments or rings to be

TABLE 5.3 Comparing ATM and Legacy LANs

Feature	*ATM*	*Legacy LANs*
Connection	Point-to-point	Connectionless shared media
Broadcast mechanism	No general broadcast mechanism	All traffic is available to all users, including unicast, broadcast, and multicast since the media is shared.
Setup	Requires point-to-point connections to be set up prior to transmission or reception of data packets.	No setup is required since all stations examine traffic on a shared-media network.

formed into a virtual LAN. Since a description of LAN emulation provides an understanding of how ATM can be used as a backbone switch for legacy LANs, we will cover LANE prior to focusing our attention upon backbone operations and switch characteristics.

LAN Emulation

LAN emulation is implemented as a client/server technology and consists of four key elements whose operation collectively makes an ATM backbone invisible to legacy LANs. Those key elements include a *LAN emulation client* (LEC), *LAN emulation server* (LES), *broadcast and unknown server* (BUS), and *LAN emulation configuration server* (LECS).

LAN Emulation Client

The LAN emulation client (LEC) is responsible for initiating requests to the ATM network for the translation of MAC addresses into ATM addresses. Each LEC has a registered MAC address for the LAN it represents, such as an Ethernet or Token-Ring six-byte MAC address. In addition, the LEC has an ATM address which enables it to communicate with other clients that are ATM stations.

LAN switches that support both legacy networks and ATM include the LEC function on an ATM adapter card installed in the switch. This is illustrated in the lower-left portion of Figure 5.9, which shows a general summary of the LAN emulation process. When a LAN switch receives a frame destined for another legacy LAN station on a different switch, the LEC transmits a MAC-to-ATM resolution request to the LAN emulation server (LES). This is illustrated in Figure 5.9 by the numeral 1.

LAN Emulation Server

The LAN emulation server (LES) is primarily responsible for registering and resolving MAC addresses to ATM addresses. When an LEC has a MAC address for which it requires an ATM address, it sends a request to the LES for the ATM address, using a protocol referred to as the *LAN Emulation Address Res-*

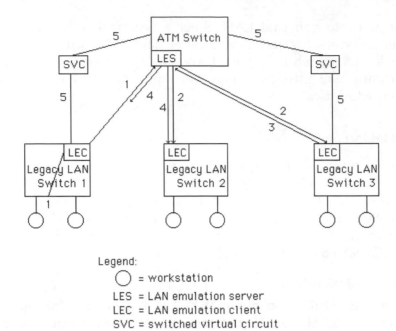

Legend:

◯ = workstation
LES = LAN emulation server
LEC = LAN emulation client
SVC = switched virtual circuit

FIGURE 5.9 The LAN emulation process.

olution Protocol (LEARP). If the LES had previously obtained the address, it will have it in cache memory and will return it to the LEC. If the LES does not have the ATM address, the LEC must use the services of the broadcast and unknown server.

Broadcast and Unknown Server

The broadcast and unknown server (BUS) is responsible for resolving unknown unicast traffic as well as providing a broadcast or multicast transmission facility via an ATM network. To locate the BUS, the LEC transmits a message to the LES requesting the ATM address associated with the all-1's MAC address which represents the broadcast address. The LES will respond to the LEC query with the ATM address of the BUS. Once the LEC knows the BUS address, it sets up a VC to the bus. Then, the LEC can send broadcast and unknown destination frames to the BUS which reconciles them by transmitting them to every ATM address in the LAN being emulated. During the address translation process the BUS, which is commonly located in an ATM switch in memory with the LES, will transmit a multicast request to every LEC in the network other than the requesting LEC. In Figure 5.9 this is indicated by the numeral 2. The LAN switch that has the destination MAC address in its address table will respond to the query as indicated by the numeral 3 in Figure 5.9, assuming that a station on LAN switch 1 is attempting to transmit data to a station on LAN switch 3. The response is received by the LES on the ATM switch which requests the BUS to broadcast the response from the LEC that had the requested MAC address to all other LECs. This is indicated by the numeral 4 in Figure 5.9. Finally, the LEC that originated the request learns the ATM address and sets up a switched virtual circuit (SVC) to the destination switch. The SVC is indicated by the numeral 5 in Figure 5.9. The previous overview of the LAN emulation process did not discuss the role of the LAN emulation configuration server, which is a key component of the LAN emulation process. Thus, in concluding this section on LANE, we will focus our attention upon the configuration server.

LAN Emulation Configuration Server

The LAN emulation configuration server (LECS) is responsible for assigning different LECs to different emulated LANs as well as for providing configuration information for the LEC. To accomplish the preceding, the LECS maintains a database of configuration information for each emulated LAN. When an LEC is powered on, one of its first actions is to set up a connection to the LECS, requesting a variety of configuration information. Such configuration information includes the address of the LES to use for a particular emulated LAN. The LECS also returns the LAN type, LAN name, maximum message length, and timeout values associated with the LAN supported by the LES. By configuring the LECS you obtain the ability to control which clients are combined to form a broadcast domain. This in turn allows you to establish multiple virtual LANs through the use of the LECS.

Backbone Operations

Similar to the use of conventional LAN switches, you can obtain a variety of networking solutions through the use of ATM switches. When used as a backbone for an existing switch-based network, there are two basic configurations that warrant attention. Those ATM backbone configurations actually are similar, with the difference between the two based upon the presence or absence of a server farm connected to a backbone ATM switch. Thus, one configuration supports distributed servers, while a second configuration is used to support the clustering of servers into a server farm.

Distributed Server Support

Figure 5.10a illustrates the use of a single ATM switch while Figure 5.10b shows the use of multiple switches to interconnect stations previously connected to legacy LAN switches. In both examples, network servers are presumed to be connected locally to the primary switch to which ring and segment network users are connected.

Quality of Service Considerations.   In examining Figure 5.10 it is important to note that since the network configuration represents a mixture of legacy LANs and ATM, there is no guaranteed quality of service (QoS) on an end-to-end basis. This means your ability to run multimedia applications to the desktop will depend upon the activity of legacy LAN switches to process frames in a timely manner. This also means that Token-Ring users will probably have fewer problems than Ethernet users when switches are heavily used. This is because Token-Ring stations can be set to limit frame length, provide a more predictable service, and support eight levels of priority, all of which are lacking in Ethernet.

Operating Rate.   If your organization is using 10-Mbps legacy LAN switches you can consider using either 25- or 155-Mbps ATM switches for your backbone network. The use of a 25-Mbps ATM backbone is more suitable for the situation where each

(a) Using a single ATM switch

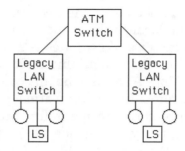

(b) Using multiple ATM switches

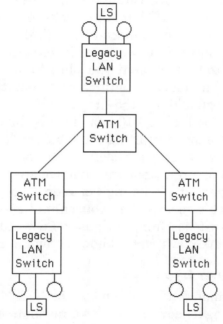

Legend:

◯ = workstations

LS = local server

FIGURE 5.10   Using ATM switches in the backbone to support distributed servers.

legacy LAN switch has its own local server which is used by workgroup stations connected to the switch, resulting in most communications being local to the legacy switch. Since the cost of a 25-Mbps ATM adapter and switches is a fraction of the cost of equivalent 155-Mbps ATM equipment for light interswitch traffic, the use of 25-Mbps ATM may be an economical method to link networks while providing a migration path to ATM. For example, in the future a requirement for multimedia support with a guaranteed quality of service could be supported by directly connecting stations to 25-Mbps ATM switch ports. The 25-Mbps ATM switches could replace the use of legacy LAN switches, providing ATM to the desktop. Then, the 25-Mbps ATM switches could be replaced by 155-Mbps ATM switches in the backbone network; however, if interswitch communications are expected to be high or if you plan to operate a centralized server form that places a sufficient amount of traffic on the backbone, you should use 155-Mbps ATM.

In examining Figure 5.10, note that by linking ATM switches you can easily expand your backbone network. In addition, since ATM signaling is standardized, it becomes possible to use switches from different vendors when constructing an ATM backbone. In comparison, signaling between legacy LAN switches is proprietary. This means that you cannot mix, as an example, 100BASE-T switches from various vendors to form a backbone similar to the ATM switch backbone shown in Figure 5.10b.

Centralized Server Support

A second common configuration by which ATM is used as a backbone for linking legacy LANs is as a mechanism for establishing a server farm. In this type of networking environment the actual relationship of ATM and legacy LAN switches would be the same as previously shown in Figure 5.10; however, instead of servers being connected to local legacy switches they would be connected to a single ATM switch to form a server farm. Doing so would enable all servers to be placed in a convenient area with respect to service, security, and upgradability.

Traffic Considerations. When ATM is used as a backbone to provide access to a server farm, all client/server sessions will flow over the backbone network. This means traffic will be considerably higher than if servers were distributed based on the switch for which they are primarily used by a workgroup served by a switch. This also means that the failure of an ATM switch performing LAN emulation renders your entire network inoperative, an important point to consider when considering ATM as a backbone mechanism to a centrally located server farm. Thus, the use of ATM as a backbone mechanism to a centrally located server farm should more than likely be accomplished at an operating rate of 155 Mbps. In addition, you should probably consider switches that support LANE version 2.0, which provides LAN emulation redundancy so that the failure of an ATM switch performing the LANE function does not take down your entire network.

ATM SWITCH FEATURES

In concluding our discussion of ATM switches we will turn our attention to ten general switch features you may wish to evaluate during the switch acquisition process. Table 5.4 lists those features in alphabetical order and provides a mechanism for you to enter your requirements for each feature and compare and contrast the products of various vendors against your ATM switch feature requirements.

ATM Ports

An examination of ATM switch characteristics should begin with the number of ports on the switch. Most ATM workgroup switches have 8, 12, or 24 ports.

ATM Port Operating Rate

This feature refers to the primary operating rate of the ATM switch and should not be confused with the high-speed port feature. ATM switches designed for use as backbone or to replace legacy LANs either operate at 25 Mbps or 155 Mbps. As previously discussed in this chapter, an operating rate of 155 Mbps

TABLE 5.4 ATM Switch Features to Consider

Feature	*Requirement*	*Vendor A*	*Vendor B*
ATM ports	_____	_____	_____
ATM port operating rate			
25 Mbps	_____	_____	_____
155 Mbps	_____	_____	_____
Backplane operating rate	_____	_____	_____
Buffering	_____	_____	_____
High-speed ports			
155 Mbps	_____	_____	_____
622 Mbps	_____	_____	_____
IP over ATM support	_____	_____	_____
LANE support	_____	_____	_____
1.0	_____	_____	_____
2.0	_____	_____	_____
Number of emulated LANs			
supported	_____	_____	_____
Port expansion			
ATM port	_____	_____	_____
Backplane	_____	_____	_____
Quality of service			
Constant bit rate	_____	_____	_____
Variable bit rate	_____	_____	_____
Unspecified bit rate	_____	_____	_____
Available bit rate	_____	_____	_____

should be considered when an ATM backbone is used to provide access to a server farm.

Backplane Operating Rate

The faster the backplane operating rate of a switch, the greater its ability to support a worst-case condition when all ports become active. Most ATM switches provide a backplane operating rate between 4 and 6 Gbps. By dividing the backplane rate by either 25 Mbps or 155 Mbps, you can determine the approximate number of ports the device can support without blocking occurring.

Buffering

When a switch cannot process cells it must have a place to temporarily store them. That place is the buffer, which can be one block of central memory or memory added to individual port cards. As a general rule with respect to ATM switches, the more memory the better. If buffers are too small they can overflow when a switch gets too busy, causing cells to be discarded which in turn forces applications to retransmit dropped traffic, further adding to an overloaded switch condition.

High-Speed Ports

Most 25-Mbps ATM switches use 155-Mbps uplink ports to link desktop switches to a backbone ATM network. However, some 25-Mbps and 155-Mbps ATM switches support the installation of 622-Mbps optical carrier 12 (OC12) adapters that provide a connection to a backbone ATM switch or a carrier's wide area network ATM switch via optical fiber.

IP over ATM Support

Although LAN emulation is the primary method used to route legacy traffic via ATM, it isn't the only method. LANE operates at the MAC layer, resulting in compatibility with layer 2 bridges, and can support any higher-level protocol. An alternative method known as *classical IP over ATM,* which is defined by the Internet Engineering Task Force (IETF) as Request for Comment (RFC) 1577, allows IP traffic to be routed via ATM. Since more vendors support LANE than IP over ATM and the latter is limited to supporting IP, many organizations prefer LAN emulation.

LANE Support

As previously discussed, LANE version 2.0 addresses the single-point-of-failure issue raised through the use of the earlier standard. Thus, users requiring redundancy and whose organizations cannot tolerate downtime should prefer support for LANE version 2.0.

Number of Emulated LANs Supported

The ability of a switch to set up more than one emulated LAN provides network managers and administrators with the ability to assign users to different workgroups. This capability enables the creation of broadcast domains that can be tailored to user activities. Since ATM does not impose limits on the distance separating end-users, they can be located in different cities and still be part of the same emulated LAN. Thus, by assigning users to different emulated LANs you obtain a virtual networking capability which, because of the distance insensitivity of ATM, permits stations associated with a vLAN to be located anywhere in a network.

Port Expansion

The number of ports that can be added to a switch can be an important consideration. Some switches permit additional chassis to be stacked onto a base unit, with an ATM port on one switch cabled to an ATM port on the first chassis and an ATM port on the first chassis then cabled to an ATM port on the second chassis in a daisy chain method. Other switches permit cascading via their proprietary backplane which, while providing a faster data transfer capability, precludes connectivity to more than one vendor product.

Quality of Service

Under the ATM standard the user-to-network interface (UNI) defines how switches set up permanent and switched virtual circuits to obtain a *quality of service* (QoS). Currently three classes of service are defined for SVCs and PVCs—*constant bit rate* (CBR), *variable bit rate* (VBR), and *unspecified bit rate* (UBR). The CBR service class results in a fixed bandwidth for transporting real-time video and voice. The VBR class of service enables the capacity on a virtual circuit to vary with traffic levels and is well suited for bursty data. The third class, UBR, provides no guarantees concerning bandwidth or delivery and is well suited for such applications as file transfers.

A fourth QoS, known as *available bit rate* (ABR), should be standardized during 1998. ABR provides a mechanism to guarantee a minimum amount of bandwidth so applications do not time out. Although the actual number of applications that support QoS was very limited at the time this book was written, such applications are expected to significantly grow and the quality of service supported by a switch should be carefully evaluated against your organization's current and projected requirements.

6

Virtual LANs

Asignificant benefit of the LAN switching revolution is the ability of manufacturers to add new functions through software that would be difficult, if not impossible, to implement without a switch. One such feature is the *virtual LAN* (vLAN), which is the focus of this chapter.

In this chapter we will first examine the basic characteristics of a virtual LAN, particularly its construction and rationale for use. Once this is accomplished we will turn to an examination of the operation of the three basic types of vLANs and a fourth specialized type of vLAN. Since standards are an important consideration when purchasing expensive network equipment, we will conclude this chapter by obtaining an overview of both de facto and de jure vLAN standards.

vLAN CHARACTERISTICS

A virtual LAN, or vLAN, can be considered a broadcast domain. This means that a transmission generated by one station on a vLAN is received only by those stations predefined by some criteria to be in the domain.

Construction Basics

A vLAN is constructed by the logical grouping of two or more network nodes on a physical topology. To accomplish this logical grouping you must use a "vLAN-aware" switching device. Those devices can include intelligent switches, which essentially perform bridging and operate at the media access control (MAC) layer, or routers, which operate at the network layer, or layer 3, of the Open Systems Interconnection (ISO) Reference Model. Although a switching device is required to develop a vLAN, in actuality it is the software used by the device that provides you with a vLAN capability. That is, a vLAN represents a subnetwork or broadcast domain defined by software and not by the physical topology of a network. Instead, the physical topology of a network serves as a constraint for the software-based grouping of nodes into a logically defined network.

Implicit versus Explicit Tagging

The actual criteria used to define the logical grouping of nodes into a vLAN can be based upon implicit or explicit tagging. Implicit tagging, which in effect eliminates the use of a special tagging field inserted into frames or packets, can be based upon MAC address, port number of a switch used by a node, protocol, or another parameter that nodes can be logically grouped into. Since many vendors offering vLAN products use different construction techniques, interoperability between vendors may be difficult, if not impossible. In comparison, explicit tagging requires the addition of a field into a frame or packet header. This action can result in incompatibilities with certain types of vendor equipment as the extension of the length of a frame or packet beyond its maximum can result in the inability of such equipment to handle such frames or packets. Based upon the preceding, the differences between implicit and explicit tagging can be characterized by the proverbial statement, "between a rock and a hard place." Although standards can be expected to resolve many interoperability problems, network managers and administrators may not have the luxury of time to wait until such standards are developed. Instead, you may wish to use existing equipment to develop vLANs to satisfy current and evolving organizational requirements. Later in this chapter I will provide detailed information necessary to assist you in selecting an appropriate vLAN construction technique. However, to provide you with an illustration of the actual construction of several vLANs, as well as to obtain the basics for discussing advantages associated with vLANs, I will illustrate the use of implicit tagging based upon switch ports.

Using Implicit Tagging

Figure 6.1 illustrates a simple eight-port Ethernet port-switching hub used to support two servers and six network nodes. The port-switching hub functions as a matrix switch, providing the

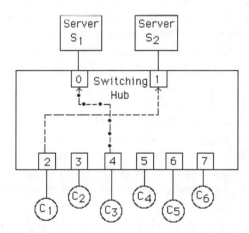

Legend:

S_1, S_2 = servers

$C_1, \ldots C_6$ = client workstations

$\boxed{n}$ = switch port n

FIGURE 6.1 Using an Ethernet port-switching hub. In a client/server communications environment, the use of a port-switching hub enhances bandwidth utilization due to the support of simultaneous cross-connections. In this example, ports 2 and 1 and 4 and 0 are cross-connected.

ability to route a frame received on any port to any other port. For simplicity, let us assume that the ports are labeled 0 through 7, with ports 0 and 1 used to connect two servers to the switch, while ports 2 through 7 are used to connect six client workstations to the switch. As indicated in Figure 6.1, the servers are labeled S_1 and S_2, while the client workstations are labeled C_1 through C_6.

In a typical client/server communications environment, the switch illustrated in Figure 6.1 would allow up to two simultaneous client/server communications to occur, in effect doubling available bandwidth through the switch in comparison to the use of a "Flat" network in which all workstations contend for access to the network along with each server. The two dashed lines in Figure 6.1 indicate two possible simultaneous client/server cross-connections or communications.

To illustrate the creation of a virtual LAN, let us assume that the organization using the switch shown in Figure 6.1 consists of employees working in the sales and administrative departments. Let us further assume that server S_1 and clients C_1, C_2, C_3, and C_4 are associated with employees in the sales department, while server S_2 and clients C_5 and C_6 are associated with the administrative department. Through the use of a vLAN-capable switch that can associate ports with virtual LAN membership, you could logically establish two vLANs. Figure 6.2 illustrates the establishment of those vLANs based upon the association of ports to membership in each virtual LAN. Here the use of port address provides an implicit tagging method for the creation of the two vLANs.

In examining Figure 6.2, note that each vLAN represents a logical grouping of ports on top of the physical topology of the network. Thus, the network previously illustrated in Figure 6.1 has been segmented by the connection of client workstations and servers to different ports on a switching hub. In this example there are two segments which represent independent broadcast domains. That is, frames transmitted by a workstation or server on one domain remain constrained to that domain. Now that we have a basic level of knowledge concerning one method used to establish virtual LANs, let's use that construction method to discuss some of the advantages associated with the use of vLANs.

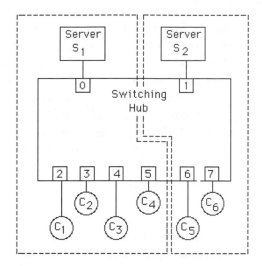

Legend:

S_1, S_2 servers
$C_1 \ldots C_6$ = client workstations
$\boxed{n}$ = port n
vLAN1 = ports 0, 2, 3, 4, 5

FIGURE 6.2   Establishing vLANs based upon the use of switch ports.

Rationale for Use

There are four key factors that can be considered as the driving force behind the development of vLANs and virtual networking. Those factors include the necessity to support virtual organizations, the ability to simplify LAN administration, more efficient utilization of network bandwidth, and enhanced network security. Let us examine each of those factors.

Supporting Virtual Organizations

A *virtual organization* is commonly defined as an organization without walls. What this means is that an organization can select its "best and brightest" employees to work on a specific project without regard to their physical location.

Prior to the development of vLANs, the primary methods used to support the virtual networking requirements of virtual organizations were commonly limited to fax, telephone, and electronic mail. While those methods are still commonly used and more than likely will continue to be used in the future, vLANs provide a mechanism to establish a subnetwork of users and servers dedicated to the support of a specific project or group of projects. Through the use of a virtual LAN, employees can be easily added or dropped from a project, and there is the ability to share access to a projects database. Thus, another reason for the desire of many organizations to obtain a virtual LAN capability concerns LAN administration.

LAN Administration

The use of equipment that supports virtual LANs can significantly simplify administrative costs associated with network additions, moves, and changes. For example, assume the employee that uses client workstation C_4 is reassigned from working in the sales department to a virtual organization group working in the administrative department. Through the use of an administrator console, the reassignment of workstation C_4 can be made automatically without having to physically modify the workstation, alter cabling, or perform other physical activity.

Figure 6.3 illustrates the effect of reassigning workstation C_4 from the sales to the administrative department. In many cases, the actual effort required to accomplish moves and changes using a vLAN-capable device is as simple as a Windows drag-and-drop operation that can be accomplished in a few seconds. With the typical cost associated with physically moving workstations by means of recabling operations ranging between $500 and $1000, a dynamic organization can severely tax the conventional method of network support as well as incur a considerable expense.

More Efficient Bandwidth Utilization

As previously noted, vLANs are created by logically segmenting a network into broadcast domains. For example, in Figures 6.2 and 6.3 two broadcast domains were created to represent logical groupings of network nodes. Once such logical groups are created, frames or packets transmitted by a member of one group are only switched between ports that are designated as belong-

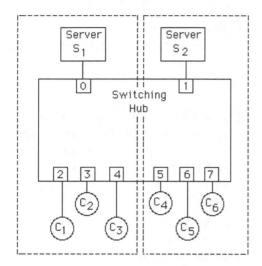

Legend:

S_1, S_2 = servers
$C_1 \ldots C_6$ = client workstations
[n] = port n

vLAN1 = ports 0, 2, 3, 4, 5
vLAN2 = ports 1, 6, 7

FIGURE 6.3 Altering vLAN membership. A vLAN capability enables workstations to be easily relocated from one broadcast domain to another, minimizing the expense associated with network adds, moves, and changes.

ing to the same virtual LAN. This results in network traffic originating within one logically created vLAN being contained to that network and results in a more efficient use of bandwidth. In addition, instead of broadcast traffic propagating throughout the physical infrastructure, such traffic is restricted to the "broadcast domains" that represent each virtually created segment. Such broadcast traffic commonly originates from servers that advertise their presence and capability to other network devices. One common example of the generation of broadcast traffic is Novell Inc.'s Service Advertisement Protocol (SAP), in which network servers advertise their presence and the type of service they provide by broadcasting a SAP packet every 60 seconds. By limiting broadcast packets or frames to a broadcast domain instead of transmitting that traffic to all network stations, network bandwidth is more efficiently used.

Improved Security

Although a vLAN is not a security device, nor should it be considered as one, it does improve security. The reason for this is the fact that transmissions are limited to broadcast domains. For example, consider Figure 6.3, which illustrates the previously discussed altered pair of vLANs. If user C_1 transmits a request to any administration department employee, the request cannot move beyond physical ports 0, 2, 3, and 4. This means that nodes outside the domain will not be capable of receiving traffic generated on the other domain. This also means that a virtual organization whose members are located in different geographical areas and are working on a confidential project can have a restful evening knowing that their traffic will not be visible outside of their virtual workgroup.

vLAN CONSTRUCTION TECHNIQUES

vLANs can be implicitly formed equivalent to layers 1 through 3 of the OSI Reference Model as well as in a rule-based manner. In this section we will primarily focus on implicit tagging. Although our examination of vLAN construction will discuss explicit tagging, we will defer a detailed examination of this topic to the following section in recognition of tagging methods falling into de facto and de jure categories of standards.

Port-grouping vLANs

As its name implies, a port-grouping vLAN represents a virtual LAN created by defining a group of ports on a switch or router to form a broadcast domain. Thus, another common name for this type of vLAN is a *port-based virtual LAN*. The hardware used to form a port-grouping vLAN can range in scope from an intelligent wiring hub to a switch or sophisticated router.

Using Intelligent Wiring Hubs

In a conventional Ethernet hub, data received on one port is repeated onto all other ports. This results in the use of a single common channel on the backplane of the hub to transmit data to all ports. A few years ago vendors borrowed a technique commonly associated with time-division multiplexing, partitioning the backplane channel by time to allow devices to access various "channels" produced by time. The resulting intelligent wiring hub lacks the switching capability associated with LAN switches; however, by associating ports to channels, a vLAN configuration capability is obtained.

Operation. When an intelligent wiring hub with vLAN creation capability is used, you can dynamically associate ports with portions of the hub's backplane channel. The backplane can be considered to represent the hub's traffic highway and an intelligent hub with vLAN creation capability subdivides the backplane by time, enabling ports to be associated with derived subchannels of bandwidth. Through the assignment of ports to specific time slots, different network segments are created, with each segment being equivalent to a workgroup.

vLAN Creation. Figure 6.4 illustrates an example of the establishment of several virtual LANs using port grouping on an intelligent hub. In Figure 6.4 the backplane's transmission capability is shown segmented into three virtual LAN time slots which repeat in sequence. Hub ports 1 and 3 are assigned to the first time slot, which equates to the first virtual LAN, while

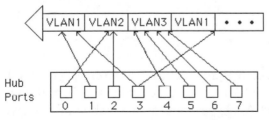

FIGURE 6.4   Port-group vLAN via an intelligent hub.

ports 0 and 2 are assigned to the second vLAN. The remaining ports, 4 through 7, are assigned to the third virtual LAN. In examining the backplane time slots, note that the fourth slot represents vLAN1 as there are a total of three virtual LANs. After the time slot for vLAN3 occurs, it is followed by the repeating sequence vLAN1, vLAN2, and so on. To illustrate that the same ports are associated with each vLAN unless a configuration change occurs, you will note that lines were drawn from ports 1 and 3 to each time slot labeled vLAN1.

Although the assignment of ports to time slots occurs electronically, in examining Figure 6.4 you will note that the lines routed from hub ports to the various time slots on the hub's backplane resemble the wiring of a patch panel. In effect, we can say that the creation of vLANs through the use of an intelligent hub represents a software-configurable wiring patch panel.

Advantages. The key advantages associated with the use of intelligent wiring hubs for the creation of vLANs are their cost and ease of use.

Cost Considerations. An intelligent wiring hub can be considered to represent a low cost port-switch. As such, the cost per port can be under $100.

Ease of Use. The creation of vLANs using an intelligent wiring hub occurs through the use of a command or graphical user interface management port. For example, assume you wish to create a virtual LAN consisting of ports 0, 1, 2, 3 and 4. Some intelligent wiring hubs include an ASSIGN statement, where the format of the statement is:

```
ASSIGN  {port n₁, n₂, . . nₙ}  to VLANn
        {port n₁,  . . nₙ   }
```

Using the preceding format and assuming you wish to configure ports 0, 1, 2, 3 and 4 to represent a broadcast domain associated with VLAN1, you could use either of the two following ASSIGN statements:

```
ASSIGN PORT 0,1,2,3 TO VLAN1
ASSIGN PORT 0 . . . 3 TO VLAN1
```

Note that the first use of the ASSIGN statement requires all ports that form the vLAN to be entered. In comparison, the second format permits a group of contiguous ports to be specified similar to the manner by which a range is specified in Lotus 1-2-3.

Disadvantages.   There are three primary disadvantages associated with the use of vLANs created through the use of intelligent wiring hubs. Those disadvantages include the inclusion of workstations being limited to those that can be directly connected to the hub, an inability to extend networking beyond the hub, and the manner by which configuration changes are effected.

Direct Connection and Extended Networking.   Since the creation of virtual LANs using a wiring hub is based upon the use of the hub's backplane, this restricts members of the vLAN to workstations that can be directly connected to the hub. In addition, since hub backplanes are independent of one another, this also means that workgroups resulting from the creation of a broadcast domain are limited to a single hub, inhibiting the connection of a hub-based vLAN to a wider network. Thus, a port-switched vLAN created from the use of a wiring hub is cut off from an extended network and requires the use of a bridge or router to obtain interoperability.

Configuration Changes.   Another problem associated with the formation of vLANs based upon port groupings concerns their configuration. Whenever a user requires recabling, a configuration change is also required to update the vLAN.

Although the preceding discussion of problems and limitations associated with the use of port grouping is considerable, this method of defining vLAN membership is quite common. For many small organizations it can provide an easy-to-implement solution to virtual networking requirements.

Using LAN Switches

A LAN switch is a much more sophisticated device than a wiring hub as it includes hardware which enables frames arriving on any port to be output to any other port. Although most switches were originally designed to operate on MAC addresses contained in frames, it was a relatively easy process for switch manufacturers to add vLAN creation based upon ports grouped into a domain.

Operation. Figure 6.5 illustrates the use of an intelligent LAN switch to create two vLANs based upon port groupings. In this example the switch was configured to create one virtual LAN consisting of ports 0, 1, 5 and 6, while a second virtual LAN was created based upon the grouping of ports 2, 3, 4 and 7 to form a second broadcast domain.

Port versus Segment Switching. In examining the vLANs created by grouping ports through the use of a LAN switch, note that although a segment-based switch is shown in Figure 6.5,

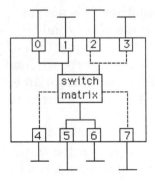

Legend:

$\boxed{n}$ = port n

⊥ = network segment

vLAN1 = ports 0, 1, 5, 6
vLAN2 = ports 2, 3, 4, 7

FIGURE 6.5 Creating port-grouping vLANs using a LAN switch.

this method of vLAN creation is also applicable to a port-based switch. When a port-based switch is used, only one station per port can be linked into a vLAN broadcast domain. In comparison, when a segment-based switch is used, multiple stations connected to a port will be grouped into a virtual LAN.

Advantages. Advantages associated with the use of LAN switches for creating vLANs include the ability to use the switching capability of the switch, the ability to support multiple stations per port, and internetworking capability.

Switch Capability. The capability of a LAN switch can include any of the large number of features discussed in Chapter 5, such as the use of fat pipes and flow control, to alleviate the potential loss of data due to a speed mismatch between ports. Thus, the use of a LAN switch to form vLANs based upon port grouping also provides a wealth of features beyond those of a conventional wiring hub.

Network Expansion. In comparison to the use of intelligent wiring hubs, the use of LAN switches provides the capability to expand a virtual network beyond one device. For example, some vendors enable switches to be interconnected so that a port-based vLAN can span hundreds of ports on multiple switches. This is commonly accomplished through the use of a management console which enables interswitch communications to be defined so that a vLAN broadcast domain can be created using ports on multiple switches linked together.

Disadvantages. Although the use of a LAN switch provides a number of advantages over the use of a wiring hub with respect to the creation of vLANs, they also have certain disadvantages associated with their use. Those disadvantages include the cost of LAN switches and the inability to associate multiple vLANs to a network segment connected to a switch port.

Cost. In comparison to the use of an intelligent wiring hub, the use of a LAN switch is considerably more expensive. This additional expense results from the fact that the switch is a much more sophisticated device than an intelligent wiring hub.

vLAN Port Support. Another limitation which is associated with both intelligent wiring hubs and LAN switches used to create port-based vLANs is the fact that they are limited to supporting one vLAN per port. This means that moves from one vLAN to another affect all stations connected to a particular port. This also means that a station requiring access to more than one vLAN must do so using multiple network interface cards if the station can support the use of multiple cards.

Supporting Inter-vLAN Communications

The use of multiple network interface cards provides an easy-to-implement solution to obtaining an inter-vLAN communications capability when only a few vLANs must be linked. This method of inter-vLAN communications is applicable to all methods of vLAN creation; however, when a built-in routing capability is included in a LAN switch, you would probably prefer to use the routing capability rather than obtain and install additional hardware.

Figure 6.6 illustrates the use of a server with multiple network interface cards to provide support to two port-based vLANs. Not only does this method of multiple vLAN support require additional hardware and the use of multiple ports on a switch or wiring hub, but, in addition, the number of NICs that can be installed in a station is typically limited to two or three. Thus, the use of a large switch with hundreds of ports config-

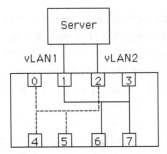

FIGURE 6.6 Overcoming the port-based constraint where stations can only join a single vLAN. By installing multiple network adapter cards in a server or workstation, a LAN device can become a member of multiple vLANs.

ured for supporting three or more vLANs may not be capable of enabling a common server to support all stations connected to the switch.

MAC-based Switching

A second type of vLAN creation is based upon the burned-in universally administered or software-configured locally administered address of each device connected to a switch. Known as MAC-based switching in recognition of the use of media access control addresses, this method of vLAN creation is also referred to as a layer-2 vLAN, since the vLAN creation occurs at the data link layer. MAC-based switching requires a true switching hub or router as the hardware platform. That platform uses software to associate MAC addresses with a broadcast domain which in turn forms a virtual LAN.

When MAC addresses are associated with the creation of virtual LANs, a vLAN-capable switch can provide a high degree of versatility. For example, selective users on a segment connected to a port, as well as individual workstations connected to other ports on a switch, can be configured into a broadcast domain representing a virtual LAN. To illustrate the advantages and disadvantages associated with layer-2 vLANs, let's first focus our attention upon the use of a LAN switch which supports layer-2 vLAN creation.

Operational Example

Figure 6.7 illustrates the use of an 18-port switch to create two virtual LANs. In this example, eighteen devices are shown connected to the switch via six ports, with four ports serving individual network segments. Thus, the LAN switch in this example is more accurately referred to as a segment switch with a MAC or layer-2 vLAN capability. This type of switch can range in capacity from small 8- or 16-port devices capable of supporting segments with up to 512 or 1024 total addresses to large switches with hundreds of ports capable of supporting thousands of MAC addresses. For simplicity of illustration we will use the six-port segment switch to denote the operation of layer-2 vLANs as well as their advantages and disadvantages.

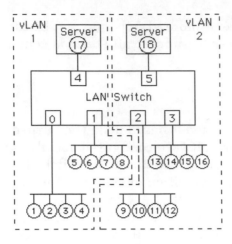

Legend:

$\boxed{n}$ = port n

$\bigcirc{n}$ = MAC address

FIGURE 6.7 Layer-2 vLAN. A layer-2 vLAN uses MAC addresses to construct broadcast domains that form a virtual LAN.

In turning our attention to the vLANs shown in Figure 6.7, note that we will use the numeric or node addresses shown contained in circles as MAC addresses for simplicity of illustration. Thus, addresses 1 through 8 and 17 would be grouped into a broadcast domain representing vLAN1, while addresses 9 through 16 and 18 would be grouped into a second broadcast domain to represent vLAN2. At this point in time you would be tempted to say "so what," since the use of MAC addresses in creating layer-2 vLANs resembles precisely the same effect as if you used a port-grouping method of vLAN creation. For example, using an intelligent hub with vLAN creation based upon port grouping would result in the same vLANs as those shown in Figure 6.7 when ports 0, 1, and 4 are assigned to one virtual LAN and ports 2, 3, and 5 to the second.

To indicate the greater flexibility associated with the use of equipment that supports layer-2 vLAN creation, let's assume users with network node addresses 7 and 8 were just transferred from the project associated with vLAN1 to the project associated with vLAN2. If you were using a port-grouping method of vLAN creation, you would have to physically recable nodes 7 and 8 to either the segment connected to port 2 or the segment connected to port 3. In comparison, when using a segment switch with a layer-2 vLAN creation capability, you would use the management port to delete addresses 7 and 8 from vLAN1 and add them to vLAN2. The actual effort required to do so might be as simple as dragging MAC addresses from one vLAN to the other when using a GUI interface, or entering one or more commands when using a command line management system. The top of Figure 6.8 illustrates the result of the previously mentioned node transfer. The lower portion of Figure 6.8 shows the two vLAN layer-2 tables, indicating the movement of MAC addresses 7 and 8 to vLAN2.

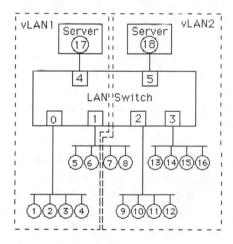

Legend:

$\boxed{n}$ = port n

$\bigcirc{n}$ = MAC address

vLAN1 = 1, 2, 3, 4, 5, 6, 17
vLAN2 = 7, 8, 9, 10, 11, 12, 13,14, 15, 16, 18

FIGURE 6.8 Moving stations when using a layer-2 vLAN.

Although the reassignment of stations 7 and 8 to vLAN2 is easily accomplished at the MAC layer, it should be noted that the "partitioning" of a segment into two vLANs can result in upper-layer problems. This is because upper-layer protocols, such as IP, require all stations on a segment to have the same network address. Some switches overcome this problem by dynamically altering the network address to correspond to the vLAN on which the station resides. Other switches without this capability restrict the creation of MAC-based vLANs to one device per port, in effect limiting the creation of vLANs to port-based switches.

Advantages

The use of MAC-based vLAN creation provides several advantages over the use of a port-grouping vLAN creation method. Those advantages include additional flexibility with respect to the reassignment of stations from one vLAN to another, greater bandwidth, and additional expandability.

Flexibility. As indicated by the movement of network nodes illustrated in Figure 6.8, a key advantage associated with the use of a layer-2 vLAN creation is flexibility. That is, unlike a port-grouping method of vLAN creation, which requires the recabling of workstations when workstation users are reassigned to a different vLAN, a layer-2 vLAN enables such reassignments via a command line entry or drag-and-move operation when using a GUI. In addition, if you simply wish to move a workstation to a different location, but wish to maintain the station's membership in the assigned vLAN, a switch performing layer-2 vLAN creation will automatically retain the station's membership. This is because membership is by MAC address, which enables the switch to retain the workstation's vLAN membership.

Bandwidth and Expandability. Other advantages of layer-2 vLAN switches concern bandwidth and expandability. As membership in a workgroup grows and its bandwidth requirements increase, the use of a layer-2 LAN switch enables workgroup members to be placed on multiple network segments while maintaining vLAN broadcast domains. The addition of extra servers to the switch which are configured into the same vLAN domain results in the ability of multiple client/server operations to occur which provides additional bandwidth. An example of this situation is illustrated in Figure 6.9. In this example a new server with the MAC address of 18 was added to vLAN1. Two in-progress client/server communications are shown occurring on vLAN1, in effect doubling the bandwidth available for users associated with that virtual LAN. In comparison, perhaps because of an absence of a requirement for additional performance, only one server is connected to vLAN2 which restricts the bandwidth available for users associated with that virtual LAN.

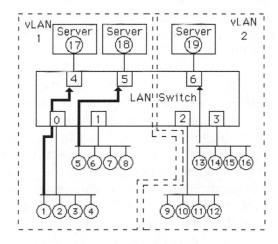

Legend:

☐ n = port n

Ⓝ = MAC address

vLAN1 = 1, 2, 3, 4, 5, 6, 7, 8, 17, 18
vLAN2 = 7, 8, 9, 10, 11, 12, 13, 14, 15, 16, 19

FIGURE 6.9 The use of a switch to form layer-2 vLANs can provide additional bandwidth by supporting multipe client/server operations.

Disadvantages

Although the use of MAC-based vLAN creation provides more flexibility and greater expandability than the use of a port-based vLAN creation method, there are certain limitations associated with the MAC-based vLAN creation process. Those limitations include the use of MAC addresses, which are not very intuitive, interswitch communications, the configuration of switches, and the difficulty associated with attempting to support mobile users attaching to fixed docking stations.

MAC Address Lists.   The creation of a MAC address list can represent a time-consuming effort. This is because a MAC address is a sequence of hexadecimal numbers burned in on the network interface card and used as such when universally administered addressing is employed or obtained from a configuration file when locally administered addressing is employed. For either situation, obtaining MAC addresses may require a visit to each workstation. The entry of those addresses into switch tables can be a long and tedious task.

Interswitch Communications.   Similar to the port-grouping method of vLAN creation, a layer-2 vLAN is normally restricted to a single switch; however, some vendors include a management platform which enables multiple switches to support MAC addresses between closely located switches. Unfortunately, neither individual nor closely located switches permit an expansion of vLANs outside of the immediate area, resulting in the isolation of the virtual LANs from the rest of the network. This deficiency can be alleviated in two ways. First, for inter-vLAN communications you could install a second adapter card in a server and associate one MAC address with one vLAN while the second address is associated with the second virtual LAN. While this method is appropriate for a switch with two vLANs, you would employ a different method to obtain interoperability when communications are required between a large number of virtual LANs. Similar to correcting the interoperability problem with the port-grouping method of vLAN creation, you would have to use routers to provide connectivity between layer-2 vLANs and the rest of your network.

Router Restrictions.   When using a router to provide connectivity between vLANs, there are several restrictions you must consider. Those restrictions typically include a requirement to use a separate switch port connection to the router for each virtual LAN and the inability to assign portions of segments to different vLANs. Concerning the former, unless the LAN switch either internally supports layer-3 routing or provides a "trunking" or "aggregation" capability that enables transmission from multiple vLANs to occur on a common port to the router, one port linking the switch to the router will be required for each vLAN. Since router and switch ports are relatively costly, internetworking of a large number of virtual LANs can become expensive. Concerning the latter, this requirement results from the fact that in a TCP/IP environment routing occurs between segments. An example of inter-vLAN communications using a router is illustrated in Figure 6.10.

When inter-vLAN communications are required the layer-2 switch transmits packets to the router via a port associated with the virtual LAN workstation requiring such communications.

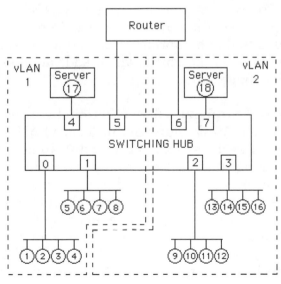

FIGURE 6.10   Inter-vLAN communications requires the use of a router.

The router is responsible for determining the routed path to provide inter-vLAN communications, forwarding the packet back to the switch via an appropriate router-to-switch interface. Upon receipt of the packet the switch uses bridging to forward the packet to its destination port.

Returning to Figure 6.10, a workstation located in vLAN1 requiring communications with a workstation in vLAN2 would have its data transmitted by the switch on port 5 to the router. After processing the packet the router would return the packet to the switch, with the packet entering the switch on port 6. Thereafter, the switch would use bridging to broadcast the packet to ports 2, 3, and 7 where it would be recognized by a destination node in vLAN2 and copied into an appropriate network interface card.

Although routing enables inter-vLAN communications, there are several disadvantages associated with the configuration shown in Figure 6.10. First, routers on a per-port cost basis are considerably more expensive than switches. Thus, the support of a large number of virtual LANs can become a budget buster. Second, from a performance perspective, the switch must forward each inter-vLAN packet twice. First the packet is forwarded from the originating node to the switch port cabled to the router that represents the originating vLAN switch-to-router connection. Next, the packet received from the router must be forwarded to its appropriate destination node. A third problem is the addition of the router which adds another device to configure and manage.

Configuration and Support. Two additional disadvantages associated with using MAC addresses to form vLANs include the configuration of switches and the inability to support the random use of docking stations. Concerning the configuration of switches, while this may not be a labor-intensive operation for a small switch, a very large network containing hundreds or thousands of users can require a considerable amount of setup time. To overcome this problem, some switches include an auto-setup feature which initializes each subnet to a default vLAN and provides graphical tools to facilitate modifying those settings.

In today's mobile environment, many organizations use docking stations with built-in LAN adapters to provide network connectivity while employees move about the office, perform sales calls, and work at home using notebooks that mate into the docking stations upon their return to the office. Since the MAC address is burned into the LAN adapter, this means that users who utilize a different docking station than the one associated with the virtual LAN they belong to may not be able to join the intended vLAN. Although this problem could be alleviated by reconfiguring the switch, rather than perform this operation each time you could override universally administrated addressing and use a configuration file in the notebook computer to establish a locally administrated address. Then each time the notebook moves to a different docking station it would retain a fixed MAC address.

Layer-3-based vLANs

A layer-3-based vLAN is constructed using information contained in the network layer header of packets. This prevents the use of LAN switches that operate at the data link layer from being capable of forming layer-3 vLANs. Thus, layer-3 vLAN creation is restricted to routers and LAN switches that provide a layer-3 routing capability.

Through the use of layer-3 operating switches and routers there are a variety of methods that can be used to create layer-3 vLANs. Some of the more common methods supported resemble the criteria by which routers operate, such as IPX network numbers and IP subnets, AppleTalk domains, and layer-3 protocols.

The actual creation options associated with a layer-3 vLAN can vary considerably based upon the capability of the LAN switch or router used to form the virtual LAN. For example, some hardware products permit a subnet to be formed across a number of ports and may even provide the capability to allow more than one subnet to be associated with a network segment connected to the port of a LAN switch. In comparison, other LAN switches may be limited to creating vLANs based upon different layer-3 protocols.

Subnet-based vLANs

Figure 6.11 illustrates the use of a layer-3 LAN switch to create two virtual LANs based upon IP network addresses. In examining the vLANs created through the use of the LAN switch, note that the first virtual LAN is associated with the subnet 198.78.55 which represents a Class C IP address, while the second vLAN is associated with the subnet 198.78.42 which represents a second Class C IP address. Also note that since it is assumed that the LAN switch supports the assignment of more than one subnet per port, port 1 on the switch consists of stations assigned to either subnet. While some LAN switches support this subnetting capability, it is also important to note that other switches do not. Thus, a LAN switch that does not support multiple subnets per port would require stations to be recabled to other ports if it was desired to associate them to a different virtual LAN.

Advantages. Three of the major advantages associated with layer-3 vLANs using subnetting include their flexibility, config-

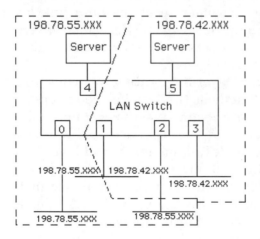

Legend:

vLAN1 = subnet 198.78.55
vLAN2 = subnet 198.78.42

FIGURE 6.11 vLAN creation based upon IP subnets.

uration, and inter-vLAN communications capability. Concerning the flexibility of layer-3 vLANs, as a user moves to another segment but retains his or her subnet number, many switches will "follow" the relocation, permitting moves to be accomplished without requiring the reconfiguration of a LAN switch.

The configuration of vLANs can be automatically formed, unlike port- and MAC-based virtual networks whose setup can be tedious and time consuming. Thus, the cost of support of a layer-3 vLAN may be less than for other types of virtual networks, and by itself can represent an important acquisition consideration.

The third advantage of a layer-3 vLAN is the fact that it supports routing. This means that it implicitly supports inter-vLAN communications, eliminating the necessity to obtain a separate router to support this capability.

Disadvantages. Although layer-3 vLANs using subnetting as a virtual LAN creation criterion address the flexibility problems of port-based vLANs and the configuration problems of MAC-based vLANs, they are not problem free. Two limitations associated with vLANs using subnetting include the configuration required to ensure network stations are using the correct protocol and network address, and the inability of some switches to support multiple subnets on a port. Although the second limitation can be overcome through the selection of a more capable LAN switch, the first limitation is associated with all types of layer-3 vLANs.

Protocol-based vLANs

In addition to forming virtual LANs based upon a network address, the use of the layer-3 transmission protocol as a method for vLAN creation provides a mechanism which enables vLAN formation to be based upon the layer-3 protocol. Through the use of this method of vLAN creation, it becomes relatively easy for stations to belong to multiple vLANs. To illustrate this concept, consider Figure 6.12, which illustrates the creation of two vLANs based upon their layer-3 transmission protocol. In examining the stations shown in Figure 6.12, note that the circles with the uppercase I represent those stations configured for

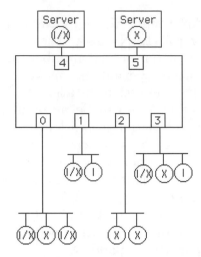

Legend:

$\boxed{n}$ = port n

$\bigcirc\!\!\!I$ = IP protocol used by station

$\bigcirc\!\!\!X$ = IPX protocol used by station

$\bigcirc\!\!\!I/X$ = IPX and IP protocols used by station

I = vLAN1 membership
X = vLAN2 membership
I/X = membership in both LANs

FIGURE 6.12 vLAN creation based upon protocol.

membership in the vLAN based upon the use of the IP protocol, while the circles containing the uppercase X represent stations configured for membership in the vLAN which uses the IPX protocol as its membership criterion. Similarly, the circles containing the characters I/X represent stations operating dual protocol stacks which enable such stations to become members of both vLANs.

Two servers are shown at the top of the LAN switch illustrated in Figure 6.12. One server is shown operating dual IPX/IP stacks, which results in the server belonging to both vLANs. In comparison, the server on the upper right of the switch is configured to support IPX and could represent a NetWare file server restricted to membership in the vLAN associated with the IPX protocol.

Advantages.   Similar to layer-3 vLANs that use subnetting, a major benefit associated with vLAN creation based upon protocol is networking flexibility. This flexibility enables stations to be moved from one network segment to another without losing their vLAN membership. Another aspect associated with networking flexibility is the ability to obtain the bandwidth advantages associated with the use of LAN switches while tailoring traffic to support different services. For example, assume a requirement to connect stations on vLAN1 to the Internet develops. To support this new requirement you could add a port to the LAN switch and connect a router to that port. Figure 6.13 illustrates the expanded LAN switch with a router connected to port 6 of the switch. Note that although you might be tempted to anticipate bandwidth problems resulting from the connection of the Internet to vLAN1, only inbound traffic directed to the network address associated with the IP-based vLAN is broadcast to the vLAN domain. In addition, as with most router-based Internet connections, you can use the filtering capability of the router to limit inbound traffic to the vLAN. In the outbound direction, only IP traffic with a network address differing from the address associated with vLAN1 will be forwarded by the router to the Internet. Thus, the basic operational capability of the router can be used to limit both inbound and outbound traffic to and from the virtual LAN connected to the Internet via the router.

Other advantages associated with the use of layer-3 protocols for vLAN creation are similar to the advantages described for subnet-based vLANs. That is, those advantages include the automatic configuration of the switch and an implicit inter-vLAN communications capability.

Disadvantages.   Layer-3 vLANs that use protocols for their creation method have disadvantages similar to those of subnet-based vLANs. That is, you must obtain equipment that supports

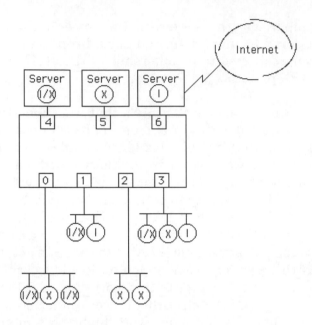

Legend:

☐n☐ = port n

①= IP protocol used by station

Ⓧ = IPX protocol used by station

Ⓘ/Ⓧ = IPX and IP protocols used by station

I = vLAN1 membership
X = vLAN2 membership
I/X = membership in both LANs

FIGURE 6.13 Expanding a vLAN to suport Internet access.

the use of protocols for vLAN creation and verifies that stations are configured correctly.

Rule-based vLANs

A recent addition to vLAN creation methods is based upon the ability of LAN switches to look inside packets and use predefined fields, portions of fields, and even individual bit settings as a mechanism for the creation of a virtual LAN.

Capabilities

The ability to create virtual LANs via a rule-based methodology provides, no pun intended, a virtually unlimited virtual LAN creation capability. To illustrate a small number of the almost unlimited methods of vLAN creation, consider Table 6.1, which lists eight examples of rule-based vLAN creation methods. Note that in addition to creating vLANs via the inclusion of specific field values within a packet, such as all IPX users with a specific network address, it is also possible to create vLANs using the exclusion of certain packet field values. The latter capability is illustrated by the next to last example in Table 6.1, which forms a vLAN consisting of all IPX traffic with a specific network address but excludes a specific node address.

Multicast Support

One rule-based vLAN creation example that deserves a degree of explanation to understand its capability is the last entry in Table 6.1. Although you might think that the assignment of a single IP address to a vLAN represents a typographical mistake, in actuality it represents the ability to enable network stations to dynamically join an IP multicast group without adversely affecting the bandwidth available to other network users assigned to the same subnet but located on different segments attached to a LAN switch. To understand why this occurs, let me digress and discuss the concept associated with IP multicast operations.

TABLE 6.1 Rule-based vLAN Creation Examples

- All IP users with a specific IP subnet address.
- All IPX users with a specific network address.
- All network users whose adapter cards were manufactured by the XYZ Corporation.
- All traffic with a specific Ethernet type field value.
- All traffic with a specific SNAP field value.
- All traffic with a specific SAP field value.
- All IPX traffic with a specific network address but not a specific node address.

IP multicast references a set of specifications that allows an IP host to transmit one packet to multiple destinations. This one-to-many transmission method is accomplished by the use of Class D IP addresses (224.0.0.0 to 239.255.255.255), which are mapped directly to data link layer-2 multicast addresses. Through the use of *IP multicasting,* a term used to reference the use of Class D addresses, the need for an IP host to transmit multiple packets to multiple destinations is eliminated. This in turn permits more efficient use of backbone network bandwidth; however, the arrival of IP Class D–addressed packets at a network destination, such as a router connected to an internal corporate network, can result in a bandwidth problem. This is because multicast transmission is commonly used for audio and/or video distribution of educational information, videoconferencing, news feeds, and financial reports, such as delivering stock prices. Due to the amount of traffic associated with multicast transmission, it could adversely affect multiple subnets linked together by a LAN switch that uses subnets for vLAN creation. By providing a "registration" capability that allows an individual LAN user to become a single user vLAN associated with a Class D address, Class D packets can be routed to a specific segment even when several segments have the same subnet. Thus, this limits the effect of multicast transmission to a single segment.

Advantages

The major advantages associated with a rule-based method of vLAN creation include its easy use of configuration and its operational flexibility. A rule-based creation method is similar to the manner by which filters are created when bridges and routers are used. Thus, the ability to configure one or more vLANs is relatively easy. Concerning flexibility, the ability to create vLANs based upon the value of a portion of a packet or the value of several fields or portions of packet fields makes vLAN creation able to satisfy just about any networking requirement a LAN manager or administrator may have. Thus, a rule-based vLAN creation capability should provide the most flexible method for creating virtual LANs.

Disadvantages

The major disadvantages associated with the use of a rule-based vLAN creation method include the configuration of vLANs and the efficiency of the switch. Due to the potential for creating vLANs based upon the value of a bit within a field of a packet, it can become a laborious task to correctly configure a complex vLAN association. Concerning switch efficiency, as the number of rules associated with the creation of a vLAN increase, the examination effort required for packets flowing through the switch increases. This in turn can result in an increase in packet latency through the LAN switch performing the rule-based comparisons.

Comparing vLAN Creation Features

We will now turn our attention to comparing the features and operational capabilities associated with the four major methods used to create vLANs. Table 6.2 provides a summary comparison

TABLE 6.2   vLAN Assignment Method Comparison

	Port-grouping		*MAC-based*	*Layer-3-based*	*Rule-based*
	Wirehub	*Switch*			
Connectivity beyond the workgroup	No*	No*	No*	Yes	Yes
Ease of station assignment	Easy	Easy	Difficult	Easy–Difficult	Easy–Difficult
Flexibility	None	None	Moderate	Moderate	High
Improved workgroup bandwidth	None	Yes	Yes	Yes	Yes
Multicast support	Inefficient	Inefficient	Inefficient	Inefficient	Inefficient
Multiple vLANs per port	No	No	Possible	Possible	Possible
Security	High	High	Low–High	Low–High	Selectable
vLAN spanning switches	No	Possible	Possible	Yes	Yes

*Installation of multiple adapters permits connectivity to other workgroups.

of the features and operational capability of port-grouping, MAC-based, layer-3-based, and rule-based vLAN creation methods. Due to a few subtle differences between the use of wiring hubs and LAN switches for the creation of port-grouping vLANs, that vLAN creation category was subdivided to reference the use of wiring hubs and LAN switches.

Connectivity beyond the Workgroup

As indicated by the footnote in Table 6.2, both port-grouping and MAC-based methods of vLAN creation can provide for station connectivity beyond a workgroup by the installation of multiple adapters in the station. In comparison, the use of a layer-3 vLAN creation method implies a built-in routing capability which allows connectivity beyond a station's workgroup.

Ease of Station Assignment

Port grouping is a relatively simple method of assigning stations to vLANs. Thus, this technique is easy to administer. In comparison, locating and entering MAC addresses can be a time-consuming and tedious task, resulting in the "difficult" entry in the table. Both layer-3 and rule-based vLAN creation methods can range from easy to difficult with respect to the ease of station assignments, with the level of difficulty based upon the actual assignment method used.

Flexibility

If we define flexibility as the ability to vary the composition of a vLAN to organizational changes, we can say that port grouping represents an inflexible method of vLAN creation. In comparison, MAC-based and layer-3-based vLAN creation methods permit stations to physically move without requiring the reconfiguration of hardware. Thus, those methods of vLAN creation provide a moderate level of flexibility. Since a rule-based vLAN creation method permits a high degree of tailoring of the composition of packets to an organization's vLAN creation requirements, it provides a higher degree of flexibility.

Improved Workgroup Bandwidth

With the exception of the use of a wiring hub, all vLAN assignment methods listed in Table 6.2 permit the use of a LAN switch.

Since a LAN switch enables multiple client/server sessions to occur simultaneously, its use can result in improved workgroup bandwidth.

Multicast Support

To effectively support the association of Class D addresses to the data link layer address requires the use of a routing capability. Thus, both layer-3 and rule-based vLAN creation methods provide an efficient method of multicast support. In addition, since a rule-based vLAN creation method also provides the ability to associate a single segment to a Class D address even when multiple segments have the same subnet, this method of vLAN creation becomes very efficient with respect to multicast support.

Multiple vLANs per Port

Although the ability to have multiple vLANs on a port is common to MAC, layer-3, and rule-based vLAN creation methods, a word of caution is warranted. As previously noted in this chapter, not all LAN switches have this capability. Thus, it is important to verify the capability of the switch to support this feature if this feature is to satisfy your organization's operational requirements.

Security

The use of a port-grouping vLAN creation method provides the highest level of security since all stations on a segment must reside on the same vLAN. In comparison, MAC and layer-3-based vLAN creation methods that permit multiple vLANs per switch port would have a low level of security, while those vLAN creation methods that do not support multiple vLANs per port would have a high level of security. The reason multiple vLANs on a segment connected to a switch port result in a low level of security is due to the fact that users associated with one vLAN could use a protocol analyzer to read frames associated with another vLAN. Thus, the ability to associate multiple vLANs to a switch port can result in a security loophole. Due to the ability of a rule-based vLAN creation method to allow the managers to create their membership criteria, security is selectable under that vLAN creation method.

vLAN Spanning

The expansion of a vLAN across multiple switches is not possible when intelligent wiring hubs are used. In comparison, the use of a LAN switch for creating a vLAN based upon port grouping, as well as the creation of a vLAN using a MAC-based creation method, may allow the expansion of the vLAN beyond a single switch. To do so switches will commonly use a management port connection to interconnect switches, which allows table entries to be transferred between switches and allows for the transmission of frames between switches. Since layer-3 and rule-based vLAN creation methods employ routing, they enable multiple switches to be linked together.

STANDARDS

As an emerging technology, you would more than likely expect vLANs to be awaiting the development of standards. Your expectation is quite correct; when this book was prepared a considerable amount of effort remained to be expended by the IEEE committee involved in developing vLAN standards.

Rather than simply stating that standards are being developed, I decided to include this section as a mechanism to provide readers with information on two types of vLAN standards—de facto and de jure. The first type of standard to be covered in this section, de facto, represents a method for providing interoperability between vLANs formed by the use of switches from a leading router and switch manufacturer. Due to the market dominance of Cisco Systems, we can consider the method by which its switches and routers recognize vLANs as a de facto standard. Thus, in the first portion of this section we will focus attention upon the Cisco Inter-Switch Link (ISL) protocol specification and that vendor's modification of the IEEE 802.10 security protocol. ISL is used by Cisco as a transport mechanism across Fast Ethernet, while the 802.10 protocol was modified by that vendor to provide a vLAN interswitch communications capability across FDDI backbones. In the second part of this section we will consider the de jure standard being developed by the IEEE. In doing so we will focus our attention upon the evolving IEEE 802.1Q standard.

De facto Standards

In this section we will examine two interswitch protocols developed by Cisco Systems that promote vLAN communications across shared LAN backbone technologies. Each protocol can be considered a de facto standard based upon several factors, such as the vendor's stance in the marketplace, its proactive approach toward vendor interoperability by sharing its specifications with other vendors, and its effort in working with IEEE standards groups concerning the development of vLAN standards. Since formal standards may be several years or more from ratification, Cisco's efforts in developing its ISL protocol and modifying the 802.10 standard may continue to provide a de facto vLAN interoperability standard for the foreseeable future.

The ISL Protocol

To obtain the ability to enable vLANs to span more than one switch, Cisco Systems developed its Inter-Switch Link (ISL) protocol as a mechanism to convey virtual LAN associations across Fast Ethernet backbone networks. ISL actually represents a frame format and protocol which enables Ethernet, FDDI, and Token-Ring frames to be transported between switches in addition to transporting their vLAN associations. Thus, ISL enables switches to support the connection of a variety of LAN modules while supporting the association of vLANs between switches.

Overview. Through the use of ISL, vLANs are explicitly identified at layer 2 via a packet-tagging process. Using explicit tagging, a switch encapsulates a frame and adds a header to each received packet which includes a field that identifies the packet's vLAN membership. This information enables the packet to be forwarded to appropriate switches and routers based upon the value of the vLAN membership identifier and the packet's MAC address. Once the packet reaches its destination, the header is removed and it is forwarded to the receiving device.

Frame Flow. Figure 6.14 illustrates the flow of ISL frames between two Cisco switches to communicate vLAN associations between those switches. Under ISL, each packet that enters a switch from a noninterswitch port that is associated with a vLAN is encapsulated into an ISL packet. That packet is then forwarded only to those switches and interconnected links that have the same vLAN address. Thus, this transmission technique can considerably reduce the flow of unnecessary broadcasts between switches and switches and routers.

Frame Composition. The ISL frame consists of three primary fields—a header, the encapsulated frame, and a 32-bit cyclic redundancy check (CRC) appended to the end of the frame. Figure 6.15 illustrates the format of the ISL frame, showing the fields within the frame and the size of each field indicated in bits placed in parenthesis in each field. In the remainder of this section we will examine the contents and use of each field.

Destination Address Field. The destination address field is 40 bits in length and represents the destination address of the frame. Since a vLAN frame must be transmitted to a broadcast domain, the address represents a multicast address. Cisco currently sets that address to hex 01-00-0C-00-00 and the contents of that field is used to inform the receiver that an ISL formatted frame is being received.

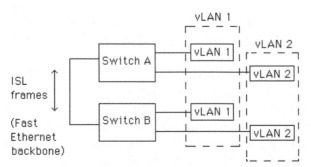

FIGURE 6.14 Using ISL to communicate vLAN associations.

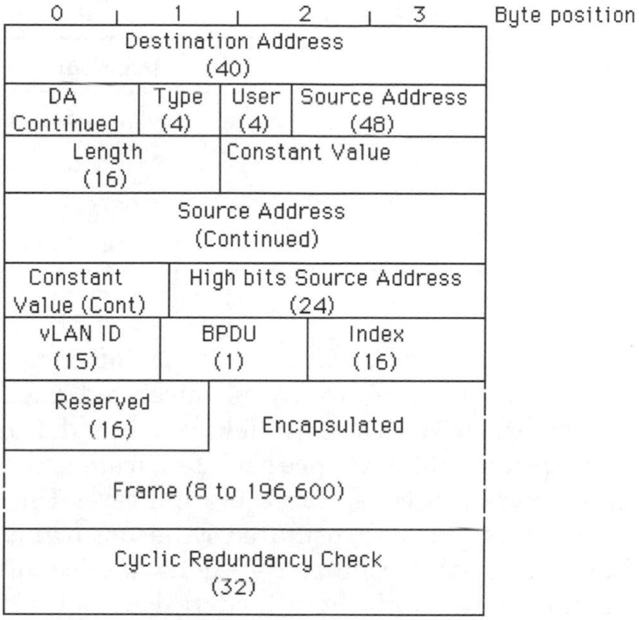

FIGURE 6.15 The Cisco Systems ISL frame format.

Type Field. The purpose of the type field is to indicate the type of frame encapsulated within the ISL frame. Currently, four type codes have been defined as indicated in Table 6.3. Since a four-bit field enables 16 type codes to be defined, support for additional encapsulations can be added in the future.

User Field. The user field represents a 4-bit extension to the type field which enables variations to the basic encapsulated frame types listed in Table 6.3 to be defined. Such definitions can be

TABLE 6.3 Type Field Definitions

Type Code	Meaning
0000	Ethernet
0001	Token-Ring
0010	FDDI
0011	ATM

TABLE 6.4 User Field Priority Assignments

User Field Bit Settings	Meanings
XX00	Normal Priority
XX01	Priority 1
XX10	Priority 2
XX11	Highest Priority

used to indicate variations in different types of encapsulated frames or to define priorities to an encapsulated packet. For encapsulated Ethernet frames, user field bits 0 and 1 are used to indicate the priority of the encapsulated frame as it flows through one or more switches. Table 6.4 indicates the assignment of user field bits for encapsulated Ethernet frames. Note that an X in the field value represents a don't-care condition.

The use of user field bits by a switch does not guarantee that a priority assignment will be honored. This is because the bit settings are used by a switch only when data can be forwarded more quickly, and the interpretation of the contents of the field does not guarantee that a frame will always have a quick path through a switch.

Source Address Field. The source address field is six bytes or 48 bits in length and contains the MAC address of the switch port transmitting the frame. Although monitoring of the values of this field can be used to determine interswitch traffic, the receiving device can ignore the contents of this field.

Length Field. The length field is two bytes or 16 bits in length. The value of this field is used to indicate a portion of the length of the ISL packet in bytes. That length excludes the destination address, type, user, source address, length, constant value, and CRC fields. Thus, the length field excludes 18 bytes in the header and represents the total length of the ISL packet minus 18 bytes.

Constant Value Field. Following the length field, the ISL packet header contains a three-byte or 24-bit field that has a constant value. The value of that field is hex AA-AA-03.

High-Bits Source Address Field. The high-bits source address field consists of three bytes or 24 bits. This field is used to represent the manufacturer portion of the source address field and is set to the value hex 00-00-0C.

vLAN Field. The vLAN field is 15 bits in length and indicates the virtual LAN ID of the packet. In Cisco terminology, the value of this field is used to refer to the "color" of the packet.

Bridge Protocol Data Unit (BPDU) Field. The BPDU field is one bit in length and is toggled to 1 when a bridge protocol data unit is encapsulated in an ISL packet. As previously indicated in this book, BPDUs are employed by the spanning tree algorithm to determine the topology of a network.

Index Field. The index field is two bytes or 16 bits in length. The contents of this field is used to indicate the port index of the source of the packet as it exits a switch. The contents of this field is used for diagnostic purposes and can be set to any value by other devices and is ignored in received packets.

Reserved Field. The reserved field is two bytes or 16 bits in length. This field is used when a Token-Ring or an FDDI frame is encapsulated. When a Token-Ring frame is encapsulated, its AC and FC field values are placed in the reserved field. When an FDDI frame is encapsulated, the FC field value of the FDDI frame is placed in the least significant byte of the reserved field. For other types of encapsulated frames the value of the reserved field is set to zero.

Encapsulated Frame. Following the previously described ISL header fields is the encapsulated frame. That frame can vary in length from 1 to 24575 bytes to accommodate Ethernet, Token-Ring, and FDDI frames. Included in the encapsulated frame is its own CRC value. Once an ISL packet is received at a switch the header and trailing CRC can be stripped, regenerating the original frame. That frame would then be used by the switch based upon certain values in the header, such as the vLAN identification.

CRC Field. The CRC appended to the end of an ISL packet is calculated on the entire packet, from its destination address field through the entire encapsulated frame. The receiving station checks this CRC field value by recomputing its own CRC. If the two do not match the frame is discarded.

It is important to note that by itself ISL is restricted to providing a mechanism for vLANs to be extended from one switch to another. However, the ability to communicate between logically defined vLANs is a layer-3 function that requires routing. Thus, the ability for vLAN membership to span switches and for devices to become members of multiple vLANs require both the ISL protocol and the use of routers that support that protocol.

Configuration Example. To illustrate the ease by which vLANs can be established across a Fast Ethernet backbone using the ISL protocol, let us return to Figure 6.14 and assume each switch is a Cisco Systems Catalyst 5000. At the time this book was prepared, each Catalyst 5000 switch was manufactured with five slots in which modules could be installed, with slot 1 always used for the supervisor module which includes a console port for switch management and two 100-Mbps Fast Ethernet ports. A variety of other modules can be installed in slots 2 through 5 to obtain 10-Mbps Ethernet and 100-Mbps Fast Ethernet support. Each port is identified by the expression X/Y, where X identifies the slot number used by a module, while Y identifies the port's position on the module. Assuming vLAN 1 on Switch A in Figure 6.14 is connected to port 1 on a module installed in slot 2, and vLAN 2 is connected to port 2, on that module you would use the Catalyst 5000's command port to configure the two vLANs by entering the following commands:

```
set vlan 1 2/1
set vlan 2 2/2
```

This first "set vlan" command creates vLAN 1 and assigns port 1 in slot 2 to it. The second command creates vLAN 2 and assigns port 2 in slot 2 to that vLAN.

To provide vLAN communications across the Fast Ethernet backbone requires the use of a trunk. When a Catalyst switch port is configured as a trunk, it automatically operates in ISL mode and uses the spanning tree protocol on all vLANs transported to ensure no closed loops occur. If we assume that port 1 on module 1 in switch A provides the trunk connection to switch B, you would enter the following trunk command to configure the port.

```
set trunk 1/1 1,2
```

Here the trunk command configures port 1 in slot 1 as a trunk and adds vLANs 1 and 2 to the trunk.

The previous commands only set up switch A. Thus, a similar series of commands would be required to be entered at the console of switch B to establish vLAN interoperability between switches. For example, assume vLAN 1 on switch B was connected to port 1 on a module in slot 3, while vLAN 2 was connected to port 2 on a module in slot 3. Then you would enter the following two commands into switch B:

```
set vlan 1 3/1
set vlan 2 3/2
```

Assuming that the Fast Ethernet backbone connection occurred on port 1 on the module in slot 1, you would then enter the trunk command as follows:

```
set trunk 1/1 1,2
```

Here the trunk command configures port 1 in slot 1 as a trunk and adds vLANs 1 and 2 to it, providing an ISL link to switch A. Thus, the entry of two series of three commands would provide vLAN interoperability between the two switches shown in Figure 6.14.

The 802.10 Security Protocol

Similar to the manner by which the ISL protocol was developed to provide vLAN connectivity across a Fast Ethernet backbone Cisco Systems modified the IEEE 802.10 Security Protocol to convey interswitch vLAN communications across FDDI backbones. In doing so, the 802.10 standardized header was modified so that a 32-bit or 4-byte vLAN ID field replaces a Security Association identifier (SAID) field.

Through the use of a unique identification mechanism vLAN information can be forwarded to switches and routers connected to one another via an FDDI backbone network. Once a packet arrives at a switch, its vLAN ID is noted as a mechanism to route the packet to an appropriate switch port, where its header is removed prior to the packet exiting the destination switch. Figure 6.16 illustrates the flow of the modified IEEE 802.10 Security Protocol between several Cisco System switches via an FDDI backbone network.

In examining Figure 6.16 it should be noted that several types of Cisco System switches are capable of supporting the modified 802.10 Security Protocol. In addition, since one Catalyst 5000 can be connected to another via an ISL link, it becomes possible to use both ISL and the modified 802.10 protocol to construct vLAN associations that cross both Fast Ethernet and FDDI backplanes.

The 802.10 Frame. The IEEE 802.10 standard was promulgated in late 1992 as a mechanism to support the security requirements of network users communicating within shared LANs,

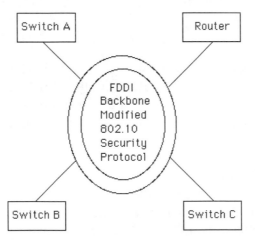

FIGURE 6.16 vLAN communications via an FDDI backbone.

such as Metropolitan Area Networks (MANs). This standard includes both encryption and authentication, which provides data confidentiality as well as the verification of the originator.

Under the 802.10 standard, a Secure Data Exchange (SDE) Protocol Data Unit (PDU) is defined. This SDE PDU represents a MAC layer frame with an 802.10 header inserted between the frame's MAC header and its information field. A special *integrity check value* (ICV) field is then appended to the end of the frame to protect against the unauthorized modification of the data in the frame. Figure 6.17 illustrates the IEEE 802.10 frame format with its header.

The header contains the destination and source address from the original frame as well as a length field whose value is incremented by 16. As indicated in Figure 6.17, the IEEE 802.10 header that follows the MAC header consists of clear and protected portions. The clear portion of the header contains three fields and is not encrypted, while the protected portion of the header also contains three fields that can be encrypted.

The first field in the clear portion of the header is the *logical SAP* (LSAP), which represents an address that defines the type of data carried in the frame. LSAPs are both administered by the IEEE and implemented by manufacturers for distinct frame

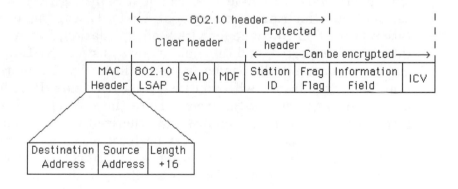

Legend:

SAID = Security Association identifier
MDF = management-defined field

FIGURE 6.17 The IEEE 802.10 rame format.

transportation purposes. Examples of IEEE-administered LSAP addresses include 06 for the ARPANET Internet Protocol (IP), 42 for the IEEE 802.1 Bridge Spanning Tree Protocol, and AA for the Sub-Network Access Protocol (SNAP). Some examples of manufacturer-implemented LSAPs include 04 for IBM SNA Path Control (individual), 05 for IBM SNA Path Control (group), E0 for Novell NetWare, and F0 for IBM NetBIOS. In the modified 802.10 frame the LSAP is expanded to three bytes and has the hex value 0A-0A-03.

The Security Association identifier (SAID) is 4 bytes in length. Under the IEEE 802.10 Protocol, it is used to provide secure data transfer across shared media, enabling the exchange of encryption keys via a look-up in a Security Management Information Base (SMIB). The SAID field is followed by a management-defined field (MDF), which is used to transport information that facilitates PDU processing and is dropped by Cisco.

The protected header replicates the source address in the original MAC frame's header. This action protects the real source of the frame from being altered and forms a mechanism to validate or authenticate the originator. In actuality the station ID field is eight bytes in length, with the first six representing the carnonical source address of the original frame. The last two bytes are flags that are undefined and are set to NULL. Following the Station ID field is a fragmentation flag that, when set, indicates the frame is a fragment. Under Cisco's implementation of the 802.10 frame for vLAN encapsulation, fragmentation is not supported, and this field is always set to NULL. The protected portion of the header is then followed by the information field of the frame, with an integrity check value (ICV) field appended to the end of the frame. Here the ICV is used as a mechanism to safeguard against unauthorized modification to the frame. To accomplish this, the protocol executes an algorithm that operates upon portions of the contents of the frame to create a binary value that functions similar to a check digit.

Cisco Systems Frame Modification. Recognizing that the IEEE 802.10 frame structure was already being routed by their products, Cisco Systems was able to easily modify the protocol to accommodate its use as a mechanism for conveying vLAN associations. To do so the 802.10 four-byte SAID field is used as the vLAN ID. This enables any device that supports the clear header portion of the 802.10 frame to become capable of supporting Cisco's method of vLAN identification. However, when used in this manner the IEEE 802.2 LSAP is changed to indicate a 802.10 vLAN frame, and the security aspect of the protocol (i.e., encryption) is not used by Cisco. Thus, although it may appear from vendor literature that this use of the 802.10 protocol represents a "standards-based" vLAN method, in actuality it does not, merely representing a proprietary extension of the protocol.

The frame format illustrated in Figure 6.17 is applicable for transporting IEEE 802.3, Ethernet 2, and Ethernet SNAP. When an 802.2 frame is transported on FDDI, or a SNAP frame originates on FDDI, the FC field of the FDDI frame is included in the MAC header as a prefix to the destination address field shown in Figure 6.17.

Through the use of a 4-byte vLAN ID field, an FDDI backbone becomes capable of supporting the transfer of information to and from billions of distinct virtual LANs, which probably exceeds by some orders of magnitude the ability of devices to support such numbers. For example, when a router or switch receives a 802.10 frame, it matches the vLAN ID against the vLANs it is configured to support. Thus, most devices have a finite and much smaller support capability than the number of vLANs that could theoretically be supported by a 4-byte field.

When the modified 802.10 frame format is used, the contents of the header govern the forwarding of the frame. When a router or switch determines that it supports the vLAN ID in the 4-byte vLAN ID field, it will remove the 802.10 header and forward the original frame to any or all ports that are associated with the virtual LAN. Similar to the use of ISP, the use of the modified IEEE 802.10 header requires a router to enable communications between vLANs.

De jure Standards

There are two de jure standards that should be considered when discussing vLANs. The first de jure standard represents the use of a switched ATM backbone for the connection of vLANs on legacy LANs. This standard is known as *LAN emulation* (LANE) and provides a transparent method of communications so that its effect is transparent to vLAN associations. The second de jure standard represents an ongoing effort of the IEEE to standardize virtual LANs. This effort involves a considerable examination of the technical aspects of vLANs and their operability within and among various types of LANs. Due to the scope of this effort, it may be several years until IEEE 802.1Q standards are actually finalized. Thus, we will focus our attention upon LAN emulation and then discuss the present state of IEEE vLAN standardization effort in the remainder of this chapter.

LAN Emulation

LAN Emulation (LANE) version 1.0 was approved by the ATM forum in February 1995 as a mechanism to enable legacy LAN traffic to communicate via an ATM backbone. To accomplish this, LANE makes a switched ATM LAN resemble a legacy local area network. Since we previously obtained an overview of the LAN emulation process in Chapter 5 when we discussed ATM switches, we will now focus our attention upon the establishment of vLANs using this technology. In doing so we will discuss both LAN emulation and IP over ATM since both mechanisms provide a virtual LAN capability over an ATM network.

vLANs and ATM. Under LAN emulation, devices register their presence on the network and become part of the same emulated LAN supported by a LAN emulation server. This action can be considered to form a MAC layer virtual LAN that defines a broadcast domain among end stations. Thus, all devices attached to an emulated LAN will appear as a bridged segment.

In addition to operating at layer 2, LANE supports layer-3 operations. To illustrate this, consider an IP workstation that has to communicate with another IP workstation via an emulated LAN. The originating station will issue an IP Address Resolution Protocol (ARP) packet to determine the MAC address of the destination. That packet will be sent to the LANE broadcast and unknown server, which will broadcast the packet to all end stations on the emulated LAN. The destination station recognizes the ARP request and responds by transmitting its MAC address. Unfortunately, the return of the MAC address, which flows to the LEC, is not what the LEC needs to set up an ATM connection. Thus, the LEC must issue a MAC-to-ATM address resolution request to the LAN emulation server and the previously described emulation process is repeated. That process is referred to as *IP over ATM address resolution* and is discussed next.

IP over ATM Address Resolution.   The actual transfer of IP over ATM is defined in RFC 1577, whose title is "Classical IP and ARP over ATM." Here the term *classical* represents the manner by which IP networks are established, in which clusters of nodes representing hosts and routers with similar subnet addresses are connected to devices outside their network by IP routers. Under RFC 1577, this classical view of IP was adhered to by the grouping of IP nodes into *logical IP subnets* (LIS). Thus, a LIS represents one or more nodes that share the same IP subnet and communicate with devices outside the subnet via an IP router.

When a LIS node is activated, it establishes a connection with another IP station or router configured to function as an ATMARP server. Since each node is configured with the ATM address of the ATMARP server, the LIS node knows where to send its request. The ATMARP server receives the LIS client request and notes its ATM address, but must learn the client's IP address to construct its tables. To do so the server transmits an *inverse* ARP request to the LIS client. Thus, as LIS clients become active, the ATMARP server can learn their ATM and IP addresses and store such information in its address table.

When the LIS client must communicate via IP, it knows the destination IP address but requires the ATM address. Thus, the client sends an ATMARP request to the server. The server responds to the request with an ATMARP reply if the ATM address associated with the destination IP address is in its address table. If not, the server returns a NAK. Since LIS clients can become active and inactive throughout the day, RFC 1577 requires the ATMARP server to periodically send out inverse ARP requests to update its tables, which provides a mechanism to eliminate non-responsive addresses from its tables.

IEEE 802.1Q

Work on the IEEE 802.1Q standard began in March 1996 with the issuance of a Project Authorization Request (PAR) titled "Standard for Virtual Bridged Local Area Networks." The PAR was assigned the 802.1Q project number and its scope was stated as follows:

> The formation of the IEEE 802.10 working group was accompanied by an initial effort which resulted in a preliminary explicit frame tagging format to provide a mechanism to identify frames that belong to different vLANs. The format was endorsed by Advanced Micro Devices, Inc., Agile Networks Inc., Bay Networks, Inc., Cisco Systems, Inc., Digital Equipment Corporation, Fore Systems, Inc., Hewlett-Packard, Intel Corporation, Plaintree Systems, Inc., xpoint Technologies, Inc., and 3Com Corporation.

Although several international meetings of the 802.10 working group occured that resulted in several revisions to an 802.10 draft document, a considerable amount of work on the standard remains to be performed. In fact, the target completion date of the PAR is May 1998.

At the time this book was prepared, the 802.1Q project was in its third draft stage. While a considerable amount of effort by members of the working group resulted in a comprehensive document, that document contained numerous sections that required further effort. Thus, readers should attempt to follow the efforts of the 802.1Q working group into 1998 as the continuing effort of the working group, through its project completion data, can be expected to fill in "to be determined" (TBD) sections as well as result in some revisions to the draft covered in this section.

Architecture. Under the 802.1Q draft standard, a 3-level model framework for vLANs was proposed. Figure 6.18 illustrates the general format of the 802.1Q architectural model.

Configuration Layer. The configuration layer of the vLAN model provides a mechanism for indicating the association of devices with different virtual LANs. The actual configuration process might occur via a variety of mechanisms, such as SNMP operating on a MIB, and configuration files on a workstation, via a server and through the use of a distribution protocol.

Distribution/Resolution Layer. The distribution/resolution layer provides the mechanism which enables switches to determine the association between a packet and a vLAN. This layer is concerned with the distribution of vLAN association between switches. To accomplish this will require a virtual LAN Mapping Protocol (VLMP) to distribute vLAN associations as well as a request/response protocol to enable specific associations to be requested.

Mapping Layer. At the third layer, mapping provides the mechanism to associate packets with vLANs. As indicated in Figure 6.18, explicit and implicit tagging as well as some possible additional mechanism will be used to provide mapping.

At the time this book was prepared, a considerable amount of effort of the 802.1Q working group had been accomplished at the mapping layer. Thus, in the remainder of this section we will primarily focus our attention upon tagging.

Frame Tagging. There are two basic types of frame tagging—implicit and explicit. Implicit tagging enables a packet to belong to a vLAN based upon the receiving port of a switch or the content of the frame. Concerning the latter, implicit tagging can be

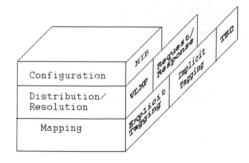

where:

```
MIB  Management Information Base
VLMP Virtual LAN Mapping Protocol
TBD  To be determined
```

FIGURE 6.18 vLAN architectural model.

based upon the MAC address, layer-3 protocol, layer-3 subnet address, and similar frame field contents. In comparison, explicit tagging requires each frame to contain an identifier that serves to classify the vLAN association of the frame.

Proposed vLAN Tagging. The explicit tagging of vLAN frames requires the addition of a header to each frame. Under the 802.1Q draft standard, that header is inserted immediately following the destination and source MAC addresses of a conventional frame.

The vLAN header consists of four fields; however, one field (user priority) remains to be defined and located in the header. Thus, the vLAN header which is shown in Figure 6.19 may be modified or, as an alternative, may have values assigned to one or more fields to encode up to 8 priority states in the header.

VPID/SVPID Fields. The *virtual LAN protocol identifier* (VPID) field is two bytes in length when an Ethernet version 2 protocol type is carried, and indicates the Ethernet protocol type trans-

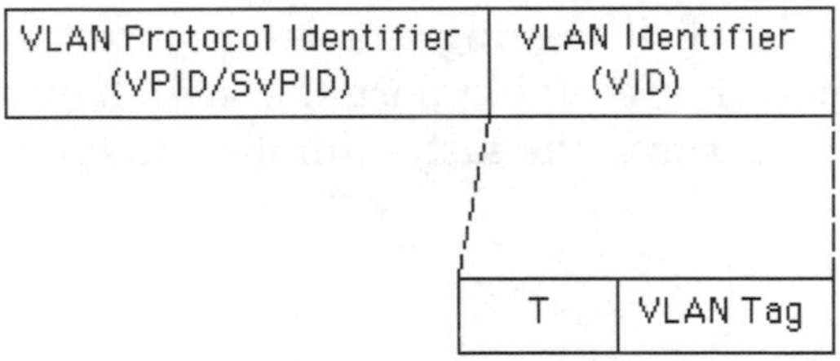

VLAN Protocol Identifier (VPID/SVPID)	VLAN Identifier (VID)

T	VLAN Tag

Legend:

VPI is 2 or 8 octets in length based upon the media type carrying the frame. SVPID defines a SNAP-encoded VPIP.

VID is 2 octets in length with a one-bit TR encapsulation bit.

T is a Token-ring encapsulation flag.

Priority field (3 bits) remains to be located.

FIGURE 6.19 The proposed vLAN header.

ported. When a SNAP-encoded vPID is transported, the field is expanded to eight octets. The first three contain the SNAP SAP header (AA-AA-03). This is followed by a three-byte OUI (00-00-00) and a two-byte vType field. Thus, the vType field in a SNAP-encoded VPID results in a prefix of the SNAP and OUI fields, with the resulting field having the mnemonic SVPIP.

VID Field. The virtual LAN identifier (VID) is two bytes in length. However, one bit, which while shown at the beginning of the field actually remains to be positioned in the field, is used to indicate whether the encapsulated frame is transported in a native Token-Ring format. That is, when the bit is set to 1, this setting will indicate that data following the VID is in a Token-Ring format. Through the setting of this bit, frames that originate as a Token-Ring frame can be transported end-to-end in their native format within a vLAN tagged frame. Doing so ensures that Token-Ring information is not translated while the frame flows across the virtual network, regardless of the type of media used to transport the vLAN frame. Although Token-Ring information is not translated, the vLAN header will be translated, if necessary, when the vLAN frame flows from one medium to another. If the source address indicates that a routing information field (RIF) is present, the RIF will prefix the SVPID field. Otherwise the source address field will be followed by either the VPID or SVPID field, with the actual field based upon the type of media the frame is transported on.

Frame Formats. Figure 6.20 illustrates examples of vLAN-tagged Ethernet, LLC, and Token-Ring frames transported on IEEE 802.31 Ethernet media. Note that the number of bytes for each field is indicated in parenthesis under the field abbreviation. When transmission occurs over FDDI or Token-Ring media there are several changes to each frame. For example, vLAN-tagged Ethernet, LLC, and Token-Ring frames transported on Token-Ring media would use a SNAP-encoded VPID (SVPID), which is eight bytes in length, in place of the byte VPID. In addition, when Token-Ring frames flow on a Token-Ring network they can contain a routing information field which is never carried on an Ethernet media-based LAN. For comparison pur-

1. vLAN-tagged Ethernet frame

DA (6)	SA (6)	VPID (2)	VID (2)	PT (2)	Data (48-1500)	CRC (4)

2. vLAN-tagged LLC frame

DA (6)	SA (6)	VPID (2)	VID (2)	LN (2)	LLC (3)	Data (0-1497)	PAD (0-43)	CRC (4)

3. vLAN-tagged Token-Ring frame.

DA (6)	SA (6)	VPID (2)	VID (2)	LN (2)	LLC (3)	TRdata (0-1497)	PAD (0-43)	CRC (4)

Legend:

DA	=	Destination MAC address
SA	=	Source MAC address
VIPD	=	VLAN Protocol ID
PT	=	Ethernet Protocol Type
LN	=	Length Field (802.3 style)
LLC	=	Logical Length Control
VID	=	vLAN identifier
Data	=	Data in native format for the medium carrying the frame.
TRdata	=	Data in native Token-Ring format.

FIGURE 6.20 vLAN-tagged frame formats for IEEE 802.3 Ethernet media.

poses, Figure 6.21 illustrates the format for three types of vLAN-tagged frames for transmission on Token-Ring and FDDI media.

In comparing the transportation of vLAN-tagged frames on IEEE 802.31 Ethernet and Token-Ring/FDDI media, note that the latter results in the prefix of each type of frame by a *ring control* (RC) field. That field is one byte in length and represents the Token-Ring access control field when the medium is a Token Ring. In comparison, when the medium is FDDI, the RC field is expanded to two bytes, with the second field representing the FDDI frame control (FC) field.

The Continuing Effort. Although a considerable amount of effort was expended defining explicit frame tagging required to identify vLANs, that effort was far from completed when this

1. vLAN-tagged Ethernet frame

RC (1/2)	DA (6)	SA (6)	SVPID (8)	VID (2)	SPT (8)	Data (46-1500)	CRC (4)

2. vLAN-tagged LLC frame

RC (1/2)	DA (6)	SA (6)	SVPID (8)	VID (2)	LLC (3)	Data (0-N)	CRC (4)

3. vLAN-tagged Token-Ring frame.

RC (1/2)	DA (6)	SA (6)	Route (0-30)	SVPID (8)	VIDtr (2)	TRdata (0-N)	CRC (4)

Legend:

RC = ring control field (AC Token Ring) and FC (FDDI)
DA = destination MAC address
SA = source MAC address
SPT = SNAP-encoded Ethernet protocol type
SVPID = SNAP-encoded VPID (vLAN protocol ID)
VID = vLAN identifier
VIDtr = vLAN identifier Token-Ring encapsulation
Route = Token-Ring source routing information
Data = Data in native format for the medium carrying the frame
TRdata = data in native Token-Ring format

FIGURE 6.21 vLAN-tagged frame formats for Token-Ring and FDDI media.

book was prepared. At that time the IEEE 802.1Q working group had not decided where and how to incorporate user priority. In addition, there were a large number of issues remaining to be resolved. Some of those issues include the use of single or multiple spanning trees per set of vLANs, the number of vLANs handled per tree, how to handle a default vLAN, and methods to support multiple links between two points in a network. In addition, the method of explicit tagging by which frames expand beyond their original standard length may present a problem if and when standard compliant switches are used in a legacy network. This is because although standard-compliant switches and routers can be expected to support the extended length of frames, legacy bridges, routers, and repeaters may not be capable of passing such frames. Due to this, proprietary-implicit vLAN creation methods that work may continue to represent a viable alternative to a standardized-explicit tagging vLAN creation method once such standards are promulgated.

Switch Management and Gigabit Networking

I n this concluding chapter we interrupt our previous tradition of focusing upon a single topic in each chapter by covering two. First we will discuss the management aspect of LAN switches from the perspective of switch performance and switch statistics the network manager and LAN administrator should note. Thus, we will focus our attention upon the type of management information generated by some LAN switches and the use of SNMP and RMON by other switches to provide meaningful statistical information or the generation of alarms in response to preset thresholds that can provide an insight into potential problems before they occur. Once this is accomplished, we will turn to a topic most suitable for concluding a book on communications technology—an evolving product. However, instead of examining specific vendor products, we will examine the operation and utilization of a generic switching product that can be expected to have an impact on local area networks. That product is the Gigabit Ethernet switch, which may provide a high degree of competition for ATM when used as a backbone to interconnect two or more local area networks within the same building.

SWITCH MANAGEMENT

Similar to the manner by which shared-media LANs have been supplemented and in many cases replaced by switches, the management capabilities of switches have also evolved. Most LAN switches were first viewed as similar to bridges based upon their operational characteristics, and vendors commonly incorporated a Simple Network Management Protocol (SNMP) and Remote Monitoring (RMON) capability into their products along with the bridge Management Information Base (MIB). While doing so provides relevant information to network managers and administrators, it does not always provide the information they seek. This is primarily a result of the installation of an RMON probe into a switch providing only traffic information on specific segments and that does not indicate the *relationship* of traffic between switch ports. Thus, although RMON information can provide valuable data concerning activity on one or a few segments, it provides only a small view of the total picture of switch activity. Recognizing this problem as well as the requirement of network managers and LAN administrators for additional information concerning switch activity, some vendors have attacked this problem by providing detailed packet-forwarding information grouped between source and destination ports. One most interesting management tool is provided by the Loral Test & Information Systems ProSwitch. The ProSwitch supports the grouping of network users into virtual LANs, which by itself represents a capability provided by other switch vendors. However, what really distinguishes the ProSwitch from other products is its ability to generate a three-dimensional display of switch source and destination activity either on an individual port-pair basis or grouped by predefined user groups.

Figure 7.1 illustrates an example of the ProSwitch three-dimensional packet-forwarding statistics display. Note that the display provides a near-instantaneous visual identification of potential cross-port activity problems as the height of the rectangular protruding areas correspond to packet activity between groups of ports. Thus, the packet-forwarding statistics screen

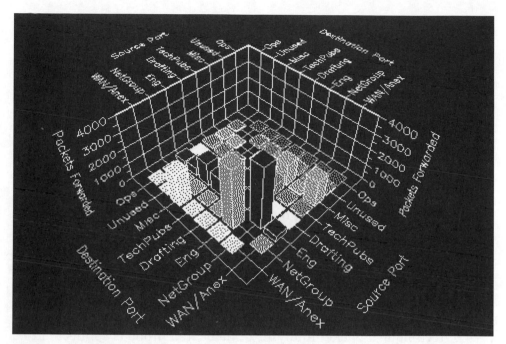

FIGURE 7.1 The ProSwitch packet-forwarding statistics display provides a three-dimensional view of activity between grouped pairs of switch ports.

display can provide an easy-to-use mechanism to obtain a feel for activity occurring through an entire switch as well as a mechanism to note potential utilization problems. From a quick examination of Figure 7.1, you can note that the three pairs labeled WAN/Anex-Misc, NetGroup-Eng, and Eng-NetGroup look like skyscrapers in a city of lots. Thus, it becomes possible to nearly instantaneously note those source-destination port pairs with the highest amount of intraswitch activity.

Management Methods

There are three basic methods used by switch manufacturers to provide cross-connection statistics, with each method having certain advantages and disadvantages that warrant a discussion. Let's turn our attention to those methods.

Integrated CPU

Some switch vendors use the CPU that powers the switch to perform management functions such as statistics gathering, sorting, and display. Those management functions are performed by borrowing cycles from the processor whose primary job should be switching traffic. Although this design method reduces the cost associated with performing management functions, the actual monitoring process as well as on-demand sorting and display functions will degrade switch performance. Thus, unless a very fast processor is used, the effect of management and switching operations being performed by a common processor can result in degraded switch performance.

Port Mirroring

Recognizing the potential performance problems associated with the use of a common processor to perform both management and switching functions, some switch manufacturers now use a port-mirroring technique to produce management data. Under this technique a packet analyzer or dedicated probe is connected to a mirrored port, enabling a user to view activity on the port. Unfortunately, this technique requires multiple analyzers or probes to simultaneously view multiple ports. In addition, this technique is essentially limited to segments connected to the port being mirrored since the attached probe or network analyzer is essentially blind to other network traffic. Thus, recognizing this limitation, vendors have incorporated a third technique into switches to provide more meaningful management data similar to the traffic display shown in Figure 7.1. That technique is achieved through the integration of an RMON probe module that works in conjunction with the backplane of the switch, enabling all traffic through the switch to be captured.

RMON Integration

Basic MAC layer RMON, commonly referred to as RMON1, is specified by two Internet Engineering Task Force (IETF) Requests for Comments (RFCs), RFC 1271 and RFC 1513. RFC 1271 defines nine Ethernet and Ethernet/Token-Ring groups while RFC 1513 defines ten specific Token-Ring RMON extensions. RMON2, which was in the process of being standardized by the IETF when this book was written, extends RMON to the network layer through the application layer, enabling the capture and generation of statistical information concerning the protocols and types of applications used.

Most switch vendors that integrate RMON into the bus of their switch provide support for a subset of the ten RMON groups. The most popular groups commonly incorporated into switches include Statistics, Host Table, Host TopN, and Traffic Matrix.

Statistics Group. The Statistics group provides information concerning packets and byte count for both Ethernet and Token-Ring. Based upon the type of traffic being monitored, additional statistical information will be based upon the type of LAN. For example, in the Ethernet Statistics group, error counts are furnished for undersizes, fragments, CRC/alignment errors, collisions, and oversize packets. In a Token-Ring environment, statistics are oriented to that LAN, providing statistics concerning beacons, purges, and various types of ring errors. For both LANs the RMON Statistics group will provide a count of packets based upon frame distribution into predefined packet lengths. Figure 7.2 provides an illustration of packet-forwarding statistics by port for a Kalpana (now part of Cisco Systems) Ethernet

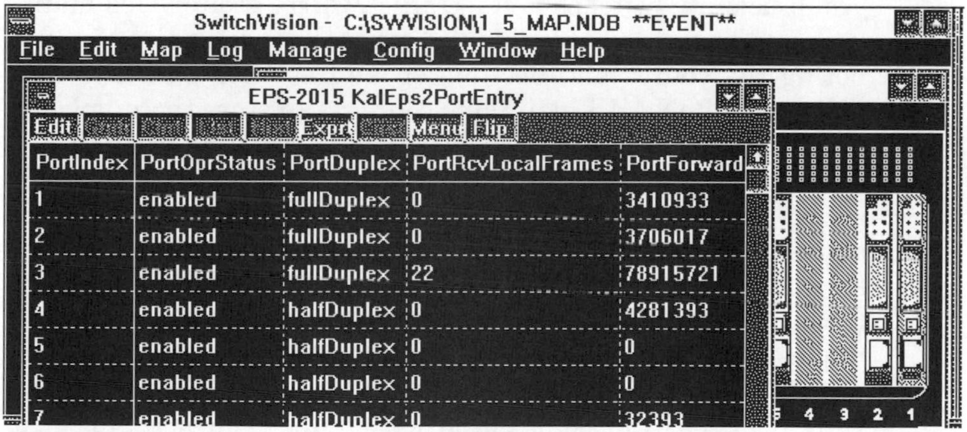

FIGURE 7.2 Using the Kalpana Ethernet switch management console to view packet-forwarding statistics on a port basis.

switch. Note the right column in the foreground window which indicates the number of packets forwarded per port.

Host Table Group. The Host Table group is incorporated in most switches that support RMON due to the statistics it accumulates. Those statistics include broadcasts, multicasts, and errored packets as well as node traffic statistics. One of the uses you can consider for this group is to determine if the use of vLANs can reduce broadcasts and enhance switch performance. For example, by noting source and destination of broadcasts you can determine the effect upon broadcasts by grouping ports into various vLANs.

Host TopN Group. The Host TopN group can be viewed as an extension of the host table as it provides sorted host statistics for N hosts. For example, you can configure the Host TopN group to maintain statistics for the top 25 nodes transmitting packets or an ordered list of all nodes based upon a specific type of error condition. In addition to defining the number of nodes you can also define the duration of the monitoring period. Thus, you could request an ordered list of all nodes based upon a predefined error condition for a predefined period of time.

Traffic Matrix Group. Perhaps the most popular RMON group used in switches is its Traffic Matrix group. This matrix gathers the amount of traffic and errors between pairs of nodes, noting the source and destination address per pair. For each pair the RMON MIB maintains counters to store the number of packets, octets, and error packets occurring between nodes. Through management software that associates ports with MAC addresses and vLAN groups with ports, you can obtain traffic statistics similar to those shown in Figure 7.1, whose use can shed an insight into switch activity not commonly obtainable through the use of other management implementation techniques. Now that we have an appreciation for some of the key switch management issues, let's conclude our examination of LAN switches by focusing our attention upon the emerging gigabit technology.

GIGABIT ETHERNET

Gigabit Ethernet is a generic name the data communications industry attached to a variety of Ethernet products being developed to extend the operation of Ethernet to a data rate of 1 Gbps (1000 Mbps). This operating rate is ten times that of Fast Ethernet and one hundred times that of the original 10-Mbps Ethernet standard. At the time this book was prepared a Gigabit Ethernet project had been approved by the Institute of Electrical and Electronics Engineers (IEEE) and was under way under the auspices of the IEEE 802.3z Task Force.

Gigabit Ethernet represents an evolving technology that is expected to provide a backbone for connecting LAN switches, servers, and routers. As such, it is being developed by various vendors as a backbone network as well as being incorporated into a Gigabit switch.

Utilization

Figure 7.3a illustrates the potential use of a Gigabit Ethernet LAN as a backbone to connect a mixed network infrastructure consisting of several 100-Mbps Ethernet switches, departmental servers, and a router. In actuality, although a bus-based LAN structure is shown Figure 7.3a, the actual implementation of Gigabit Ethernet is via a hub, similar to but operating 10 times faster than a 100BASE-T hub. Thus, a Gigabit LAN can be expected to provide a backbone capability for Fast Ethernet similar to the manner by which Fast Ethernet provides a backbone for 10BASE-T Ethernet.

Figure 7.3b illustrates the use of a Gigabit Ethernet switch as a backbone to interconnect 100-Mbps switches, departmental servers, and a router. The key advantage of the use of a Gigabit Ethernet switch over a Gigabit Ethernet LAN is the same as that for other switches—the ability to support multiple cross-connections through a switch. With six ports it becomes possible for the Gigabit Ethernet switch to support three simultaneous cross-connections for a total bandwidth of 3 Gbits. In comparison, the Gigabit Ethernet LAN shown in Figure 7.3a is limited

a. Backbone Gigabit Ethernet LAN

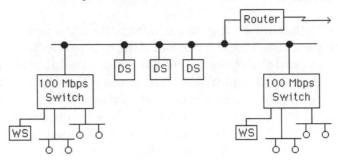

b. Using a Gigabit switch.

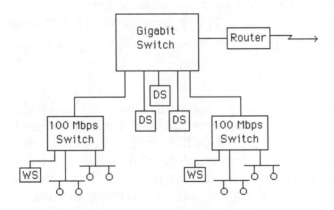

Legend:

○ ⟋⟍ = segment and workstations

WS = workgroup server
DS = departmental server

FIGURE 7.3   Using Gigabit Ethernet as a backbone.

to one cross-connection at a time, which results in a maximum bandwidth of 1 Gbits.

Evolving Technology

Although Gigabit Ethernet was not standardized when this book was written, several vendors had announced switches based upon this evolving technology. Unlike some Fast Ethernet and Ethernet switches that can easily be expanded to accommodate additional interfaces, the backplane operating rate required for a Gigabit Ethernet switch begins at such a high rate for a two-port connection that it limits the number of high-speed ports for nonblocked operations. For example, to support 32 Gigabit Ethernet ports a Gigabit Ethernet switch would require a backplane operating rate of 32 Gbps, which is presently beyond the capability of switch design. However, one vendor announced a switch with a backplane capacity of 16 Gbits during 1997. This switch provides sufficient bandwidth to support up to 16 separate Gigabit Ethernet, 128 Fast Ethernet, or 384 Ethernet ports.

When comparing backplane operating rates, raw speed can be deceptive. For example, another vendor that announced a switch with a 19.5-Gbits backplane was designed so that it can only support up to 88 switched Fast Ethernet and 176 switched Ethernet ports. Thus, users considering Gigabit Ethernet for use in a multi-tier network should carefully examine the number of ports of the various types of LANs supported instead of raw backplane bandwidth.

Although it is a favorite expression of stock brokers that the past does not guarantee future events, it is also certain that, if reasonably priced, Gigabit Ethernet will adversely affect ATM-based LAN installations. ATM is a much more complex technology while Gigabit Ethernet permits existing legacy networks to be used without LAN emulation. Although Gigabit Ethernet still lacks the quality of service that ATM has, its 1-Gbps operating rate may provide sufficient capacity that guaranteed bandwidth may not be necessary to effectively deliver

ATM to the desktop. As we move toward the new century we can say with assurance that "time will tell," and the cost and operation of Gigabit Ethernet should definitely be considered by network managers and LAN administrators as a mechanism to satisfy organizational networking requirements.

Index